ITALIAN
STEP BY STEP

STEP BY STEP

CHARLES BERLITZ

Charles Berlitz, world-famous linguist and author of more than 100 language teaching books, is the grandson of the founder of the Berlitz Schools. Since 1967, Mr. Berlitz has not been connected with the Berlitz Schools in any way.

Wynwood
A DIVISION OF
Baker Book House Co
Grand Rapids, MI

Library of Congress Cataloging-in-Publication Data

Berlitz, Charles, 1914–
    Italian step-by-step / by Charles Berlitz.
        p.   cm.
    ISBN 0-922066-42-6
    1. Italian language—Conversation and phrase books—English.
I. Title.
PC1121.B46   1990
458.3'421—dc20   90-12128
                                                         CIP

Copyright © 1990, 1979 by Charles Berlitz
Published by Wynwood ® Press
a division of Baker Book House Company
P.O. Box 6287, Grand Rapids, MI 49516-6287

Eighth printing, January 2001

Printed in the United States of America

For current information about all releases from
Baker Book House, visit our web site:
http://www.bakerbooks.com

INTRODUCTION

Here's your passport to travel pleasure. Charles Berlitz, whose grandfather founded the internationally acclaimed Berlitz Language Schools, now offers a new and simplified learning technique to foreign language.

Using Berlitz's method, you'll be conversant in the language; you'll be able to read signs and newspapers with ease; and most important, you'll be comfortable and knowledgeable speaking or hearing the language.

How often have we not risked speaking a foreign tongue for fear of making a mistake or "doing it wrong"? With ITALIAN STEP-BY-STEP, accent and pronunciation problems are solved forever. There will be no need to fear appearing gauche before a waiter or salesperson, no terror at buying a train ticket or sending back a steak cooked rare instead of medium. You will discover the music and rhythm of language as spoken by those born into the culture and tradition of a nation.

Charles Berlitz has determined that we use approximately 2,000 words in daily speech in *any* language. So he includes in his program a vocabulary of 2,600 words chosen especially for their frequency of use.

By familiarizing yourself with these words, accompanied by the easily understood methods of pronunciation described herein, you will come to feel at ease in a new tongue, in the context of everyday life situations.

Make sure your travel—whether it's business, vacation, or the trip of a lifetime—isn't spoiled by an inability to savor the pleasures of the native tongue.

ITALIAN STEP-BY-STEP will be your personal guide to an unforgettable, truly satisfying journey to a welcoming, accessible land.

CONTENTS

Contents

            Present tense of the most important regular and ir-
            regular verbs — present tense used as the
            progressive — use of verbs without subject
            pronouns

            Singular and plural forms of demonstratives — the
            intensive form of the adjective — combinations of
            "with" with the article — special forms of pro-
            nouns after "of"

            Letters and their pronunciations — spelling — the
            written accent — use of the impersonal pronoun —
            the reflexive form of verbs — "to be named" or
            "to be called" — useful exclamations

            The present participle — use of the progressive —
            direct object pronouns and position with verbs —
            "to know" and "to be acquainted with"

Contents

Contents

HOW TO PRONOUNCE ITALIAN

Every sentence in the lessons and dialogues of this book is written three times — first in Italian, then in easy-to-read syllables that show you how to pronounce it, and finally in English, so you can understand the meaning.

To pronounce the Italian correctly, say the second line out loud; read the separate syllables as if they were English and presto! — they come out Italian.

Here is an example. Note that the syllables in capital letters are to be stressed:

Come sta Lei?
KO-may sta lay?
How are you?

As you progress, you should try to pronounce the Italian without looking at the second line — but it will still be there if you need it.

The Italian pronunciation of many letters and combinations of letters differs considerably from English. The following list will help you to remember the differences.

ITALIAN SPELLING	ENGLISH SOUND
a	ah
e	ay
i	ee
o	oh
u	oo
c (before e or i)	ch
c (before other vowels)	k
ch	k
g (before e or i)	j
g (before other vowels)	g (as in "go")
gh	g (as in "go")

ITALIAN SPELLING	ENGLISH SOUND
gl	lli (as in "million")
gn	ny (as in "canyon")
h	always silent
r	r (a single r should be lightly rolled (trilled); a double r is strongly rolled)
s	s (but pronounced as a z when it comes between vowels)
sc (before e or i)	sh
sc (before other vowels)	sk
sch	sk
z (beginning a word)	dz
z (within a word)	ts
zz	ts and sometimes dz

Note that in the phonetics, "oh" is used instead of "o" only within a syllable or after t or d, to avoid confusion with English sounds.

After reading each lesson for the first time, it is most important that you read the text and the instant conversation aloud. Read slowly at first, and then gradually increase your speed to a normal conversational rate, reading the Italian line instead of the pronunciation line. This is an excellent and proven technique, not only to help your pronunciation, but also the way to imprint the key expressions firmly in your mind. Whether you are studying alone or with someone else, try reading the different roles within the lessons, and specially in the "instant conversations," aloud, with expression and even gestures, and with increasing speed. By accustoming yourself to speaking naturally and easily, you will attain an exuberant flow and rhythm, which is the essence of speaking Italian like the Italians.

ITALIAN
STEP BY STEP

INSTANT CONVERSATION: IN A CAFÉ

The following phrases can be of immediate use in any Italian café. A dash before a sentence indicates a change of speakers.

— Buon giorno, signore.
Bwohn JOR-no, seen-YO-ray.
Good morning, sir.

The Important Second Line
The second line, which gives the Italian pronunciation, is meant to be read as if you were reading English syllables, and the result will come out as understandable Italian. For complete value of each Italian letter see Preface.

— Buon giorno.
Bwohn JOR-no.
Good morning.

È libero questo tavolo?
Ay LEE-bay-ro KWEHS-toh TA-vo-lo?
Is this table free?

A question of translation
The literal translation of *È libero questo tavolo?* is "Is free this table?". However, in the translations, we give the closest English approximation rather than a word-for-word translation so that you will become used to saying the whole expression in a natural way without hesitation.

— Sí, signore. Prego, si accomodi.
See, seen-YO-ray. PRAY-go, see ahk-KO-mo-dee.
Yes, sir. Please, sit down.

— Con permesso.
Kohn pehr-MESS-so.
With (your) permission.

Oh, scusi, signora.
Oh, SKOO-zee, seen-YO-ra.
Oh, excuse me, madam.

— Non fa niente, signore.
Nohn fa N'YEN-tay, seen-YO-ray.
It is nothing, sir.

_____

— Cameriere, un caffè nero, per piacere.
Ka-mehr-YAY-ray, oon kahf-FAY NAY-ro, pehr p'ya-CHAY-ray.
Waiter, one black coffee, please.

Masculine and feminine
All nouns are masculine or feminine. When "a"
or "one" are used with a masculine noun, it is
translated by *un* and occasionally by *uno*, and
when the noun is feminine, it is *una* or *un'*. Masculine nouns generally end in -*o*, while most
feminine nouns end in -*a*.

— Sì, signore, subito.
See, seen-YO-ray, SOO-bee-toh.
Yes, sir, right away.

— Ah, signor Dinardo. Come sta?
Ah, seen-YOHR Dee-NAHR-doh. KO-may sta?
Ah, Mr. Dinardo. How are you?

— Molto bene, grazie. E Lei?
MOHL-toh BAY-nay, GRAHTS-yay. Ay Lay?
Very well, thank you. And you?

— Così, così. Si accomodi un momento, per piacere.
**Ko-ZEE, ko-ZEE. See ahk-KO-mo-dee oon mo-MEN-toh, pehr
                              p'ya-CHAY-ray.**
So-so. Sit down a moment, please.

Ecco una sedia.
EK-ko OO-na SEHD-ya.
Here is a chair.

4

— Con piacere.
Kohn p'ya-CHAY-ray.
With pleasure.

— Cameriere, per piacere, un altro caffè.
Ka-mehr-YAY-ray, pehr p'ya-CHAY-ray, oo-NAHL-tro kahf-FAY.
Waiter, please, another coffee.

— Molte grazie.
MOHL-tay GRAHTS-yay.
Thank you very much.

— Questo caffè è buono, vero?
KWESS-toh kahf-FAY eh BWO-no, VAY-ro?
This coffee is good, isn't it?

Non è vero?
Vero, which means "true," is used for a word
for "right," "don't you agree?," "isn't it?".
Vero is really a shortened form for *non è*
vero? — "isn't it true?"

— Sì, non c'è male.
See, nohn chay MA-lay.
Yes, it's not bad.

_____

— Cameriere, il conto, per favore.
Ka-mehr-YAY-ray, eel KOHN-toh, pehr fa-VO-ray.
Waiter, the bill, please.

— Ecco, signore.
EK-ko, seen-YO-ray.
Here you are, sir.

Ecco!
Ecco can mean a variety of things, such as:
"there it is," "there you are," or "here it is,"
"here you are," as well as "here is," "here
are," or "there is," "there are" depending on
the context.

— Grazie per il caffè.
GRAHTS-yay pehr eel kahf-FAY.
Thank you for the coffee.

Several words for "the"

For the word "the," *il, l'* and occasionally *lo* are used for the masculine singular, and *la* or *l'* for the feminine singular. The reason why there are several words for "the" for both the masculine and feminine is that this depends on the first letter of the noun that the "the" goes with. If it is a vowel, the *il* or *la* are abbreviated to *l'*, while the masculine word for "the" — *lo* — is used only in front of *sp, st,* and *z-* ("the mirror" — *lo specchio;* "the sugar" — *lo zucchero*). The reason for these changes is to make Italian sound more musical — a notable characteristic of this beautiful language.

The word for "this" is *questo* for the masculine and *questa* for the feminine.

It is important to know whether a noun is masculine or feminine because the word for "a," "the," as well as many adjectives have masculine and feminine forms. Among the nouns you have just seen *tavolo, caffè,* and *momento* are masculine, while *signora* and *sedia* are feminine. Compare:

> *un momento* — a moment
> *il momento* — the moment
> *questo momento* — this moment

> *una sedia* — a chair
> *la sedia* — the chair
> *questa sedia* — this chair

— Prego. Arrivederci!
PRAY-go. Ah-rree-vay-DEHR-chee!
You're welcome. Goodbye!

— Arrivederci e a presto!
Ah-rree-vay-DEHR-chee eh ah PRESS-toh!
Good bye and till soon!

TEST YOUR ITALIAN

Match these phrases. Score 10 points for each correct answer. See answers below.

1. Good morning.	Con permesso.
2. Please, sit down.	Scusi, signora.
3. With your permission.	Buon giorno.
4. Excuse me, madam.	Arrivederci, e a presto.
5. It is nothing, sir.	Si accomodi, per piacere.
6. Waiter, one black coffee, please.	Come sta?
7. Yes, sir, right away.	Molto bene, grazie, e Lei?
8. How are you?	Cameriere, un caffè nero, per piacere.
9. Very well, thank you — and you?	Sì, signore, subito.
10. Goodbye, and see you soon.	Non fa niente, signore.

Answers: Numbers going down on right should be: 3 4 1 10 2 8 9 6 7 5

SCORE _____%

7

step 1
NAMES OF OBJECTS AND PLACES

Un albergo, un ristorante,
OO-nahl-BEHR-go, oon ree-sto-RAHN-tay,
A hotel, a restaurant,

un teatro, una banca.
oon tay-AH-tro, OO-na BAHN-ka.
a theater, a bank.

Linguistic rhythm
You will note that a letter in the phonetics syllables is sometimes transferred onto a following
word when that word starts with a vowel. This
will give your phonetic reading a more natural
Italian sound.

È un ristorante?
Ay oon ree-sto-RAHN-tay?
Is it a restaurant?

An easy question
A declarative or affirmative sentence can be
made into an interrogative by simply raising the
voice toward the end of the sentence. È
means "is," or as it is used here, "it is" or "is
it . . . ?".

Sì. È un ristorante.
See. Ay oon ree-sto-RAHN-tay.
Yes. It's a restaurant.

È un albergo?
Ay oo-nahl-BEHR-go?
Is it a hotel?

No, signore. Non è un albergo.
No, seen-YO-ray. No-NAY oo-nahl-BEHR-go.
No, sir. It is not a hotel.

Non-not
Non, the word for "not," comes before the
verb. "It is not" — *Non è.*

Che cos'è?
Kay ko-ZAY?
What is it?

Cos'è? = What is it?
Che cos'è?, the expression for "what is it?" or
"what is this?," is a contraction for *che cosa
è?* — "what thing is it?" At times, this is further
abbreviated, with the same meaning, to *cos'è?*

È un teatro.
Ay oon tay-AH-tro.
It is a theater.

Un tassì, un autobus.
Oon tass-SEE, oon ow-toh-booss.
A taxi, a bus.

È un tassì o un autobus?
Ay oon tass-SEE oh oon ow-toh-booss?
Is it a taxi or a bus?

È un tassì.
Ay oon tass-SEE.
It is a taxi.

Un cinema, un negozio, un museo.
Oon CHEE-nay-ma, oon nay-GOHTS-yo, oon moo-ZAY-oh.
A movie theater, a store, a museum.

È un negozio? Sì, è un negozio.
Ay oon nay-GOHTS-yo? See, ay oon-nay-GOHTS-yo.
Is it a store? Yes, it is a store.

È un museo? No, non è un museo.
Ay oon moo-ZAY-oh? No, no-NAY oon moo-ZAY-oh.
Is it a museum? No, it is not a museum.

Cos'è?
Ko-ZAY?
What is it?

È un cinema.
Ay oon CHEE-nay-ma.
It is a movie theater.

Una via, una piazza, una statua.
OO-na VEE-ah, OO-na P'YAHTS-sa, OO-na STA-twa.
A street, a square, a statue.

Che via è questa?
Kay VEE-ah ay KWESS-ta?
What street is this?

È Via Garibaldi.
Ay VEE-ah Ga-ree-BAHL-dee.
It is Garibaldi Street.

Che piazza è questa?
Kay P'YAHTS-sa ay KWESS-ta?
What square is this?

È Piazza Vittorio Emanuele II.
Ay P'YAHTS-sa Veet-TOHR-yo Ay-ma-NWEH-lay Say-KOHN-doh.
It is the Square of Vittorio Emanuele (the) Second.

Che statua è questa?
Kay STA-twa ay KWESS-ta?
What statue is this?

È la statua di San Pietro.
Ay la STA-twa dee Sahn P'YAY-tro.
It is the statue of Saint Peter.

Che ristorante è questo?
Kay ree-sto-RAHN-tay ay KWESS-toh?
What restaurant is this?

È il Ristorante Capri.
Ay eel ree-sto-RAHN-tay KA-pree.
It is the Restaurant Capri.

INSTANT CONVERSATION: A RIDE IN A TAXI

— Tassì, è libero?
Tahs-SEE, ay LEE-bay-ro?
Taxi, are you free?

— Sì, signore. Per dove?
See, seen-YO-ray. Pehr DOH-vay?
Yes, sir. Where to?

— All' Albergo Narciso. È lontano?
Ahl-lahl-BEHR-go Nahr-CHEE-zo. Ay lohn-TA-no?
To the Hotel Narciso. Is it far?

Combinations with "a" (to)
A means "to" and combines with the article —
al teatro, alla banca. Albergo, a masculine noun
beginning with a vowel, takes the article lo
which is shortened to l'. When a is combined
with lo, it becomes allo, as in the case of allo
spettacolo — "to the show," but when it comes
before a noun beginning with a vowel, it drops
the -o, as in all'albergo.

— No, signore. Non è lontano. È vicino.
No, seen-YO-ray. No-NAY lohn-TA-no. Ay vee-CHEE-no.
No, sir. It is not far. It is near.

— Scusi. Dov'è l'Hotel Tevere?
SKOO-zee. Doh-VAY lo-TEL TAY-vay-ray?
Excuse me. Where is the Hotel Tevere?

— Lì, a sinistra.
Lee, ah see-NEE-stra.
Over there, on the left.

— È un buon albergo?
Ay oon bwohn ahl-BEHR-go?
Is it a good hotel?

> **Dropping the "o"**
> Certain adjectives such as *buono* drop the -o
> when used before the masculine noun, as in
> *buon albergo.*

— Sì, signore, molto buono . . . e molto caro.
See, seen-YO-ray, MOHL-toh BWO-no . . . ay MOHL-toh KA-ro.
Yes, sir, very good . . . and very expensive.

— Dov'è il Museo Nazionale?
Doh-VAY eel Moo-ZAY-oh Nats-yo-NA-lay?
Where is the National Museum?

— Alla fine di questa via, a destra.
AHL-la FEE-nay dee KWESS-ta VEE-ah, ah DESS-tra.
At the end of this street, on the right.

È quel grande edificio, lì.
Ay kwehl GRAHN-day ay-dee-FEE-cho, lee.
It's that big building, over there.

Ecco l'albergo, signore.
EK-ko lahl-BEHR-go, seen-YO-ray.
Here's the hotel, sir.

— Molto bene. Grazie. Quant' è?
MOHL-toh BAY-nay. GRAHTS-yay. Kwan-TAY?
Very good. Thank you. How much is it?

— Duemila e cinquecento lire.
Doo-ay-MEE-la ay CHEEN-kway-CHEN-toh LEE-ray.
Two thousand five hundred lire.

— Vediamo — mille, duemila, uno, due, tre, quattro, . . . e cinque.
Vehd-YA-mo — MEE-lay, DOO-ay-MEE-la, OO-no, DOO-ay, tray,
                    KWAHT-tro . . . ay CHEEN-kway.
Let's see — one thousand, two thousand, one, two, three, four . . . and
                                                                        five.

E questo è per Lei.
Ay KWESS-toh ay pehr lay.
And this is for you.

— Molte grazie, signore.
MOHL-tay GRAHTS-yay, seen-YO-ray.
Many thanks, sir.

— Prego.
PRAY-go.
You're welcome.

The question of gender
People who study Italian for the first time often ask why nouns are masculine or feminine. There is no simple answer as to why — but it will help you to remember that masculine nouns usually end in *o* and feminine nouns in *a*. As for the others, you must learn their gender as you meet them and, after using them a number of times, you will remember the gender automatically, just as Italians do.

TEST YOUR ITALIAN

Match the following phrases. Score 10 points for each correct answer. See answers below.

1. È un buon albergo?		Are you free?
2. È vicino?		How much is it?
3. È lontano?		Where is it?
4. Non è lontano.		Is it a good hotel?
5. È libero?		What square is this?
6. È a sinistra.		Is it far?
7. Dov'è?		It's the left.
8. A destra.		Is it near?
9. Quant'è?		It's not far.
10. Che piazza è questa?		To the right.

Answers: Numbers going down on right should be: 5 9 7 1 10 3 6 4 2 8

SCORE _____%

HOW TO USE THE PRESENT TENSE OF VERBS

Alcuni esempi del verbo *essere:*
Ahl-KOO-nee ay-ZEHM-pee del VEHR-bo *EHS-seh-ray:*
Some examples of the verb "to be:"

È italiano Lei o americano?
Ay ee-tahl-YA-no lay oh ah-may-ree-KA-no?
Are you Italian or American?

Io sono italiano e anche mia moglie è italiana.
EE-oh SO-no ee-tahl-YA-no ay AHN-kay MEE-ah MOLL-yay ay ee-tahl-YA-na.
I am Italian and my wife too is Italian.

Adjectives follow gender
Adjectives take the gender of the noun or pronoun they refer to. The feminine form of an adjective is formed by changing the final -o to an -a:

italiano, italiana — Italian (masc. and fem.)
americano, americana — American (masc. and fem.)
spagnolo, spagnola — Spanish (masc. and fem.)
tedesco, tedesca — German (masc. and fem.)

If the adjective ends in -e, instead of in -o, the ending does not change in the feminine:

francese — French (masc. and fem.)
inglese — English (masc. and fem.)

È italiano egli?
Ay ee-tahl-YA-no ELL-yee?
Is he Italian?

No, egli non è italiano; è francese.
No, ELL-yee no-NAY ee-tahl-YA-no; ay frahn-CHEH-zay.
No, he's not Italian; he's French.

È italiana ella?
Ay ee-tahl-YA-na El-la?
Is she Italian?

No, ella non è italiana; è inglese.
No, EL-la no NAY ee-tahl-YA-na; ay een-GLAY-zay.
No, she's not Italian; she's English.

Di dov'è Lei?
Dee doh-VAY Lay?
Where are you from?

Sono di Sorrento.
SO-no dee So-RREN-toh.
I'm from Sorrento.

Che bella città!
Kay bel-la cheet-TA!
What a beautiful city!

— Scusi, dove sono i signori Bernardi?
SKOO-zee, doh-vay SO-no ee seen-YO-ree Behr-NAR-dee?
Excuse me, where are Mr. and Mrs. Bernardi?

"To be" — "essere"
Italian verbs change their endings according to the person, that is the subject. Here is how *essere* — "to be," looks in table form.

io sono	I am
Lei, egli, ella è	you (sing.) are; he, she, it is
noi siamo	we are
Loro, loro sono	you (pl.) are; they (masc. and fem.) are

The verb form for *Lei, egli* and *ella* as well as the equivalent form of "it" is the same. "It" is usually not used as a separate pronoun, since the nouns for anything as well as any person are either masculine or feminine, the corresponding pronouns would then always be either "he" or "she."

Loro with a capital *L* means "you" in the plural, while *loro* with a small *l* means "they," both for the masculine and the feminine. Since, when you hear it, you can't know how it is written, the meaning will be clear to you according to the context.

— Sono nella sala da pranzo dell'albergo.
SO-no NEL-la SA-la da PRAHND-zo del-lahl-BEHR-go.
They are in the dining room of the hotel.

The plural
The Italian plural is not formed with an -*s*, but with an -*i* for the masculine plural and an -*e* for the feminine plural. The plural of *signore* is *signori* and that of *signora* is *signore*, but when masculine and feminine genders are mixed as in Mr. and Mrs. Bernardi, the masculine gender is used: *i signori Bernardi.*

When "the" refers to objects in the plural, *i* is used for the masculine and *le* for the feminine. In the case of some masculine nouns, however — before words beginning with *z*-, a vowel, or *sp*, or *st*, *gli* is used instead of *i*. If a feminine noun already ends in -*e*, such as *la madre* — "the mother," then the plural is formed by changing the -*e* to -*i*: *le madri* — "the mothers."

— Dove sono i loro bambini?
DOH-vay SO-no ee LO-ro bahm-BEE-nee?
Where are their children?

Possessives

The following chart will help you to identify the possessives — the equivalent of "my," "your," "his," etc.

	SINGULAR		PLURAL	
	masc.	fem.	masc.	fem.
my	*mio*	*mia*	*miei*	*mie*
your	*Suo*	*Sua*	*Suoi*	*Sue*
his, her, its	*suo*	*sua*	*suoi*	*sue*
our	*nostro*	*nostra*	*nostri*	*nostre*
your	*Loro*	*Loro*	*Loro*	*Loro*
their	*loro*	*loro*	*loro*	*loro*

Note that *suo* and *loro* are capitalized when they mean "your."

— Sono nel parco.
SO-no nel PAR-ko.
They're in the park.

— Dove sono Francesca e Giannina?
DOH-vay SO-no Frahn-CHAYS-ka ay J'yahn-NEE-na?
Where are Francesca and Giannina?

— Sono in viaggio.
SO-no een V'YAHD-jo.
They're on a trip.

Il verbo *parlare:*
Eel VEHR-bo *pahr-LA-ray:*
The verb "to speak":

Parlare

The verb *parlare* is a first conjugation verb, which means that its infinitive "to speak" — *parlare* — ends in *-are.* Here are the important verb forms in the present tense:

io parlo
Lei parla
egli, ella parla
noi parliamo
Loro parlano
loro parlano

From here on, you will notice that frequently the pronouns which would be used with the verbs in English are dropped, as the form of the verb generally indicates who is performing the action.

I speak — *io parlo,* or simply *parlo*
We speak — *noi parliamo,* or *parliamo*

Io parlo italiano.
EE-oh PAHR-lo ee-tahl-YA-no.
I speak Italian.

Parla inglese Lei?
PAHR-la een-GLAY-zay Lay?
Do you speak English?

Mia moglie non parla bene l'italiano.
MEE-ah MOLL-yay nohn PAHR-la BAY-nay lee-tahl-YA-no.
My wife doesn't speak Italian well.

No word for "do" or "does"
The auxiliary "do" or "does," used for asking questions or "do not" or "does not" for negative statements, have no counterpart in Italian. To ask a question, where you would use "do . . . ?" or "does . . . ?" in English, in Italian just reverse the position of the verb.

You speak — *Lei parla*
Do you speak? — *Parla Lei?*

To make the negative with "do not" or "does not," use *non* before the verb.

He doesn't speak — *Egli non parla*
We don't speak — *Noi non parliamo*

Noi parliamo italiano con i nostri amici italiani.
NO-ee pahrl-YA-mo ee-tahl-YA-no kohn ee NOSS-tree ah-MEE-chee
　　　　　　　　　　　　　　　　　　　　ee-tahl-YA-nee.
We speak Italian with our Italian friends.

Loro parlano molto rapidamente.
LO-ro PAHR-la-no MOHL-toh ra-pee-da-MEN-tay.
They speak very rapidly.

Words ressembling English
The ending -*mente* corresponds to the English
equivalent -*ly*. Many Italian adverbs are easily
recognizable if you remember this point.

rapidamente — rapidly
raramente — rarely
naturalmente — naturally
possibilmente — possibly
probabilmente — probably
generalmente — generally

Una presentazione:
OO-na pray-zenn-tahts-YO-nay:
A presentation:

— Signora Camaro . . . il mio amico Carlo Rossini.
**Seen-YO-ra Ka-MA-ro . . . eel MEE-oh ah-MEE-ko KAHR-lo
Ross-SEE-nee.**
Mrs. Camaro . . . my friend, Carlo Rossini.

— Piacere, signore.
P'ya-CHAY-ray, seen-YO-ray.
Pleased to meet you, sir.

— Il piacere è mio, signora.
Eel p'ya-CHAY-ray ay MEE-oh, seen-YO-ra.
The pleasure is mine, madam.

— Il Suo nome è italiano,
Eel SOO-oh NO-may ay ee-tahl-YA-no,
Your name is Italian,

ma Lei è americano, non è vero?
ma LAY ay ah-may-ree-KA-no, no-NAY VAY-ro?
but you are American, aren't you?

— Sì, i miei genitori sono italiani.
See, ee m'yay jay-nee-TO-ree SO-no ee-tahl-YA-nee.
Yes, my parents are Italian.

— Interessante!
Een-tay-ress-SAHN-tay!
(How) interesting!

Di che parte sono?
Dee kay PAHR-tay SO-no?
What part are you from?

— Mio padre è di Firenze,
MEE-oh PA-dray ay dee Fee-REHNT-say,
My father is from Florence,

e mia madre è di Roma.
ay MEE-ah MA-dray ay dee RO-ma.
and my mother is from Rome.

Io sono di Nuova York,
EE-oh SO-no dee NWO-va Yohrk,
I am from New York,

ma anche laggiù si parla molto l'italiano.
ma AHN-kay lahd-JOO see PAHR-la MOHL-toh lee-tahl-YA-no.
but there too Italian is spoken a lot.

> **Si parla italiano**
> When *si* is used with the form of the verb which goes with *egli* and *ella*, it means "one" in the general sense. Here is a sign you may have seen in shops:
>
> *Qui si parla italiano.* — Here one speaks Italian, or Here Italian is spoken.

— Sì, è vero.
See, ay VAY-ro.
Yes, it's true.

E Lei, signora, parla inglese?
Ay Lay, seen-YO-ra, PAHR-la een-GLAY-zay?
And you, madam, do you speak English?

— Parlo soltanto un poco.
PAHR-lo sohl-TAHN-toh oon PO-ko.
I speak only a little.

L'inglese è molto difficile.
Leen-GLAY-zay ay MOHL-toh deef-FEE-chee-lay.
English is very difficult.

Ma con Lei, signore,
Ma kohn Lay, seen-YO-ray,
But with you, sir,

non è necessario parlare inglese.
no-NAY nay-chess-SAHR-yo pahr-LA-ray een-GLAY-zay.
it is not necessary to speak English.

Lei parla italiano molto bene
Lay PAHR-la ee-tahl-YA-no MOHL-toh BAY-nay
You speak Italian very well

e con un buon accento.
ay kohn oon bwohn aht-CHEN-toh.
and with a good accent.

— Molte grazie, signora.
MOHL-tay GRAHTS-yay, seen-YO-ra.
Thank you very much, madam.

Lei è molto gentile.
Lay ay MOHL-toh jen-TEE-lay.
You are very kind.

INSTANT CONVERSATION: IN AN OFFICE

Il signor Martino è di Nuova York.
Eel seen-YOHR Mahr-TEE-no ay dee NWO-va Yohrk.
Mr. Martino is from New York.

È americano, però parla italiano.
Ay ah-may-ree-KA-no, peh-RO PAHR-la ee-tahl-YA-no.
He is American, but he speaks Italian.

È nell' ufficio del signor Ferrucci.
Ay nel-loof-FEE-cho del seen-YOHR Fay-RROOT-chee.
He is in Mr. Ferrucci's office.

"In" + the article
"In" is the same word in Italian and in English, except, of course, for the difference in pronunciation. However, *in* combines with the articles in the following way:

in + *il* = *nel*
in + *lo* = *nello,* or *nell'* (if the next word begins with a vowel)
in + *la* = *nella,* or *nell'* (if the next word begins with a vowel)
in + *i* = *nei*
in + *gli* = *negli* or *negl'* (before a word beginning with *i*-)
in + *le* = *nelle*

Parla con la segretaria del signor Ferrucci.
PAHR-la kohn la say-gray-TAHR-ya del seen-YOHR Fay-RROOT-chee.
He speaks with Mr. Ferrucci's secretary.

SIGNOR MARTINO:

Buon giorno, signorina.

Bwohn JOR-no, seen-yo-REE-na.

Good morning, Miss.

È questo l'ufficio del signor Ferrucci?

Ay KWESS-toh loof-FEE-cho del seen-YOHR Fay-RROOT-chee?

Is this Mr. Ferrucci's office?

Di + the article

The possessive of nouns is expressed by *di:*

l'auto di Giorgio — George's automobile

Di combines with the article in much the same manner as *in.*

di + il = del
di + lo = dello, or *dell'* (if the next word begins with a vowel)
di + la = della, or *dell'* (if the next word begins with a vowel)
di + i = dei
di + gli = degli or *degl'* (before a word beginning with *i-*)
di + le = delle

LA SEGRETARIA:

Sì, signore. Sono la sua segretaria.

See, seen-YO-ray. SO-no la SOO-ah say-gray-TAHR-ya.

Yes, sir. I am his secretary.

SIGNOR MARTINO:

Sono il signor Martino —

SO-no eel seen-YOHR Mahr-TEE-no —

I am Mr. Martino —

sono un suo amico.

SO-no oon SOO-oh ah-MEE-ko.

I am a friend of his.

Ecco il mio biglietto.

EK-ko eel MEE-oh beel-YEHT-toh.

Here is my card.

È molto occupato adesso?
Ay MOHL-toh ohk-koo-PA-toh ah-DESS-so?
Is he very busy now?

Un momento, signore.
Oon mo-MEN-toh, seen-YO-ray.
One moment, sir.

(Ella parla al telefono.)
(El-la PAHR-la ahl tay-LAY-fo-no.)
(She speaks on the telephone.)

Scusi, signore.
SKOO-zee, seen-YO-ray.
Excuse me, sir.

È molto occupato adesso?
Ay MOHL-toh ohk-koo-PA-toh ah-DESS-so?
Are you very busy now?

Il signor Martino è qui nell'ufficio.
Eel seen-YOHR Mahr-TEE-no ay kwee nel-loof-FEE-cho.
Mr. Martino is here in the office.

Va bene. Subito.
Va BAY-nay. SOO-bee-toh.
Very well. Right away.

Sta bene, signor Martino.
Sta BAY-nay, seen-YOHR Mahr-TEE-no.
It's all right, Mr. Martino.

Il signor Ferrucci è nel suo ufficio.
Eel seen-YOHR Fay-RROOT-chee ay nel SOO-oh oof-FEE-cho.
Mr. Ferrucci is in his office.

Prego, da questa parte.
PRAY-go, da KWESS-ta PAHR-tay.
Please, this way.

25

SIGNOR MARTINO:

Grazie. Lei è molto gentile, signorina.

GRAHTS-yay. Lay ay MOHL-toh jen-TEE-lay, seen-yo-REE-na.

Thank you. You are very kind, Miss.

LA SEGRETARIA:

È un piacere, signore.

Ay oon p'ya-CHAY-ray, seen-YO-ray.

It's a pleasure, sir.

TEST YOUR ITALIAN

Match these phrases. See answers below. Score 10 points for each correct answer.

1. Do you speak English?	Piacere.
2. I speak Italian.	Questo è interessante.
3. Where do you come from?	Prego, da questa parte.
4. They are on a trip.	È molto occupato?
5. Pleased (to meet you).	Lei è molto gentile.
6. This is interesting.	Parlo italiano.
7. Please, this way.	Parla inglese Lei?
8. Are you very busy?	Sono in viaggio.
9. You are very kind.	Lei parla italiano molto bene.
10. You speak Italian very well.	Di dov'è Lei?

Answers: Numbers on the right should be: 5 6 7 8 9 2 1 4 10 3

SCORE _____%

NUMBERS AND HOW TO USE THEM

I Numeri:
Ee NOO-may-ree:
The numbers:

1	2	3	
uno	due	tre	
OO-no	**DOO-ay**	**tray**	

4	5	6	
quattro	cinque	sei	
KWAHT-tro	**CHEEN-kway**	**say**	

7	8	9	10
sette	otto	nove	dieci
SEHT-tay	**OHT-toh**	**NO-vay**	**D'YAY-chee**

Da dieci a quindici:
Da D'YAY-chee ah KWEEN-dee-chee:
From 10 to 15:

11	12	13
undici	dodici	tredici
OON-dee-chee	**DOH-dee-chee**	**TRAY-dee-chee**

14	15
quattordici	quindici
kwaht-TOHR-dee-chee	**KWEEN-dee-chee**

e poi:
eh PO-ee:
and then:

16	17	18
sedici	diciassette	diciotto
SAY-dee-chee	**dee-chass-SEHT-tay**	**dee-CHOHT-toh**

19	20
diciannove	venti
dee-chahn-NO-vay	**VEN-tee**

Dopo il venti:
DOH-po eel VEN-tee:
After (the) 20:

21	22	23
ventuno	ventidue	ventitrè
ven-TOO-no	**ven-tee-DOO-ay**	**ven-tee-TRAY**

24
ventiquattro
ven-tee-KWAHT-tro

25	eccetera, fino a	30
venticinque	**eht-CHAY-tay-ra, FEE-no ah**	trenta
ven-tee-CHEEN-kway	etc., until	**TREN-ta**

e dopo	31	40
ay DOH-po	trentuno	quaranta
and, after	**tren-TOO-no**	**kwa-RAHN-ta**

50	60	70
cinquanta	sessanta	settanta
cheen-KWAHN-ta	**sess-SAHN-ta**	**seht-TAHN-ta**

80	90
ottanta	novanta
oht-TAHN-ta	**no-VAHN-ta**

Da cento a mille:
Da CHEN-toh ah MEEL-lay:
From 100 to 1000:

100	200
cento	duecento
CHEN-toh	**doo-ay-CHEN-toh**

300	400
trecento	quattrocento
tray-CHEN-toh	**kwaht-tro-CHEN-toh**

29

500	600
cinquecento	seicento
cheen-kway-CHEN-toh	**say-CHEN-toh**
700	800
settecento	ottocento
seht-tay-CHEN-toh	**oht-toh-CHEN-toh**
900	1.000
novecento	mille
no-vay-CHEN-toh	**MEEL-lay**
100.000	1.000.000
cento mila	un milione
CHEN-toh MEE-la	**oon-meel-YO-nay**

Remember
Periods are used for large numbers. The comma is used as a decimal point.

I numeri sono importanti —
Ee NOO-may-ree SO-no eem-pohr-TAHN-tee —
Numbers are important —

nei negozi . . .
nay nay-GOHT-see . . .
in stores . . .

Adjectives change gender and number
Adjectives agree with the noun they modify according to the gender, masculine or feminine, and to the number, singular or plural.
the important store — *il negozio importante*
the important stores — *i negozi importanti*
the expensive car — *la macchina cara*
the expensive cars — *le macchine care*

Un cliente: Quanto costa?
Oon klee-EN-tay: KWAHN-toh KOSS-ta?
A customer: How much is it?

La commessa: Seicento cinquanta lire, signore.
La kohm-MESS-sa: Say-CHEN-toh cheen-KWAHN-ta LEE-ray,
                              seen-YO-ray
The saleslady: Six hundred and fifty lire, sir.

al telefono . . .
ahl tay-LAY-fo-no . . .
on the telephone . . .

Una voce: Pronto! Chi parla?
OO-na VO-chay: PROHN-toh! Kee PAHR-la?
A voice: Hello! Who is speaking?

Seconda voce: È questo il numero 78-45-83?
**Say-KOHN-da VO-chay: Ay KWESS-toh eel NOO-may-ro seht-tahn-
TOHT-toh kwa-rahn-ta-CHEEN-kway oht-tahn-ta-TRAY?**
Second voice: Is this the number 78-45-83?

Prima voce: No, signore, Questo è il 78-43-85.
**PREE-ma VO-chay: No, seen-YO-ray. KWESS-toh ay eel seht-tahn-
TOHT-toh kwa-rahn-ta-TRAY oht-tahn-ta-CHEEN-kway.**
First voice: No, sir. This is 78-43-85.

Seconda voce: Oh! Scusi! È uno sbaglio!
Seh-KOHN-da VO-chay: Oh! SKOO-zee! Ay OO-no SBAHL-yo!
Second voice: Oh! Excuse me! It's a mistake!

per domandare indirizzi . . .
pehr doh-mahn-DA-ray een-dee-REETS-see . . .
to ask for addresses . . .

> **In order to**
> *Per* means "for," "through," or "in order to."
> *per domandare* — in order to ask for
>
> *Domandare* is a verb of the first conjugation and
> follows the same pattern as *parlare* in Step 2.

Un signore: Qual'è il Suo indirizzo?
Oon seen-YO-ray: Kwa-LAY eel SOO-oh een-dee-REETS-so?
A gentleman: What is your address?

Una signora: Via Veneto, numero 14,
**OO-na seen-YO-ra: VEE-ah VAY-nay-toh, NOO-may-ro
kwaht-TOHR-dee-chee,**
A lady: Veneto Street, Number 14,

al secondo piano.
ahl say-KOHN-doh P'YA-no.
on the second floor.

Ordinal numbers
Here are the ordinal numbers from 1 to 10 if
you use them for asking for your floor in eleva-
tors, remember that floors start with what in
America is called the "second."

primo	— first	*sesto*	— sixth
secondo	— second	*settimo*	— seventh
terzo	— third	*ottavo*	— eighth
quarto	— fourth	*nono*	— ninth
quinto	— fifth	*decimo*	— tenth

Telephone numbers
Italian telephone numbers are given in pairs, except for a case like 07, which would be said
zero sette.

per sapere l'ora . . .
pehr sa-PAY-ray LO-ra . . .
to know the time . . .

Che ora è?
Kay OH-ra ay?
What time is it?

È l'una.
Ay LOO-na.
It's one o'clock.

Che ora è? (or) Che ore sono?
In telling time, the feminine plural article *le* is
used with the noun meaning "the hour" —
l'ora — which is after one o'clock in the plural — *le ore*. However, the word *ore* is not said,
and all that remains is the article. In order to
say "it's one o'clock," the singular is used — *è
l'una*, for "its two o'clock" *sono le due* etc.
Most official times, such as train or plane
schedules, radio and TV announcements and
news bulletins, are given on a 24-hour system.
"At three in the afternoon" would be *alle
quindici*.

Sono le due.
SO-no lay DOO-ay.
It's two o'clock.

Sono le due e cinque. . . le due e dieci.
SO-no lay DOO-ay ay CHEEN-kway. . . lay DOO-ay ay D'YAY-chee.
It's five past two. . . ten past two.

Sono le due e un quarto.
SO-no lay DOO-ay ay oon KWAHR-toh.
It's a quarter past two.

Sono le due e venti . . . le due e venticinque.
**SO-no lay DOO-ay ay VEN-tee . . . lay DOO-ay ay
ven-tee-CHEEN-kway.**
It's twenty past two . . . twenty-five past two.

Sono le due e mezzo.
SO-no lay DOO-ay ay MEHDZ-so.
It's half past two.

Sono le due e trentacinque . . . le tre meno venti.
**SO-no lay DOO-ay ay tren-TA-CHEEN-kway . . . lay tray MAY-no
VEN-tee.**
It's twenty-five to three . . . twenty to three.

Sono le tre meno un quarto.
SO-no lay tray MAY-no OON KWAHR-toh.
It's a quarter to three.

Sono le tre meno dieci . . . le tre meno cinque.
**SO-no lay tray MAY-no D'YAY-chee . . . lay tray MAY-no
CHEEN-kway.**
It's ten to three . . . five to three.

Sono le tre.
SO-no lay tray.
It's three o'clock.

per fare appuntamenti . . .
pehr FA-ray ahp-poon-ta-MEN-tee . . .
To make appointments . . .

— Va bene per domani — alle cinque?
Va BAY-nay pehr doh-MA-nee — AHL-lay CHEEN-kway?
It is all right for tomorrow — at five?

— Come? A che ora?
KO-may? Ah kay OH-ra?
What? At what time?

— Alle cinque del pomeriggio.
AHL-lay CHEEN-kway del po-may-REEDJ-jo.
At five in the afternoon.

— Sì, come no — però dove?
See, KO-may no — pay-RO DOH-vay?
Yes, certainly — but where?

— Davanti alla Fontana di Trevi.
Da-VAHN-tee AHL-la Fohn-TA-na dee TRAY-vee.
In front of the Trevi Fountain.

— Benone. Però se non ci sono
Bay-NO-nay. Pay-RO say nohn chee SO-no
Very good. But if I'm not there

alle cinque in punto,
AHL-lay CHEEN-kway een POON-toh,
at exactly 5 o'clock,

mi aspetti, va bene?
mee ah-SPEHT-tee, va BAY-nay?
wait for me, all right?

INSTANT CONVERSATION: AT A UNIVERSITY

Un giovane parla con una giovane:
Oon JO-va-nay PAHR-la kohn OO-na JO-va-nay:
A young man speaks with a young woman:

> **Watch the article**
> Sometimes the same word is masculine or femi-
> nine. In such a case, you can tell its gender
> only by the article, as in *un giovane* and *una
> giovane.*

— Buon giorno, signorina.
Bwohn JOHR-no, seen-yo-REE-na.
Good morning, Miss.

Lei è una nuova studentessa qui, vero?
Lay ay OO-na NWO-va stoo-den-TESS-sa kwee, VAY-ro?
You are a new student here, right?

> **Si ricordi! (remember)**
>
> | | MASCULINE | FEMININE |
> |---|---|---|
> | student | lo studente | la studentessa |
> | professor | il professore | la professoressa |
> | doctor | il dottore | la dottoressa |
> | champion | il campione | la campionessa |

— Sì, è il mio primo anno qui.
See, ay eel MEE-oh PREE-ma AHN-no kwee.
Yes, it's my first year here.

— Molto bene. Io sono il segretario
MOHL-toh BAY-nay. EE-oh SO-no eel say-gray-TA-r'yo
Very good. I am the secretary

dell' Università.
del-loo-nee-vehr-see-TA.
of the University.

Easy to recognize
Many words ending in -*tà* have their English counterparts in "-ty" and are easily recognizable.

università — university
città — city
qualità — quality
quantità — quantity
libertà — liberty
unità — unity
nazionalità — nationality

These words are all feminine and in the plural they do not change: *le città* — "the cities."

Mario Bentrovato.
MAHR-yo Ben-tro-VA-toh.
Mario Bentrovato.

— Piacere, signore.
P'ya-CHAY-ray, seen-YO-ray.
Pleased to meet you, sir.

— Prego, qual'è il Suo nome e cognome?
PRAY-go, kwa-LAY eel SOO-oh NO-may ay kohn-YO-may?
Excuse me, what is your first and last name?

Qual'è?
When asking for telephone numbers, addresses, etc., *qual'è* . . . , literally "which is . . ." is frequently used instead of *che*, which is used directly with the noun: *che strada?* — "what street?," *che numero?* — "what number?"

— Lucrezia Rotolo.
Loo-KRAYTS-ya RO-toh-lo.
Lucrezia Rotolo.

— Grazie. E qual'è il Suo numero di telefono?
GRAHTS-yay. Ay kway-LAY eel SOO-oh NOO-may-ro dee tay-LAY-fo-no?
Thank you. And what is your telephone number?

— Il mio numero è 31-94-69.
**Eel MEE-oh NOO-may-ro ay tren-TOO-no, no-vahn-ta-KWAHT-tro,
sess-sahn-ta-NO-vay.**
My number is 31-94-69.

— Capito. E il Suo indirizzo?
Ka-PEE-toh. Ay eel SOO-oh een-dee-REETS-so?
Understood. And your address?

— Corso della Vittoria, numero 24.
KOHR-so DEL-la Veet-TOHR-ya, NOO-may-ro ven-tee-KWAHT-tro.
Avenue of Victory, number 24.

Terzo piano.
TEHRT-so P'YA-no.
Third floor.

— Benissimo. È tutto.
Bay-NEESS-see-mo. Ay TOOT-toh.
Very good. That's all.

Grazie, e a presto!
GRAHTS-yay, ay ah PRESS-toh!
Thank you, and until soon!

Un amico della giovane: Che tipo!
Oon ah-MEE-ko DEL-la JO-va-nay: Kay TEE-po!
A friend (male) of the young woman: What a character!

LA GIOVANE:
Non è un tipo.
No-NAY oon TEE-po.
He is not a character.

È il segretario
Ay eel say-gray-TAHR-yo
He is the secretary

dell' Università.
del-loo-nee-vehr-see-TA.
of the University.

37

L'AMICO:
Che bugiardo!
Kay boo-JAHR-doh!
What a liar!

Non è vero.
No-NAY VAY-ro.
That's not true.

È uno studente come tutti noi.
Ay OO-no stoo-DEN-tay KO-may TOOT-tee NO-ee.
He is a student like all of us.

For sound
Un becomes *uno* when used before a noun
starting with *z-* or with *s-* followed by a second
consonant.

Attenzione. . . .
Aht-tents-YO-nay. . . .
Be careful. . . .

TEST YOUR ITALIAN

Translate these sentences into English. Score 10 points for each correct answer. See answers below.

1. Quanto costa? _____

2. Seicento cinquanta lire, signore. _____

3. Chi parla? _____

4. Qual'è il Suo indirizzo? _____

5. Che ore sono? _____

6. Sono le tre meno un quarto. _____

7. Alle cinque del pomeriggio. _____

8. Qual'è il Suo nome e cognome? _____

9. Qual'è il Suo numero di telefono? _____

10. Non è vero. _____

SCORE _____%

Step 4   ITALIAN: LOCATING THINGS AND PLACES

Ecco alcuni esempi delle espressioni
EK-ko ahl-KOO-nee ay-ZEHM-pee DEL-lay ay-spress-YO-nee
Here are some examples of the expressions

c'è e *ci sono* (*vi sono*):
chay ay *chee SO-no* (*vee SO-no*):
"there is" and "there are":

— C'è qualcuno in quest'ufficio?
Chay kwahl-KOO-no een kway-stoof-FEE-cho?
Is there anyone in this office?

— Sì, c'è qualcuno.
See, chay kwahl-KOO-no.
Yes, there's somebody.

> **C'è, ci sono, vi sono**
> "There is" or "is there" is expressed by *c'è*
> and "there are" or "are there" by *ci sono* or *vi
> sono*. There is no difference in the use of *ci
> sono* and *vi sono*; you simply take your choice.

— Quante persone ci sono?
KWAHN-tay pehr-SO-nay chee SO-no?
How many people are there?

— Ci sono sette persone.
Chee SO-no SEHT-tay pehr-SO-nay.
There are seven people.

— Quante scrivanie ci sono nella camera?
KWAHN-tay skree-va-NEE-ay chee SO-no NEL-la KA-may-ra?
How many desks are there in the room?

40

Quanto?
"How much" and "how many" are both translated by the same word *quanto*, which changes according to the number and gender of the noun it modifies:

quanto denaro? — how much money?
quanta frutta? — how much fruit?
quanti uomini? — how many men?
quante donne? — how many women?

— Ci sono due scrivanie.
Chee SO-no DOO-ay skree-va-NEE-ay.
There are two desks.

— Quante sedie vi sono?
KWAHN-tay SAYD-yay vee SO-no?
How many chairs are there?

— Vi sono quattro sedie.
Vee SO-no KWAHT-tro SAYD-yay.
There are four chairs.

— Cosa c'è sul muro?
KO-za chay sool MOO-ro?
What is on the wall?

Su and its combinations
"On" is *su*, which combines with the article as follows:

su + il = *sul*
su + lo = *sullo* or *sull'* (before nouns beginning with a vowel)
su + la = *sulla* or *sull'* (before nouns beginning with a vowel)
su + i = *sui*
su + gli = *sugli* or *sugl'* (before nouns beginning with *i-*)
su + le = *sulle*

— Sul muro vi sono alcuni quadri
Sool MOO-ro vee SO-no ahl-KOO-nee KWA-dree.
On the wall there are some pictures

e un orologio.
ay oo-no-ro-LOHJ-jo.
and a clock.

— Ora sono le cinque e mezzo.
OH-ra SO-no lay CHEEN-kway ay MEHDZ-zo.
Now it's five thirty.

C'è qualcuno nell'ufficio?
Chay kwahl-KOO-no nel-loof-FEE-cho?
Is there anyone in the office?

— No, adesso non c'è nessuno.
No, ah-DESS-so nohn chay ness-SOO-no.
No, now there is nobody there.

A double negative
Notice that a literal translation of the above
would be "there isn't nobody there," as a double negative is not only permissible, but the only
correct way to use *nessuno* ("nobody") and
niente ("nothing") with a verb.

— C'è qualche cosa sul tavolo?
Chay KWAHL-kay KO-za sool TA-vo-lo?
Is there anything on the table?

— Sì, c'è qualche cosa.
See, chay KWAHL-kay KO-za.
Yes, there is something.

— Cosa c'è?
KO-za chay?
What is there?

Vi sono varie cose,
Vee SO-no VAHR-yay KO-zay,
There are various things,

dei fiori, della frutta, e una bottiglia di vino.
day F'YO-ree, DEL-la FROOT-ta, eh OO-na boht-TEEL-ya dee VEE-no
flowers, fruits, and a bottle of wine.

"Di" and its combinations

"Some" or "any" is formed by combining *di* with the definite article:

di + il = del
di + i = dei
di + l' = dell'
di + lo = dello
di + gli = degli
di + la = della
di + le = delle

della frutta — (some) fruit
del caffè — (some) coffee
delle matite — (some) pencils
dello zucchero — (some) sugar
dei fiori — (some) flowers

Remember that you must use the *di* and the article for this partitive construction. You cannot simply say — "flowers," "fruits," "coffee," etc. as in English.

C'è qualcosa sulla sedia?
Chay kwahl-KO-za SOOL-la SAYD-ya?
Is there anything on the chair?

No, non c'è niente — niente affatto.
no, nohn chay N'YEN-tay — N'YEN'tay ahf-FAHT-toh.
No, there is nothing — nothing at all.

C'è e ci sono sono utili
Chay ay chee SO-no SO-no OO-tee-lee
"There is" and "there are" are useful

per fare domande.
pehr FA-ray doh-MAHN-day.
for asking questions.

43

Per esempio:
Pehr ay-ZEHMP-yo:
For example:

Scusi, signore. C'è un buon
SKOO-zee, seen-YO-ray. Chay oon bwohn
Excuse me, sir. Is there a good

ristorante qui vicino?
ree-sto-RAHN-tay kwee vee-CHEE-no?
restaurant nearby?

Dov'é una banca?
DOH-vay OO-na BAHN-ka?
Where is there a bank?

Dov'é una farmacia?
DOH-vay OO-na fahr-ma-CHEE-ah?
Where is there a drug-store?

C'è un telefono pubblico qui?
Chay oon tay-LAY-fo-no POOB-blee-ko kwee?
Is there a public telephone here?

Dov'è una buca postale?
DOH-vay OO-na BOO-ka po-STA-lay?
Where is there a mailbox?

Altre espressioni:
AHL-tray ay-spresso-YO-nee:
Other expressions:

All'albergo:
Ahl-lahl-BEHR-go:
At the hotel:

Un viaggiatore: C'è una camera libera?
Oon v'yahd-ja-TOH-ray: Chay OO-na KA-may-ra LEE-bay-ra?
A traveler: Is there a room free?

Il direttore: Mi dispiace.
Eel dee-reht-TOH-ray: Mee dees-P'YA-chay.
The manager: I'm sorry.

Mi dispiace
Learn this phrase now as a complete idiomatic expression, in constant use. We will take up the reason for this construction in Step 13.

È tutto occupato.
Ay TOOT-toh oh-koo-PA-toh.
Everything is taken.

In casa:
Een KA-za:
At home:

Il ragazzo: C'è qualcosa da mangiare?
Eel ra-GAHTS-so: Chay-kwahl-KO-za da mahn-JA-ray?
The boy: Is there anything to eat?

"Da" = "from," "to," "for" etc.
Although *da* means "from," it has a variety of other idiomatic uses. Here it means "to" or "for," in the sense of "to eat" or "for eating."

Ho fame.
Oh FA-may.
I'm hungry.

"To have" instead of "to be"
In Italian, you literally say "I have hunger," instead of "I am hungry." The different "persons" of the verb *avere*, "to have," are:

io ho	— I have
Lei, egli, ella ha	— you (sing.), he, she, (it) has
noi abbiamo	— we have
Loro, loro hanno	— you (pl.), they have

La madre: Sì, c'è del pane, del burro.
La MA-dray: See, chay del PA-nay, del BOO-rro.
The mother: Yes, there is some bread, some butter.

e della carne nella cucina.
ay DEL-la KAHR-nay NEL-la koo-CHEE-na.
and some meat in the kitchen.

Il marito: Che c'è da bere?
Eel ma-REE-toh: Kay chay da BAY-ray?
The husband: What is there to drink?

Ho sete.
Oh SAY-tay.
I'm thirsty.

> **More on "avere" (to have)**
> Here is another case where the literal transla-
> tion would be "I have thirst," instead of "I am
> thirsty." The following expressions also use
> *avere:*
>
> *Ho fretta* — I'm in a hurry
>   *Ha fretta?* — Are you in a hurry?
> *Ho caldo* — I'm hot
>   *Ha caldo?* — Are you hot?
> *Ho freddo* — I'm cold
>   *Ha freddo?* — Are you cold?

C'è della birra e del vino.
Chay DEL-la BEE-rra ay del VEE-no.
There is some beer and some wine.

In ufficio:
Een oof-FEE-cho:
At the office:

Il capo: C'è qualcosa d'importante nella posta?
Eel KA-po: Chay kwahl-KO-za deem-pohr-TAHN-tay NEL-la PO-sta?
The boss: Is there anything important in the mail?

La segretaria: No, non c'è niente d'importante.
**La say-gray-TAHR-ya: No, nohn chay N'YEN'tay
                     deem-pohr-TAHN-tay.**
The secretary: No, there is nothing of importance.

Fra amici:
Fra ah-MEE-chee:
Among friends:

Paolo: Ciao! Che c'è di nuovo?
PA-oh-lo: Chow! Kay chay dee NWO-vo?
Paul: Hi! What's new?

Michele: Oh! Niente di straordinario.
Mee-kay-lay: Oh! N'YEN-tay dee stra-ohr-dee-NAHR-yo.
Michael: Oh! Nothing extraordinary.

Qualcosa d'importante
Di is used to introduce the following adjective in phrases like the above.

niente di nuovo. — nothing new.
qualcosa di buono. — something good
qualcosa d'importante — something important.
niente d'interessante — nothing interesting

47

INSTANT CONVERSATION: GETTING MAIL AND MESSAGES

UN SIGNORE:
Oon seen-YO-ray:
A GENTLEMAN:

La mia chiave, per favore.
La MEE-ah K'YA-vay, pehr fa-VO-ray.
My key, please.

Ho fretta.
Oh FREHT-ta.
I'm in a hurry.

Ci sono lettere per me?
Chee SO-no LEHT-tay-ray pehr may?
Are there letters for me?

> **The changing pronouns**
> When pronouns come *after* prepositions such as *per* — "for," *tra* or *fra* — "among" or "between," *io* becomes *me, egli* becomes *lui; ella* becomes *lei;* while *Lei, noi, loro* and *Loro* do not change.

UN IMPIEGATO:
Oo-neem-p'yay-GA-toh:
AN EMPLOYEE:

Sì, signore. Ci sono due lettere,
See, seen-YO-ray. Chee SO-no DOO-ay LEHT-tay-ray,
Yes, sir. There are two letters,

una cartolina postale
OO-na kahr-toh'LEE-na po-STA-lay
a postcard

e un pacco abbastanza grande.
ay oon PAHK-ko ahb-ba-STRAHND-za GRAHN-day.
and a rather large package.

Una delle lettere è dall'estero.
OO-na DEHL-lay LEHT-tay-ray ay dahl-LESS-tay-ro.
One of the letters is from abroad.

> **Da is combined with the article**
> *Da* is combined here with the word for
> "abroad," *l'estero.* It combines with the definite
> articles in the following way:
>
> *da + il* = *dal*
> *da + lo* = *dallo* or *dall'* (before nouns begin-
> ning with a vowel)
> *da + la* = *dalla* or *dall'* (before nouns begin-
> ning with a vowel)
> *da + i* = *dai*
> *da + gli* = *dagli* or *dagl'* (before nouns begin-
> ning with *i-*)
> *da + le* = *dalle*

I francobolli sono molto belli, no?
Ee frahn-ko-BOHL-lee SO-no MOHL-toh BEHL-lee, no?
The stamps are very beautiful, aren't they?

IL SIGNORE:
Sì, molto. Questo è tutto?
See, MOHL-toh. KWESS-toh ay TOOT-toh?
Yes, very. Is this all?

L'IMPIEGATO:
No, signore. Ci Sono due messaggi telefonici.
No, seen-YO-ray. Chee SO-no DOO-ay mess-SAHD-jee
                    tay-lay-FO-nee-chee.
No, sir. There are two telephone messages.

È tutto scritto su questo foglio.
Ay TOOT-toh SKREET-toh soo KWESS-toh FOHL-yo.
Everything is written on this sheet of paper.

IL SIGNORE:
Grazie. C'è altro?
GRAHTS-yay. Chay AHL-tro?
Thank you. Is there anything more?

L'IMPIEGATO:
No, signore. Non c'è altro.
No, seen-YO-ray. Nohn chay AHL-tro.
No, sir. There's nothing more.

IL SIGNORE:
Bene. E adesso, per favore,
BAY-nay. Ay ah-DESS-so, pehr fa-VO-ray,
Good. And now, please,

dieci francobolli da cento lire
D'YAY-chee frahn-ko-BOHL-lee da CHEN-toh LEE-ray.
ten one hundred lire stamps

> **"Da" as *at* or *of***
> Here *da* is used as "at" or "of" to describe the
> value of something.

e delle buste per posta aerea.
Ay DEHL-lay BOO-stay pehr PO-sta ah-AY-ray-ah.
and some air mail envelopes.

L'IMPIEGATO:
Subito, signore.
SOO-bee-toh, seen-YO-ray.
Right away, sir.

TEST YOUR ITALIAN

Translate these phrases into English. Score 10 points for each correct answer. See answers below.

1. C'è qualcosa da mangiare?

2. Sì, c'è del pane, del burro e della carne.

3. Che c'è da bere?

4. C'è della birra e del vino.

5. Che c'è di nuovo?

6. Oh, niente di straordinario.

7. La mia chiave, per favore.

8. Ci sono lettere per me?

9. Questo è tutto?

10. Non c'è altro.

Answers: 1. Is there anything to eat? 2. Yes, there is some bread, some butter and some meat. 3. What is there to drink? 4. There is some beer and some wine. 5. What is new? 6. Oh, nothing extraordinary. 7. My key, please. 8. Are there letters for me? 9. Is this all? 10. There is nothing more.

SCORE _____%

step 5

HOW TO USE THE PRESENT TENSE OF THE THREE VERB CONJUGATIONS

In italiano ci sono
Een ee-tahl-YA-no chee SO-no
In Italian there are

tre coniugazioni di verbi.
tray kohn-yoo-gahts-YO-nee dee VEHR-bee.
three conjugations of verbs.

To learn Italian through Italian
You will notice that in the first part of each step we frequently use Italian to explain verbs or other constructions. While this information is repeated more fully in the English notes, seeing it first in Italian is a more natural and direct approach and you will be learning Italian through the use of Italian. This will be of special value to you when you review without following the English text.

I verbi come *studiare, parlare,*
Ee VEHR-bee KO-may *stood-YA-ray, pahr-LA-ray,*
Verbs like "to study," "to speak,"

visitare, stare, ritornare e altri
vee-zee-TA-ray, STA-ray, ree-tohr-NA-ray **ay AHL-tree**
"to visit," "to stay," "to return" and others

sono verbi della prima coniugazione.
SO-no VEHR-bee DEL-la PREE-ma kohn-yoo-gahts-YO-nay.
are verbs of the first conjugation.

Verbs ending in "-are"
The first conjugation means the verbs whose infinitives end in -are, which are the majority of Italian verbs. All of these verbs have the same

52

present tense endings as *parlare* in Step 2. The appropriate endings are simply added to the stem of the verb after the *-are* is taken off. Here is *abitare* — "to live."

> *io abito* — I live
> *Lei, (egli, ella) abita* — you, he, she lives
> *noi abitamo* — we live
> *Loro, (loro) abitano* — you, they live

"He," "she," "it," "they"
In addition to *egli* and *ella* for "he" and "she," there are two other words equally used: *lui* for "he" and *lei* for "she." Although this *lei* for "she" could be easily confused with the *Lei* for "you" especially as it uses the same verb form, it is usually clear from the context. There is even a third set of "he" and "she" pronouns — *esso* and *essa* which form their plural in *essi* and *esse* respectively. These plurals can be used for "they" instead of *loro*.

Ecco degli esempi di questi verbi:
EK-ko DELL-yee ay-ZEHM-pee dee KWESS-tee VEHR-bee:
Here are some examples of these verbs:

Studio l'italiano
STOOD-yo lee-tahl-YA-no
I study Italian

ma lo parlo soltanto un poco.
ma lo PAHR-lo sohl-TAHN-toh oon PO-ko.
but I speak it only a little.

Visito Roma per la prima volta.
VEE-zee-toh RO-ma pehr la PREE-ma VOHL-ta.
I am visiting Rome for the first time.

Stiamo all' Albergo Nazionale.
ST'YA-mo ahl-lahl-BEHR-go Nats-yo-NA-lay.
We are staying at the National Hotel.

Dove abita Lei?
DO-vay AH-bee-ta Lay?
Where do you live?

Parla inglese?
PAHR-la een GLAY-zay?
Do you speak English?

Che cosa studiano quest' anno
Kay KO-za STOOD-ya-no kwess-TAHN-no
What are you studying this year

nella classe di musica?
NEL-la KLAHS-say dee MOO-zee-ka?
in the music class?

Studiamo la musica di Verdi.
Stood-YA-mo la MOO-zee-ka dee VEHR-dee.
We are studying the music of Verdi.

> **"Parlo," "I speak" or "I am speaking"**
> The present tense can also be translated by the
> progressive. *Studiamo* can mean either "we
> study" or "we are studying." The phrase *Chi
> parla?* — "Who is speaking?" is in constant
> use on the telephone.

Quando comincia il concerto?
KWAHN-doh ko-MEEN-cha eel kohn-CHEHR-toh?
When does the concert begin?

Fra poco. Entriamo.
Fra PO-ko. En-TR'YA-mo.
In a little while. Let's go in.

> **How to say "let's"**
> The present tense of the verb used with *noi* can
> have the sense of "let's (do something)." *An-
> diamo* — "let's go." *Parliamo* — "Let's talk."

Arriva molta gente, vero?
Ahr-REE-va MOHL-ta JEHN-tay, VAY-ro?
A lot of people are arriving, aren't they?

Sì, tutti aspettano l'entrata del direttore.
See, TOOT-tee ah-SPEHT-ta-no len-TRA-ta del dee-reht-TO-ray.
Yes, they are all waiting for the entrance of the conductor.

Ah, eccolo. Adesso cominciano.
Ah, EHK-ko-lo. Ah-DESS-so ko-MEEN-cha-no.
Ah, there he is. Now they are beginning.

> **There she is! = Eccola!**
> The masculine pronoun *lo* for "him" is attached
> to *ecco* and it becomes *eccolo* — "there he
> is." There are also *eccola* — "there she is,"
> *eccoli* — "there they (masc.) are," and *ec-
> cole* — "there they (fem.) are."

I verbi come *vivere, prendere, mettere,*
Ee VEHR-bee KO-may *VEE-vay-ray, PREN-day-ray, MEHT-tay-ray,*
Verbs like "to live," "to take," "to put,"

chiudere, vedere, perdere e altri
***K'YOO-day-ray, vay-DAY-ray, PEHR-day-ray* ay AHL-tree**
"to close," "to see," "to lose" and others

sono della seconda coniugazione.
SO-no DEL-la say-KOHN-da kohn-yoo-gahts-YO-nay.
are of the second conjugation.

> **Verbs ending in "-ere"**
> Verbs of the second conjugation form the pres-
> ent tense by dropping -ere from the infinitive
> and adding -o for *io*, -e for *Lei, egli, ella*, -iamo
> for *noi* and -ono for *Loro, loro, essi*, and *esse.*

	prendere	mettere	vivere
io	*prendo*	*metto*	*vivo*
Lei,			
(*egli,ella*)	*prende*	*mette*	*vive*
noi	*prendiamo*	*mettiamo*	*viviamo*
Loro, (*loro*)	*prendono*	*mettono*	*vivono*

Ecco alcuni esempi:
EK-ko ahl-KOO-nee ay-ZEHM-pee:
Here are some examples:

55

La signora Ricci vive a Roma.
La sccn-YO-ra REET-chee VEE-vay ah RO-ma.
Mrs. Ricci lives in Rome.

I suoi genitori vivono a Milano.
Ee swoy jay-nee-TO-ree VEE-vo-no ah Mee-LA-no.
Her parents live in Milan.

Oggi prende il treno per Milano
OHD-jee PREHN-day eel TRAY-no pehr Mee-LA-no
Today she is taking the train for Milan

con i suoi bambini.
kohn ee swoy bahm-BEE-nee.
with her children.

Prendono un tassì per la stazione.
PREHN-do-no oon tass-SEE pehr la stahts-YO-nay.
They take a taxi to the station.

L'autista mette le valige dentro
Lah-oo-TEE-sta MEHT-tay lay vah-LEE-jay DEN-tro
The driver puts the suitcases inside

e chiude lo sportello.
ay K'YOO-day lo spor-TEL-lo.
and closes the (car) door.

Ma la signora vede un grande orologio
Ma la seen-YO-ra VAY-day oon GRAHN-day oh-ro-LO-jo
But the lady sees a big clock

all'angolo di una strada.
ahl-LAHN-go-lo dee OO-na STRA-da.
at the corner of a street.

"È tardi. Presto, per favore,
"Ay TAHR-dee. PRESS-toh, pehr fa-VO-ray,
"It's late. Hurry, please,

o perdiamo il treno."
oh pehrd-YA-mo eel TRAY-no."
or we'll lose (miss) the train."

56

Nella terza coniugazione ci sono
NEL-la TEHRT-sa kohn-yoo-gahts-YO-nay chee SO-no
In the third conjugation there are

verbi come *partire, aprire, seguire,*
VEHR-bee KO-may *pahr-TEE-ray, ah-PREE-ray, say-GWEE-ray,*
verbs like "to leave," "to open," "to follow,"

finire, capire e *dire.*
fee-NEE-ray, ka-PEE-ray **ay** *DEE-ray.*
"to finish," "to understand" and "to say."

Verbs ending in "-ire"

The third conjugation includes verbs that end in -ire. Some of these verbs like *partire, aprire* and *seguire* have the same forms as those that we have examined in the second conjugation, but some of them such as *finire* and *capire,* although having the same endings, show a different spelling pattern when they are conjugated, characterized by the addition of -isc- to the stem.

finire	capire
finisco	capisco
finisce	capisce
finiamo	capiamo
finiscono	capiscono

Dire, although belonging to the third conjugation, is an irregular verb, meaning that it changes the spelling of its base.

io	dico
Lei, (egli, ella)	dice
noi	diciamo
Loro, (loro)	dicono

I turisti seguono la guida.
Ee too-REE-stee SAY-gwo-no la GWEE-da.
The tourists follow the guide.

Egli apre il cancello dei giardini.
ELL-yee AH-pray eel kan-CHEL-lo day jahr-DEE-nee.
He opens the gate of the gardens.

Tutti dicono: "Che bello!"
TOOT-tee DEE-ko-no: "Kay BEL-lo!"
They all say: "How beautiful!"

Ma alcuni non capiscono tutte
Ma ahl-KOO-nee nohn ka-PEE-sko-no TOOT-tay
But some don't understand all

le sue spiegazioni.
lay SOO-ay sp'yay-gahts-YO-nee.
his explanations.

Uno dice: "Più piano, per favore.
OO-no DEE-chay: "P'yoo P'YA-no, pehr fa-VO-ray.
One says: "More slowly, please.

Non capisco tutto."
Nohn ka-PEE-sko TOOT-toh."
I don't understand everything."

Un altro dice: "Quando finisce quest'escursione?"
Oo-NAHL-tro DEE-chay: "KWAN-doh fee-NEE-shay
                              KWESS-tess-koors-YO-nay?
Another one says: "When does this excursion end?

A che ora partiamo?"
Ah kay OH-ray pahrt-YA-mo?"
At what time do we leave?"

Dire è un verbo irregolare.
Dee-ray **ay oon VEHR-bo ee-rray-go-LA-ray.**
"To say" is an irregular verb.

Altri verbi irregolari sono
AHL-tree VEHR-bee ee-rray-go-LA-ree SO-no
Other irregular verbs are

andare, sapere, venire e *fare.*
ahn-DA-ray, sa-PAY-ray, vay-NEE-ray **ay** *FA-ray.*
"to go," "to know," "to come" and "to do."

Some irregular (and important) verbs

Although each of these verbs belongs to a conjugation, which means that they should follow the same pattern as the others, they all show certain irregularities as they are conjugated, and for this reason are called irregular verbs. How can you know when a verb is irregular? The answer is — you don't — You simply have to learn them through usage just as Italian children do when they learn their language. The main forms of these four verbs are as follows:

andare	sapere	venire	fare
vado	so	vengo	faccio
va	sa	viene	fa
andiamo	sappiamo	veniamo	facciamo
vanno	sanno	vengono	fanno

— Cosa fa quest'estate?
KO-sa fa kwess-tess-TA-tay?
What are you doing this summer?

— Faccio un viaggio in Italia.
FAHT-cho oon V'YAHD-jo een Ee-TAHL-ya.
I am making a trip to Italy.

— Va solo?
Va SO-lo?
Are you going alone?

— No, non vado solo.
No, nohn VA-doh SO-lo.
No, I'm not going alone.

Vengono anche mia moglie e i bambini.
VEN-go-no AHN-kay MEE-ah MOHL-yay ay ee bahm-BEE-nee.
My wife and children are coming also.

— Ah, tutti fanno il viaggio insieme!
Ah, TOOT-tee FAHN-no eel V'YAHD-jo eens-YAY-may!
Ah, you are all making the trip together!

È meglio così.
Ay MELL-yo ko-ZEE.
It's better like that.

— E Lei, sa quando va di nuovo in Italia?
Ay Lay, sa KWAN-doh va dee NWO-vo een Ee-TAHL-ya?
And you, do you know when you are going to Italy again?

— Non so. Presto, spero.
Nohn so. PRESS-toh, SPAY-ro.
I don't know. Soon, I hope.

INSTANT CONVERSATION: AN INVITATION TO THE MOVIES

— Buona sera, ragazze. Dove vanno?
BWO-na SAY-ra, ra-GAHTS-say. DO-vay VAHN-no?
Good evening, girls. Where are you going?

— Andiamo al cinema.
Ahnd-YA-mo ahl CHEE-nay-ma.
We're going to the movies.

— A che cinema vanno?
Ah kay CHEE-nay-ma VAHN-no?
To what movie theater are you going?

— Andiamo al Corso.
Ahnd-YA-mo ahl KOR-so.
We're going to the Corso.

— Che film danno oggi?
Kay feelm DAHN-no OHD-jee?
What movie are they giving today?

— Un nuovo film.
Oon NWO-vo feelm.
A new picture.

Dicono che è molto divertente.
DEE-ko-no kay ay MOHL-toh dee-vehr-TEN-tay.
They say it's very funny.

Non viene con noi?
Nohn V'YAY-nay kohn NO-ee?
Aren't you coming with us?

— Non so se ho tempo.
Nohn so say oh TEM-po.
I don't know if I have time.

Quando comincia?
KWAHN-doh ko-MEEN-cha?
When does it start?

Fra poco. Alle otto e mezzo.
Fra PO-ko. AHL-lay OHT-toh ay MEHDZ-zo.
Soon. At eight thirty.

Abbiamo quindici minuti per arrivare.
Ahb-B'YA-mo KWEEN-dee-chee mee-NOO-tee pehr ah-rree-VA-ay.
We have fifteen minutes to get there.

— E sanno quando finisce?
Ay SAHN-no KWAHN-do fee-NEE-shay?
And do you know when it ends?

— Finisce alle dieci e mezzo, più o meno.
Fee-NEE-shay AHL-lay D'YAY-chee ay MEHDZ-za, p'yoo oh
MAY-no.
It ends at ten thirty, more or less.

— Non è tardi.
No-NAY TAHR-dee.
It's not late.

Allora ho tempo.
Ahl-LO-ra oh TEM-po.
Then I have time.

Vengo con Loro, ma pago io i biglietti.
VEN-go kohn LO-ro, ma PA-go EE-oh ee beell-YEHT-tee.
I'll come with you, but I'll pay for the tickets.

— Ma che dice! Siamo troppi.
Ma kay DEE-chay! S'YA-mo TROHP-pee.
But what are you saying! We are too many.

Ognuno paga per sè.
Ohn-YOO-no PA-ga pehr say.
Each one pays for himself.

Masculine predominates (grammatically)
Although the group speaking with the generous young man is composed entirely of girls, they use the masculine form — *ognuno,* instead of the feminine form *ognuna,* because they're including the young man. No matter how many girls are in a group, if it includes just one man, the whole group, grammatically at least, is considered masculine.

TEST YOUR ITALIAN

Fill in the correct verb forms. Score 10 points for each correct answer. See answers below.

1. I am visiting Rome for the first time.
   _____ Roma per la prima volta.

2. I don't understand.
   Non _____.

3. Where do you live?
   Dove _____ Lei?
      (abitare)

4. Her parents live in Milan.
   I suoi genitori _____ a Milano.
              (vivere)

5. They take a taxi.
   _____ un tassì.

6. The turists follow the guide.
   I turisti _____ la guida.

7. At what time do we leave?
   A che ora _____?

8. I'm not going alone.
   Non _____ da solo.

9. What movie are they giving today?
   Che film _____ oggi?

10. Do you know when it ends?
    _____ quando _____?

SCORE ____%

step 6 FAMILY RELATIONSHIPS

La famiglia:
La fa-MEEL-ya:
The family:

marito e moglie
ma-REE-toh ay MOHL-yee
husband and wife

padre e figlio
PA-dray ay FEEL-yo
father and son

fratello e sorella
fra-TEL-lo ay so-REL-la
brother and sister

nonno e nipote
NOHN-no ay nee-PO-tay
grandfather and grandson

genitori e figli
jay-nee-TOH-ree ay FEEL-yee
parents and children

madre e figlia
MA-dray ay FEEL-ya
mother and daughter

nonni e nipoti
NOHN-nee ay nee-PO-tee
grandparents and grandchildren

nonna e nipote
NOHN-na ay nee-PO-tay
grandmother and granddaughter

This could lead to confusion
"Granddaughter" and "grandson" are both
translated by *nipote, Nipote* also means
"niece" or "nephew." Its meaning depends on
whether the article used with it is feminine.

Il signor Ragusa è un uomo d'affari.
Eel seen-YOHR Ra-GOO-za ay oon WO-mo dahf-FA-ree.
Mr. Ragusa is a businessman.

Ha il suo ufficio a Genova.
Ah eel SOO-oh oof-FEE-cho ah JAY-no-va.
He has his office in Genoa.

I Ragusa hanno due figli,
Ee Ra-GOO-za AHN-no DOO-eh FEEL-yee,
The Ragusas have two children,

> **No plural for family names**
> The family name does not change its form for
> the plural.

un figlio e una figlia.
oon FEEL-yo ay OO-na FEEL-ya.
a son and a daughter.

Suo figlio, Guglielmo, è studente.
SOO-oh FEEL-yo, Gool-YEL-mo, ay stoo-DEN-tay.
His son, William, is a student.

Va a scuola.
Va ah SKWO-la.
He goes to school.

Lucia, la sorella di Guglielmo,
Loo-CHEE-ah, la so-REL-la dee Gool-YEL-mo,
Lucy, William's sister,

studia arte.
STOOD-ya AHR-tay.
studies art.

È fidanzata.
Eh fee-dahnt-SA-ta.
She is engaged.

Il suo fidanzato è avvocato.
Eel SOO-oh fee-dahnt-SA-toh ay ahv-vo-KA-toh.
Her fiancé is a lawyer.

Il padre del signor Ragusa,
Eel PA-dray del seen-YOHR Ra-GOO-za,
Mr. Ragusa's father,

il nonno di Guglielmo e Lucia,
eel NOHN-no dee Gool-YEL-mo ay Loo-CHEE-ah,
William's and Lucy's grandfather,

è in pensione.
ay een pens-YO-nay.
is retired.

È un ex-ufficiale dell'Esercito.
Eh oo-NEHKS-oof-fee-CHA-lay del-eh-ZEHR-chee-toh.
He is a former officer of the Army.

In una famiglia ci sono anche
Een OO-na fa-MEEL-ya chee SO-no AHN-kay
In a family there are also

gli zii e le zie,
l'yee DZEE-ee ay lay DZEE-ay,
the uncles and the aunts,

i cugini e le cugine,
ee koo-JEE-nee ay lay koo-JEE-nay,
the cousins (masculine and feminine),

e anche
eh AHN-kay
and also

il suocero e la suocera,
eel SWO-chay-ro ay la SWO-chay-ra,
the father-in-law and the mother-in-law,

il cognato e la cognata,
eel kohn-YA-toh ay la kohn-YA-ta,
the brother-in-law and the sister-in-law,

il genero e la nuora.
eel JAY-nay-ro ay la NWO-ra.
the son-in-law and the daughter-in-law.

INSTANT CONVERSATION:
TALKING ABOUT ONE'S FAMILY

— È sposata Lei?
Ay spo-ZA-ta Lay?
Are you married?

— Sì; quel signore è mio marito.
See; kwel seen-YO-ray ay MEE-oh ma-REE-toh.
Yes; that gentleman is my husband.

— Quello con la barba?
KWEL-lo kohn la BAHR-ba?
The one with the beard?

> **Questo**
> *Questo* means "this one" or "the one near-by."
> *Quello* means "that one" or "the one over
> there." Both have the regular four forms of an
> adjective — masculine and feminine singular
> and plural:
>
> | | | | |
> |---|---|---|---|
> | *questo* | *questa* | *questi* | *queste* |
> | *quello* | *quella* | *quelli* | *quelle* |

— No, l'altro; quello coi baffi
No, LAHL-tro; KWEL-lo KO-ee BAHF-fee.
No, the other one; the one with the moustache.

> **Con**
> *Con* is frequently combined with the articles *il*
> and *i*. Thus,
>
> con *i* can also be *coi*
> con *il* can also be *col*
> con *gli* can also be *cogli*
>
> Unlike combinations of the definite articles with
> *su, di, a, in, da*, this combination is a matter of
> choice.

— Ha figli?
Ah FEEL-yee?
Do you have children?

— Ne abbiamo quattro,
Nay ahb-B'YA-mo KWAHT-tro,
We have four,

"Ne" è importantissimo
Ne is a very important and useful word, meaning "of it," "of them," "any" or "some," if the word referred to has already been mentioned. *Ne* is one of the little words that are in constant conversational use in Italian, and are sometimes considered bewildering to the student. Actually, if you remember that *ne* means any one of several things — and then fit in its appropriate meaning, there's really nothing to it.

tre figli e una figlia.
tray FEEL-yee ay OO-na FEEL-ya.
three sons and a daughter.

E Lei?
Ay Lay?
And you?

— Non ho figli — sono scapolo.
No-NO FEEL-yee — SO-no SKA-po-lo.
I don't have children — I'm a bachelor.

I Suoi figli sono qui?
Ee SWO-ee FEEL-yee SO-no kwee?
Are your children here?

— No. Uno vive in Inghilterra.
No. OO-no VEE-vay een Een-geel-TEHR-ra.
No. One lives in England.

When to capitalize
Nationalities are written in small letters. As you have noticed the word for "you" — *Lei is capitalized, while "I"* — *io* is written with a small letter. Even the possessive adjective for "your" — *Sou* — is written with a capital letter.

È sposato con un'inglese.
Ay spo-ZA-toh kohn oo-neen-GLAY-zay.
He is married to an English girl.

Gli altri ragazzi e la ragazza
L'yee AHL-tree ra-GAHTS-see ay la ra-GAHTS-sa
The other boys and the girl

sono ancora in collegio.
SO-no ahn-KO-ra een kohl-LAY-jo.
are still in boarding school.

Ecco una foto di loro.
EK-ko OO-na FO-toh dee LO-ro.
Here is a picture of them.

— Che bei ragazzi!
Kay bay ra-GAHTS-see!
What beautiful children!

Quanti anni hanno?
KWAHN-tee AHN-nee AHN-no?
How old are they?

How old are you?
In describing ages, *avere* is used:
Quanti anni ha? — "How old are you?"
(literally, "How many years have you?")
Ne ho 21 — "I am 21" (literally, "I have 21 of them")

— Pietro ha quattordici anni
P'YAY-tro ah kwaht-TOHR-dee-chee AHN-nee
Peter is fourteen years old

e Giorgio ne ha dodici.
ay JOHR-jo nay ah DOH-dee-chee.
and George is twelve.

The useful "ne"
As explained above, *ne* can be used as here when the item you're discussing — years, in this case — has already been mentioned.

E questa è Teresa.
Eh KWESS-ta ay Tay-RAY-za.
And this one is Teresa.

Ha quasi diciassette anni.
Ah KWA-zee dee-chass-SEHT-tay AHN-nee.
She is almost seventeen.

— Che bella!
Kay BEL-la!
How beautiful!

E che begli occhi!
Ay kay bell-YOHK-kee!
And what beautiful eyes!

The many forms of "bello"
Like other adjectives, *bello* changes gender and number to agree with the noun, but it differs from other adjectives in that it uses the forms of the definite articles. Observe:

bel — masculine singular
bello — masculine singular before nouns beginning with *z-*, or *s-* plus another consonant.
bella — feminine singular
bell' — masculine or feminine singular before nouns beginning with a vowel.
bei — masculine plural
begli — masculine plural before nouns beginning with *z-*, *sp*, *st*, or a vowel.
begl' — masculine plural before nouns beginning with *i-*.
belle — feminine plural

A che scuola vanno?
Ah kay SKWO-la VAHN-no?
What school do they go to?

— I ragazzi vanno a un collegio a Pisa.
Ee ra-GAHTS-see VAHN-no ah oon kohl-LAY-jo ah PEE-za.
The boys go to a boarding school in Pisa.

Però nostra figlia studia
Pe-RO NOSS-tra FEEL-ya STOOD-ya
But our daughter studies

in una scuola per ragazze, a Padova.
een OO-na SKWO-la pehr ra-GAHTS-say, ah PA-doh-va.
in a school for girls, in Padua.

Abbiamo parenti lì
Ahb-B'YA-mo pa-REN-tee lee
We have relatives there

È differente
Note the difference:

parents — *genitori*
relatives — *parenti*

e vive con loro.
ay VEE-vay kohn LO-ro.
and she lives with them.

— Veramente?
Vehr-ra-MEN-tay?
Really?

È contenta di stare tanto lontana
Ay kohn-TEN-ta dee STA-ray TAHN-toh lohn-TA-na
Is she happy to stay so far away

dai suoi genitori?
DA-ee SWO-ee jay-nee-TOH-ree?
from her parents?

— Come no!
KO-may no!
Of course!

È contentissima.
Ay kohn-ten-TEESS-si-ma.
She is very happy.

"Pianissimo" and other expressions
The ending *-issimo* (*-issima* for the feminine)
adds an intensive quality to an adjective.

bravissimo — very (extremely) good
fortissimo — very strong (or loud)
pianissimo — very slow (or soft)

— Senza dubbio parla molto bene l'italiano, vero?
SENT-sa DOOB-b'yo PAHR-la MOHL-toh BAY-nay lee-tahl-YA-no, VEHR-ro?
She undoubtedly speaks Italian very well, right?

— Certamente! Meglio di me.
Chehr-ta-MEN-tay! MEHL-yo dee may.
Certainly! Better than I.

"Di" can mean "than"
When a comparative adverb is used as here comparing how people do something or perform an action, "than" is translated by *di*. Also, after *di*, the personal pronoun changes as well, in the following way:

io becomes *me*
egli becomes *lui*
ella becomes *lei*

But *Lei, noi* and *Loro* don't change. The same is true of all prepositions.

davanti a me — in front of me
dietro di me — behind me
dietro di lui — behind him

— Però Lei parla italiano perfettamente.
Peh-RO Lay PAHR-la ee-tahl-YA-no pehr-feht-ta-MEN-tay.
But you speak Italian perfectly.

— Mille grazie.
MEEL-lay GRAHTS-yay.
A thousand thanks.

Lei è molto gentile.
Lay ay MOHL-toh jen-TEE-lay.
You are very kind.

Oh, ecco mio marito.
Oh, EK-ko MEE-oh ma-REE-toh.
Oh, here is my husband.

Probabilmente è ora di andare via.
Pro-ba-beel-MEN-tay ay OH-ra dee ahn-DA-ray VEE-ah.
It's probably time to leave.

Via!
Andare via — "to leave" or "to go off," is a useful idiom. *Andare* means simply "to go," but when *via* is added to it, it gives a sense of "to go away" or "to be off." *Via*, which is basically the word for "street," can mean "Go away!" or, more colloquially, "Beat it!"

TEST YOUR ITALIAN

Translate these sentences into Italian. Score 10 points for each correct translation. See answers below.

1. Are you (feminine) married?

_____

2. Yes; that gentleman is my husband.

_____

3. Do you have children?

_____

4. We have four — three sons and a daughter.

_____

5. What beautiful children!

_____

6. How old are they?

_____

7. She is almost seventeen.

_____

8. I am single.

_____

9. She is very happy.

_____

10. A thousand thanks.

_____

Answers: 1. È sposata Lei? 2. Sì; quel signore è mio marito. 3. Ha figli? 4. Ne abbiamo quattro — tre figli e una figlia. 5. Che bei ragazzi! 6. Quanti anni hanno? 7. Ha quasi diciassette anni. 8. Sono scapolo. 9. È contentissima. 10. Mille grazie.

SCORE _____%

75

THE ALPHABET —
READING — WRITING —
TELEPHONING

Quali sono le lettere
KWA-lee SO-no lay LEHT-tay-ray
What are the letters

dell'alfabeto italiano? Eccole:
del-lahl-fa-BAY-toh ee-tahl-YA-no? EHK-ko-lay:
of the Italian alphabet? Here they are:

A	B	C	D	E	F
ah	bee	chee	dee	ay	EHF-fay

G	H	I	L	M	N
jee	AHK-ka	ee	EL-lay	EM-may	EN-nay

O	P	Q	R	S	T
oh	pee	koo	EHR-rr	ESS-say	tee

U	V	Z
oo	vee	DZAY-ta

L'alfabeto italiano
Lahl-fa-BAY-toh ee-tahl-YA-no
The Italian alphabet

ha ventun lettere.
ah ven-TOON LEHT-tay-ray.
has twenty-one letters.

> The Italian alphabet has properly only 21 letters, although the missing letters j, k, w, x, and y are used in words of foreign origin.

L'alfabeto inglese ha
Lahl-fa-BAY-toh een-GLAY-zay ah
The English alphabet has

ventisei lettere.
VEN-tee-SAY LEHT-tay-ray.
twenty-six letters.

L'alfabeto italiano ha meno
Lahl-fa-BAY-toh ee-tahl-YA-no ah MAY-no
The Italian alphabet has fewer

lettere che l'alfabeto inglese.
LEHT-tay-ray kay lahl-fa-BAY-toh een-GLAY-zay.
letters than the English alphabet.

> Quante di meno? Cinque di meno.
> **KWAN-tay dee MAY-no? CHEEN-kway dee MAY-no.**
> How many less? Five less.

L'alfabeto inglese
Lahl-fa-BAY-toh een-GLAY-zay
The English alphabet

ha più lettere
ah p'yoo LEHT-tay-ray
has more letters

che l'alfabeto italiano.
kay lahl-fa-BAY-toh ee-tahl-YA-no.
than the Italian alphabet.

> Quante di più? Cinque di più.
> **KWAN-tay dee p'yoo? CHEEN-kway dee p'yoo.**
> How many more? Five more.

J, K, W,
ee-LOON-go, KAHP-pa, DOHP-p'ya VOO,
J, K, W,

X e Y non sono
eeks ay ee GRAY-ka nohn SO-no
X and Y are not

lettere italiane, ma sono
LEHT-tay-ray ee-tahl-YA-nay, ma SO-no
Italian letters, but they are

necessarie per scrivere
nay-chess-SAHR-yay pehr SKREE-vay-ray
necessary in order to write

nomi e parole straniere.
NO-mee ay pa-RO-lay strahn-YAY-ray.
foreign names and words.

L'italiano ha un accento scritto.
Lee-tahl-YA-no ah oon aht-CHEN-toh SKREET-toh.
Italian has a written accent.

Si scrive solamente sull'ultima
See SKREE-vay so-la-MEN-tay sool-LOOL-tee-ma
It is written only on the last

> **The impersonal "si"**
> *Si scrive* is impersonal and can mean "one
> writes," "you write," "we write," or "it is writ-
> ten," according to the text. It is similar in use to
> *si parla* — "one speaks" or "it is spoken,"
> which we examined in Step 2. Another useful
> expression with *si* is *si dice* — "one says" or
> "it is said."

sillaba della parola:
SEEL-la-ba DEL-la pa-RO-la:
syllable of the word:

così, città, quantità, università.
ko-ZEE, cheet-TA, kwan-tee-TA, oo-nee-vehr-see-TA.
thus, city, quantity, university.

— Scusi, signora. Come si chiama?
SKOO-zee, seen-YO-ra. KO-may K'YA-ma?
Excuse me, madam. What is your name?

> **How do you call yourself?**
> *Si chiama* means "you call youself" or "you are
> called." *Chiamare* is "to call"; *chiamarsi* — "to
> call oneself" is the regular word for "to be
> called" or "to be named." When the infinitive of
> a verb has a *-si* affixed to it in the place of the
> final *-e* of the infinitive, this means that this re-

flexive verb follows the pattern below. Here are the four basic forms of *chiamarsi:*

> *mi chiamo* — "my name is" or "I am called"
> *Si (si) chiama* "your (his, her) name is" or "you (he, she) is called"
> *ci chiamiamo* — "our name is" or "we are called"
> *Si (si) chiamano* — "your (their) name is" or "you (they) are called"

It would also be correct to say *il mio nome è —* "my name is," *il Suo (suo) nome è —* "your (his, her) name is," *i nostri nomi sono —* "our names are," and *il Loro (loro) nomi sono —* "your (their) names are," as either of the two choices would be correct.

— Mi chiamo Maria Dixon.
Mee K'YA-mo Ma-REE-ah DEEK-sohn.
My name is Maria Dixon.

— Come si scrive il Suo cognome?
KO-may see SKREE-vay eel SOO-oh kohn-YO-may?
How do you write your last name?

— Si scrive così:
See SKREE-vay ko-ZEE:
It's written this way:

D I X O N.
dee, ee, eeks, oh, EN-nay.
D I X O N.

— Come si chiamano questi signori?
KO-may see K'YA-ma-no KWESS-tee seen-YO-ree?
What are the names of these gentlemen?

— Essi si chiamano Roberto Della Valle
ESS-see see K'YA-ma-no Ro-BEHR-toh DEL-la VAHL-lay
Their names are Robert Della Valle

e Antonio Vittorini.
ay Ahn-TOHN-yo Veet-toh-REE-nee.
and Anthony Vittorini.

79

I loro nomi sono italiani.
Ee LO-ro NO-mee SO-no ee-tahl-YA-nee.
Their last names are Italian.

Come si chiama questo?
While on the subject of *chiamarsi,* learn this
useful question: "What is this called in Italian?"
Come si chiama questo in italiano?

Noi scriviamo lettere
NO-ee skreev-YA-mo LEHT-tay-ray
We write letters

ai nostri amici.
AH-ee NOSS-tree ah-MEE-chee.
to our friends.

Scriviamo il nome e l'indirizzo
Skreev-YA-mo eel NO-may ay leen-dee-REETS-so
We write the name and address

sulla busta,
SOOL-la BOO-sta,
on the envelope,

mettiamo la lettera dentro
meht-T'YA-mo la LEHT-tay-ra DEN-tro
we put the letter inside

e poi chiudiamo la busta.
ay poy k'yood-YA-mo la BOO-sta.
and then we close the envelope.

Dopo, vi mettiamo dei francobolli.
DOH-po, vee meht-T'YA-mo day frahn-ko-BOHL-lee.
After, we put stamps on it.

INSTANT CORRESPONDENCE:
A THANK-YOU NOTE
AND A POSTCARD

Una lettera a un amico:
OO-na LET-tay-ra ah oon ah-MEE-ko:
A letter to a friend:

Caro Roberto,
KA-ro Ro-BEHR-toh,
Dear Robert,

molte grazie per i fiori.
MOHL-tay GRAHTS-yay pehr ee F'YO-ree.
Many thanks for the flowers.

Sono bellissimi!
SO-no bel-LEESS-see-mee!
They are very beautiful!

Le rose gialle sono
Lay RO-zay JAHL-lay SO-no
Yellow roses are

i miei fiori perferiti.
ee m'yay F'YO-ree pray-fay-REE-tee.
my favorite flowers.

Grazie di nuovo.
GRAHTS-yay dee NWO-vo.
Thank you again.

A presto.
Ah PRESS-toh.
Until soon.

Affettuosi saluti, Lucia
Ahf-feht-T'WO-zee sa-LOO-tee, loo-CHEE-ya
Affectionate greetings, Lucia

Una cartolina postale a un'amica:
OO-na kahr-toh-LEE-na po-STA-lay ah oo-na-MEE-ka:
A post card to a friend:

The disappearing "a"
Amica is feminine, but when *una* is used with it, the *a* of *una* is dropped as *amica* also begins with an *a-*.

Cara Beatrice,
KA-ra BAY-ah-TREE-chay,
Dear Beatrice,

Tanti saluti da Palermo.
TAHN-tee sa-LOO-tee da Pa-LEHR-mo.
Many greetings from Palermo.

Tutto qui è molto bello.
TOOT-toh kwee ay MOHL-toh BEL-lo.
Everything here is very beautiful.

Il clima è magnifico
Eel KLEE-ma ay mahn-YEE-fee-ko
The climate is magnificent

e la gente è molto interessante.
ay la JEN-tay ay MOHL-toh een-tay-ress-SAHN-tay.
and the people are very interesting.

Ma Lei non è qui . . . che peccato!
Ma Lay no-NAY kwee . . . kay pehk-KA-toh!
But you are not here . . . what a shame!

Exclamations with "Che"
In addition to *che peccato!*, the following phrases will be useful to express your conversational reactions:

che fortuna! — what luck!
che sfortuna! — what a misfortune!
che bello! — how beautiful!
che brutto! — how ugly! how awful!
che strano! — how strange!
che gioia! — how great! how nice!
che meraviglia! — how marvelous!

Con affetto, Riccardo
Kohn ahf-FEHT-toh, Reek-KAHR-doh
Affectionately, Richard

TEST YOUR ITALIAN

Translate these sentences into English. Score 10 points for each correct translation. See answers below.

1. Molte grazie per i fiori.

2. Sono bellissimi!

3. Le rose gialle sono i miei fiori preferiti.

4. Grazie di nuovo.

5. A presto.

6. Tanti saluti da Palermo.

7. Tutto qui è molto bello.

8. Il clima è magnifico.

9. La gente è molto interessante.

10. Affettuosi saluti.

SCORE _____%

step 8

BASIC VERBS RELATING TO SENSES

Ecco degli altri
EK-ko dell-YAHL-tree
Here are some other

verbi molto importanti:
VEHR-bee MOHL-toh eem-pohr-TAHN-tee:
very important verbs:

vedere, guardare, leggere,
vay-DAY-ray, gwahr-DA-ray, LEHD-jay-ray,
"to see," "to look at," "to read,"

scrivere, ascoltare, sentire,
SKREE-vay-ray, ah-skohl-TA-ray, sen-TEE-ray,
"to write," "to listen to," "to hear,"

mangiare, bere e molti altri.
mahn-JA-ray, BAY-ray ay MOHL-tee AHL-tree.
"to eat," "to drink" and many others.

New verbs? Add the endings you already know.
By applying the verb endings which you learned in Step 5 according to the conjugation pattern, you will immediately be able to use the correct form of any new verb as it appears, unless it is irregular. The only verb in the group of infinitives that we have just given you which is irregular is *bere*, which goes as follows: *bevo, beve, beviamo, bevono.*

Vediamo con gli occhi.
Vehd-YA-mo kohn L'YOHK-kee.
We see with our eyes.

Io La vedo.
EE-oh La VAY-doh.
I see you.

Direct object pronouns
The direct object pronoun comes before the verb. "I see you" — *io La vedo*, is literally "I you see." For the negative, the *non* comes before the direct object pronoun. "I don't see you" — *non La vedo*. Here are the direct object pronouns:

me	— *mi*
him, it (masc.)	— *lo*
her, it (fem.)	— *la*
you	— *La*
us	— *ci*
you (m. pl.), them (masc.)	— *Li, li*
you (f. pl.), them (fem.)	— *Le, le*

Lei mi vede.
Lay mee VAY-day.
You see me.

Noi vediamo dei film.
NO-ee vehd-YA-mo day feelm.
We see some movies.

Guardiamo gli attori alla televisione.
Gwahrd-YA-mo ll'yaht-TOH-ree ahl-la tay-lay-veez-YO-nay.
We watch the actors on (the) television.

Leggiamo con gli occhi.
Lehd-JA-mo kohn L'YOHK-kee.
We read with our eyes.

L'uomo sta leggendo un giornale.
L'WO-mo sta lehd-JEN-doh oon johr-NA-lay.
The man is reading a newspaper.

The progressive
The present participle corresponds to the English ending "-ing." This ending is -*ando* for the first conjugation, and -*endo* for the second and

85

third. For the present progressive tense, we use the present of *stare* combined with the present participle of the verb.

sto ascoltando — I'm listening
ella sta scrivendo — she is writing
non stiamo leggendo — we are not reading
stanno mangiando — they are eating

But remember that in Italian, the present indicative can also be translated as the progressive. *Egli scrive* means "he writes" or "he is writing," but *egli sta scrivendo* is only "he is writing."

La donna non sta leggendo un giornale,
La DOHN-na nohn sta lehd-JEN-doh oon johr-NA-lay,
The woman is not reading a newspaper,

ma una rivista.
ma OO-na ree-VEE-sta.
but a magazine.

Scriviamo con una matita o con una penna.
Skreev-YA-mo kohn OO-na ma-TEE-ta oh kohn OO-na PEN-na.
We write with a pencil or a pen.

Io scrivo lettere a mano.
EE-oh SKREE-vo LEHT-tay-ray ah MA-no.
I write letters by hand.

La segretaria sta scrivendo
La say-gray-TAHR-ya sta skree-VEN-doh
The secretary is writing

una lettera a macchina.
OO-na LEHT-tay-ra ah MAHK-kee-na.
a letter on the typewriter.

Con le orecchie sentiamo
Kohn lay oh-REHK-k'yay sent-YA-mo
With our ears we hear

molti suoni e rumori differenti.
MOHL-tee SWO-nee ay roo-MO-ree deef-fay-REN-tee.
many different sounds and noises.

Ascoltiamo la radio.
Ah-skohlt-YA-mo la RAHD-yo.
We listen to the radio.

Ascoltiamo musica, notizie,
Ah-skohlt-YA-mo MOO-zee-ka, no-TEETS-yay,
We listen to music, news,

e avvisi pubblicitari.
ay ahv-VEE-zee poob-blee-chee-TA-ree.
and commercials.

Una signora sta cantando.
OO-na seen-YO-ra sta kahn-TAHN-doh.
A lady is singing.

La gente sta ascoltando.
La JEN-tay sta ah-skohl-TAHN-doh.
The people are listening.

Quando finisce, tutti dicono: "Brava!"
KWAHN-doh fee-NEE-shay, TOOT-tee DEE-ko-no: "BRA-va!"
When she finishes, they all say: "Brava!"

"Molto bene, eccellente!"
"MOHL-toh BAY-nay, eht-chel-LEN-tay!"
"Very good, excellent!"

"Come canta bene!"
"KO-may KAHN-ta BAY-nay!"
"How well she sings!"

Si respira col naso.
See ray-SPEE-ra kohl NA-zo.
We breathe with our nose.

Col naso si odora anche.
Kohl NA-zo see oh-DOH-ra AHN-kay.
We also smell with the nose.

Si mangia con la bocca e coi denti.
See MAHN-ja kohn la BOHK-ka ay KO-ee DEN-tee.
We eat with our mouth and our teeth.

> **More on the impersonal "si"**
> The impersonal *si* corresponds closely to the
> use of "one" as here, where it could be trans-
> lated as "one eats" or "we eat." We some-
> times translate the impersonal *si* as "one,"
> sometimes as "we," "you" or "they," so that
> you can appreciate and get accustomed to the
> flexibility of its use.

Mangiamo del pane, della carne,
Mahn-JA-mo del PA-nay, DEL-la KAHR-nay,
We eat bread, meat,

della verdura e della frutta.
DEL-la vehr-DOO-ra ay DEL-la FROOT-ta.
vegetables and fruit.

Beviamo del caffè, del tè, della birra,
Behv-YA-mo del kahf-FAY, del tay, DEL-la BEE-rra,
We drink coffee, tea, beer,

del vino . . . e dell'acqua.
del VEE-no . . . ay del-LAHK-kwa.
wine . . . and water.

Luigi non beve acqua, ma vino.
LWEE-jee nohn BAY-vay AHK-kwa, ma VEE-no.
Louis does not drink water, but wine.

Camminiamo e corriamo
Kahm-meen-YA-mo ay ko-RR'YA-mo
We walk and run

con le gambe e i piedi.
kohn lay GAHM-bay ay ee P'YAY-dee.
with the legs and the feet.

Questi ragazzi stanno correndo
KWESS-tee ra-GAHTS-see STAHN-no ko-RREN-doh
These boys are running

rapidamente, però i cani stanno
ra-pee-da-MEN-tay, pay-RO ee KA-nee STAHN-no
quickly, but the dogs are

correndo più rapidamente.
ko-RREN-doh p'yoo ra-pee-da-MEN-tay.
running more quickly.

Questi giovani stanno ballando.
KWESS-tee JO-va-nee STAHN-no bahl-LAHN-doh.
These young people are dancing.

Quando si balla, si muove tutto il corpo.
KWAHN-doh see BAHL-la, see MWO-vay TOOT-toh eel KOHR-po.
When we dance, we move the whole body.

Col corpo sentiamo delle sensazioni.
Kohl KOHR-po sen-TYA-mo DEL-lay sen-sahts-YO-nee.
With the body, we feel sensations.

Sentiamo il caldo e il freddo,
Sent-YA-mo eel KAHL-doh ay eel FRED-doh,
We feel heat and cold,

la fame e la sete,
la FA-may ay la SAY-tay,
hunger and thirst,

il dolore e il piacere.
eel doh-LO-ray ay eel p'ya-CHAY-ray.
pain and pleasure.

Ecco alcuni esempi dell'uso del pronome
EK-ko ahl-KOO-nee ay-ZEHM-pee del-LOO-zo del pro-NO-may
Here are some examples of the use of the pronoun

come oggetti del verbo.
KO-may ohd-JEHT-tee del VEHR-bo.
as objects of the verb.

Examples of object pronouns
This following account, using the direct pronoun objects, also reminds you that there is no separate pronoun form for "it." "It" uses the same

89

verb form as "he" and "she," and as an object, takes the pronoun "him" or "her," depending on the gender of whatever the "it" may be.

Giovanni è in campagna.
Jo-VAHN-nee ay een kahm-PAHN-ya.
John is in the country.

Guarda gli uccelli e gli alberi.
GWAHR-da ll'yoot-CHEL-lee ay LL'YAHL-bay-ree.
He looks at the birds and the trees.

Li guarda.
Lee GWAHR-da.
He looks at them.

Guarda le nuvole.
GWAHR-da lay NOO-vo-lay.
He looks at the clouds.

Le guarda.
Le GWAHR-da.
He looks at them.

Un toro sta mangiando dell'erba.
Oon TOH-ro sta mahn-JAHN-doh del-LEHR-ba.
A bull is eating grass.

La sta mangiando.
La sta mahn-JAHN-doh.
He's eating it.

Giovanni non vede il toro.
Jo-VAHN-nee nohn VAY-day eel TOH-ro.
John doesn't see the bull.

Non lo vede.
Nohn lo VAY-day.
He doesn't see it.

Però il toro vede Giovanni.
Pay-RO eel TOH-ro VAY-day Jo-VAHN-nee.
But the bull sees John.

Lo vede.
Lo VAY-day.
It sees him.

Giovanni sente il toro.
Jo-VAHN-nee SEN-tay eel TOH-ro.
John hears the bull.

Lo sente e lo vede.
Lo SEN-tay ay lo VAY-day.
He hears it and sees it.

Giovanni corre verso il recinto.
Jo-VAHN-nee KO-rray VEHR-so eel ray-CHEEN-toh.
John runs toward the fence.

Lo salta.
Lo SAHL-ta.
He jumps (over) it.

Giovanni è salvo. È contento.
Jo-VAHN-nee ay SAHL-vo. AY kohn-TEN-toh.
John is safe. He is happy.

Ma il toro non è contento.
Ma eel toh-ro nohn eh kohn-TEN-toh.
But the bull is not happy.

È scontento.
Ay skohn-TEN-toh.
He is dissappointed.

La "s" è importante

The letter s- at the beginning of a word often has a negative, or opposite, connotation:

piacevole	pleasant
spiacevole	unpleasant
gradevole	agreeable
sgradevole	disagreeable
apparire	to appear
sparire	to disappear
fortunato	fortunate
sfortunato	unfortunate

INSTANT CONVERSATION: AT A DISCO

MARCO:
MAR-KO:
MARK:

Vede quella ragazza?
VAY-day KWEL-la ra-GAHTS-sa?
Do you see that girl?

PIETRO:
P'YAY-tro:
PETER:

Come dice?
KO-may DEE-chay?
What are you saying?

> **"Dire" — "to say"**
> Dire is irregular in the present, which means
> that, although its endings are the same as other
> third conjugation verbs, its stem changes. The
> present tense of dire is dico, dice, diciamo,
> dicono.

Non La sento molto bene.
Nohn La SEN-toh MOHL-toh BAY-nay.
I don't hear you very well.

C'è molto rumore qui.
Chay MOHL-toh roo-MO-ray kwee.
There is a lot of noise here.

MARCO:

Vede quella giovane?
VAY-day KWEL-la JO-va-nay?
Do you see that young lady?

PIETRO:
Quale? Ne vedo molte.
KWA-lay? Nay VAY-doh MOHL-tay.
Which one? I see many.

MARCO:
Quella che sta vicino al microfono.
KWEL-la kay sta vee-CHEE-no ahl mee-KRO-fo-no.
The one who's near the microphone.

PIETRO:
La biondina che sta cantando
La b'yohn-DEE-na kay sta kahn-TAHN-doh
The blonde who's singing

o l'altra che sta suonando il piano?
oh LAHL-tra kay sta swo-NAHN-doh eel P'YA-no?
or the other one who's playing the piano?

MARCO:
No, quella carina, con i capelli neri.
No, KWEL-la ka-REE-na, kohn ee ka-PEL-lee NAY-ree.
No, the pretty one, with the black hair.

Porta un vestito rosso.
POHR-ta oon vay-STEE-toh ROHS-so.
She's wearing a red dress.

> **Che vestito porta?**
> *Portare* means "to carry" or "to wear," depending on how it is used.

PIETRO:
Quella che sta ballando
KWEL-la kay sta bahl-LAHN-doh
The one who's dancing

con quel vecchio?
kohn kwel VEHK-k'yo?
with that old fellow?

MARCO:
Sì, quella.
See, KWEL-la.
Yes, that one.

PIETRO:

È molto bella! E come balla bene!
Ay MOHL-toh BEL-la! Ay KO-may BAHL-la BAY-nay!
She's very beautiful! And how well she dances!

La conosce?
La ko-NO-shay?
Do you know her?

MARCO:

No, non la conosco. Sa chi è?
No, nohn la ko-NO-sko. Sa kee ay?
No, I don't know her. Do you know who she is?

"Conoscere" and "sapere"
Compare *conoscere* — "to know (a person) or
"to be familiar with something," and *sapere* —
"to know a fact" or "to know how to do something." The basic verb forms are as follows:

conosco	*so*
conosce	*sa*
conosciamo	*sappiamo*
conoscono	*sanno*

PIETRO:

No, non so chi è. Lei lo sa?
No, nohn so kee ay. Lay lo sa?
No, I don't know who she is. Do you know?

MARCO:

Macchè! Si capisce
Ma KAY! See ka-PEE-shay
Oh, come on! It's obvious

che non la conosco!
kay nohn la ko-NO-sko!
that I don't know her!

Perciò sto domandando!
Pehr-CHO sto doh-mahn-DAHN-doh!
That's why I'm asking!

PIETRO:

Va bene! Va Bene!
Va BAY-nay! Va BAY-nay!
All right! All right!

Vedo che Lei è molto interessato.
VAY-doh kay Lay ay MOHL-toh een-tay-ress-ah-to.
I see that you are very interested.

Andiamo a vedere il mio amico Peppino.
Ahnd-YA-mo ah vay-DAY-ray eel MEE-oh ah-MEE-ko Pep-PEE-no.
Let's go see my friend Peppino.

È uno che conosce tutti quanti.
Ay OO-no kay ko-NO-shay TOOT-tee KWAHN-tee.
He's one that knows everybody

TEST YOUR ITALIAN

Match these phrases. Score 10 points for each correct answer. See answers below.

1. I see you.

Sentiamo il caldo e il freddo.

2. You see me.

Vede quella ragazza?

3. We listen to the radio.

Non La sento molto bene.

4. We feel heat and cold.

Sa chi è?

5. Do you see that girl?

La conosce?

6. What are you saying?

Lei mi vede.

7. I don't hear you very well.

C'è molto rumore qui.

8. There's a lot of noise here.

Come dice?

9. Do you know her?

Io La vedo.

10. Do you know who she is?

Ascoltiamo la radio.

Answers: 4 5 7 10 9 8 2 6 9 1 3

SCORE _____%

step 9   PROFESSIONS AND OCCUPATIONS

Per sapere la professione di una persona
Pehr sa-PAY-ray la pro-fess-YO-nay dee OO-na pehr-SO-na
In order to know the profession of a person

o il posto che ha, diciamo:
oh eel PO-sto kay ah, dee-CHA-mo:
or the position which he has, we say:

"Dove lavora Lei?"
"DOH-vay la-VO-ra Lay?"
"Where do you work?"

o, "Qual'è la Sua professione?"
oh, "Kwa-LAY la SOO-ah pro-fess-YO-nay?"
or, "What is your profession?"

Shared words — English-Italian
Many Italian words ending in -*ione* are the same in meaning (though not in pronunciation) as English words ending in *"-ion."* They are all feminine, but form their plural by changing the final **-e** to **-i**. Here are some others:

unione	impressione
visione	occasione
sessione	discussione
dimensione	illusione
televisione	decisione

Eccone alcune:
EK-ko-nay ahl-KOO-nay:
Here are some of them:

Un uomo d'affari lavora in un ufficio.
Oo-NWO-mo dahf-FA-ree la-VO-ra ee-noo-noof-FEE-cho.
A businessman works in an office.

Gli operai lavorano nelle fabbriche.
L'yo-pay-RA-ee la-VO-ra-no NEL-lay FAHB-bree-kay.
The workers work in the factories.

I dottori curano i malati.
Ee doht-TOH-ree KOO-ra-no ee ma-LA-tee.
The doctors take care of the sick.

> **Curare**
> *Curare* means both "to take care of" and "to cure," a rather optimistic combination of meanings.

Gli attori e le attrici
L'-yaht-TOH-ree ay lay aht-TREE-chee
The actors and actresses

lavorano nel teatro o nel cinema.
la-VO-ra-no nel tay-AH-tro oh nel CHEE-nay-ma.
work in the theater or in the movies.

Un pittore dipinge quadri.
Oon peet-TOH-ray dee-PEEN-jay KWA-dree.
A painter paints pictures.

Un autore scrive libri.
Oo-na-oo-TOH-ray SKREE-vay LEE-bree.
An author writes books.

Un musicista suona il piano
Oon moo-zee-CHEE-sta SWO-na eel P'YA-no
A musician plays the piano

> **To ring (or) to play**
> *Suonare* means "to play (an instrument)" or "to ring," according to the context.
> *Suona il violino.* — She plays the violin.
> *Qualcuno sta suonando il campanello.* — Somebody is ringing the doorbell.

o qualche altro strumento.
oh KWAHL-kay AHL-tro stroo-MEN-toh.
or some other instrument.

Un meccanico fa delle riparazioni.
Oon mehk-KA-nee-ko fa DEL-lay ree-pa-rahts-YO-nee.
A mechanic makes repairs.

Un portalettere distribuisce la posta.
Oon pohr-ta-LEHT-tay-ray dee-stree-boo-EE-shay la PO-sta.
A mailman delivers the mail.

Un conducente guida un autobus o un tram.
Oon kohn-doo-CHEN-tay gwee-da ay oo-NA-oo-toh-booss oh oon trahm.
A driver drives a bus or a street-car.

> **Condurre**
> *Condurre* has an irregular *infinitive*. Its present tense is *conduco, conduce, conduciamo, conducono.*

Un autista di tassì guida tassì.
Oon ow-TEE-sta dee tass-SEE gwee-da tass-SEE.
A taxi driver drives taxis.

> **La città**
> Words which have a written accent on the last syllable do not change for the plural:
> *la città* — the city
> *le città* — the cities

I pompieri spengono incendi.
Ee pohmp-YAY-ree SPEN-go-no een-CHEN-dee.
Firemen put out fires.

> **Spegnere**
> *Spegnere* is irregular in the present. Its forms are *spengo, spegne, spegniamo, spengono.*

La polizia dirige ill traffico
La po-leet-SEE-ah dee-REE-jay eel TRAHF-fee-ko
The police directs the traffic

e arresta i criminali.
ay eh-RRAY-sta ee kree-mee-NA-lee.
and arrests criminals.

INSTANT CONVERSATION: AT A PARTY

— Che festa piacevole!
Kay FAY-sta p'ya-CHAY-vo-lay!
What a pleasant party!

— Sì. Gl'invitati sono molto interessanti.
See. L'-yeen-vee-TA-tee SO-no MOHL-toh een-tay-ress-SAHN-tee.
Yes. The guests are very interesting.

— È vero. La signora Facciolla
Ay VAY-ro. La seen-YO-ra Faht-CHOHL-la
It's true. Mrs. Facciolla

ha degli amici molto diversi.
ah DELL-ya-MEE-chee MOHL-toh dee-VEHR-see.
has some quite varied friends.

In quel gruppo lì,
Een kwel GROOP-po lee,
In that group over there,

> *Qui* and *qua* both mean "here," as *lì* and *là* mean "there." *Laggiù* means "over there," "down there," while "up there" is *lassù*.

vicino alla finestra,
vee-CHEE-no AHL-la fee-NAY-stra,
near the window,

c'è un avvocato, un compositore,
chay oo-nahv-vo-KA-toh, oon kohm-po-see-TOH-ray,
there is a lawyer, a composer,

un ingegnere, un architetto,
oo-neen-jehn-YAY-ray, oo-nahr-kee-TEHT-toh,
an engineer, an architect,

un dentista e un giocatore di calcio.
oon den-TEE-sta ay oon jo-ka-TOH-ray dee KAHL-cho.
a dentist and a football player.

— È un gruppo abbastanza vario.
Eh oon GROOP-po ahb-ba-STAHNTS-ah VAHR-yo.
It's quite a diverse group.

— Chissà di che stanno discutendo! ...
Keess-SA dee kay STAHN-no dee-skoo-TEN-doh! ...
Who knows what they're discussing! ...

> **Who knows?**
> *Chissà* originally was written *chi sa* — "who knows," but now is written together as one word. *Chissà* also means "perhaps."

Architettura, musica, legge ...
Ahr-kee-teht-TOO-ra, MOO-zee-ka, LEHD-jay ...
Architecture, music, law ...

— Il calcio, senza dubbio.
Eel KAHL-cho, SENT-sa DOOB-b'yo.
Football, no doubt.

> **Lo sport = sport**
> The football referred to is soccer, not American football.

— Sa chi è quella bella signora?
Sa kee ay KWEL-la BEL-la seen-YO-ra?
Do you know who that beautiful lady is?

Porta un vestito bellissimo.
POHR-ta oon ve-STEE-toh bel-LEESS-see-mo.
She's wearing a very beautiful dress.

— È un soprano dell'Opera.
Eh oon so-PRA-no del-LO-pay-ra.
She's a soprano from the Opera.

> **Masculine gender for a female person**
> Even though the soprano is a girl, the word *soprano* is a masculine noun, and therefore takes the masculine article and adjective.

Si chiama Laura Ardito.
See K'YA-ma LA-oo-ra Ahr-DEE-toh.
Her name is Laura Ardito.

— E i due signori che sono con lei?
Ay ee DOO-ay seen-YO-ree kay SO-no kohn lay?
And the two gentlemen who are with her?

Pronouns with prepositions
When pronouns are used as objects of prepositions, there are special forms, some of which
are different from the pronoun forms used as
objects of verbs. After prepositions such as *a,
con, per* and *da,* the following forms are used:

me	*me*
you	*Lei*
him	*lui*
her	*lei*
us	*noi*
you (pl.)	*Loro*
them	*loro*

— Il signore piuttosto anziano
Eel seen-YO-ray p'yoot-TOH-sto ahnts-YA-no
The rather elderly gentleman

è un critico d'arte,
ay oon KREE-tee-ko DAHR-tay,
is an art critic,

e quello più giovane e più attraente
ay KWEL-lo p'yoo JO-va-nay ay p'yoo ah-tra-YEN-tay
and the younger and better-looking one

è un attore.
ay oo-naht-TOH-ray.
is an actor.

Ma guardi chi sta entrando adesso.
Ma GWAHR-dee kee sta en-TRAHN-doh ah-DESS-so.
But look who is coming in now.

— È Alberto Di Sicone,
Ay Ahl-BEHR-toh Dee See-KO-nay,
It's Albert Di Sicone,

il famoso regista.
eel fa-MO-zo ray-JEE-sta.
the famous movie director.

— Davvero? C'è un articolo su lui
Dahv-VAY-ro? Chay oo-nahr-TEE-ko-lo soo LOO-ee
Really? There's an article about him

nel giornale di oggi.
nel johr-NA-lay dee OHD-jee.
in today's newspaper.

È molto bravo, non crede?
Ay MOHL-toh BRA-vo, nohn KRAY-day?
He's very good, don't you think?

— Certo. A proposito, lo conosco.
CHEHR-toh. Ah pro-PO-zee-toh, lo ko-NO-sko.
Certainly. By the way, I know him.

Andiamo a chiacchierare un poco con lui.
Ahnd-YA-mo ah k'yahk-k'yay-RA-ray oon PO-ko kohn LOO-ee.
Let's go chat a while with him.

TEST YOUR ITALIAN

Match these people to the work they do. Score 10 points for each correct answer. See answers below.

1. Un uomo d'affari	guida un autobus o un tram. (A)
2. I dottori	spengono incendi. (B)
3. Un pittore	distribuisce la posta. (C)
4. Gli operai	arresta i criminali. (D)
5. Un musicista	dipinge quadri. (E)
6. Un portalettere	suona il piano. (F)
7. I pompieri	lavorano nel cinema. (G)
8. Un conducente	lavora in un ufficio. (H)
9. La polizia	lavorano nelle fabbriche. (I)
10. Gli attori e le attrici	curano i malati. (J)

Answers: 1-H; 2-J; 3-E; 4-I; 5-F; 6-C; 7-B; 8-A; 9-D; 10-G.

SCORE _____%

step 10

HOW TO ASK AND GIVE DIRECTIONS — CAR TRAVEL

Ecco degli esempi
EHK-ko DELL-yee ay-ZEHM-pee
Here are some examples

del modo in cui dare degli ordini,
del MO-doh een KOO-ee DA-ray dell-YOHR-dee-nee,
of the way in which to give commands,

e anche dell'uso dei pronomi
ay AHN-kay del-LOO-zo day pro-NO-mee
and also of the use of pronouns

con gli ordini.
kohn L'-YOHR-dee-nee.
with orders.

L'uomo nell' automobile
L'WO-mo nel-la-oo-toh-MO-bee-lay
The man in the automobile

parla con un pedone.
PAHR-la kohn oon pay-DOH-nay.
speaks to a pedestrian.

Gli domanda: "È questa
L'-yee doh-MAHN-da: "Ay KWESS-ta
He asks him: "Is this

Indirect object pronouns

Gli — "to him" or "him," is an indirect object pronoun. Here are the others:

"me" or "to me"	— *mi*
"you" or "to you" (sing.)	— *Le*
"Him" or "to him"	— *gli*
"her" or "to her"	— *le*

"us" or "to us"	— *ci*
"you" or "to you" (pl.)	— *Loro*
"them" or "to them"	— *loro*

These indirect object pronouns come before the verb, with the exception of *Loro*, which always comes after the verb.

la via per Ostia?"
la VEE-ah pehr OHST-ya?"
the road for Ostia?"

Il pedone gli risponde:
Eel pay-DOH-nay l'yee-ree-SPOHN-day:
The pedestrian answers him:

"No, signore. Non è questa.
"No, seen-YO-ray. No-NAY KWESS-ta.
"No, sir. This is not it.

Continui diritto per due isolati ancora.
Kohn-TEE-nwee dee-REET-toh pehr DOO-ay ee-zo-LA-tee ahn-KO-ra.
Continue straight for two more blocks.

For giving orders
To give commands, simply change the *-a* ending of the first conjugation to *-i:*

> *Lei parla* — you speak
> *Parli!* — speak!

and, for the second and third conjugation, change the *-e* ending to *-a:*

> *Lei scrive* — you write
> *Scriva!* — write!
> *Lei sente* — you listen
> *Senta!* — listen!

However, when the *io* form of the verb ends in *-go* or *-co*, it keeps this form for the imperative, which then ends in *-ga* or *-ca*. Therefore, the imperatives for *uscire* — "to go out," *venire* — "to come," and *dire* — "to say," are *esca!*, *venga!*, and *dica!*. Other important exceptions are for *essere* — "to be," *andare* — "to go," fare — "to do," or "to make" and *avere* — "to have," whose imperatives are *sia, vada, faccia,* and *abbia.*

Poi volti a sinistra,
Poy VOHL-tee ah see-NEE-stra,
Then turn left,

fino al semaforo.
FEE-no ahl seh-MA-fo-ro.
up to the traffic light.

Poi prenda la destra.
Poy PREN-da la DESS-tra.
Then take a right.

Segua quella via. È la giusta.
SAY-gwa KWEL-la VEE-ah. Ay la JOO-sta.
Follow that road. It's the correct one.

Però faccia attenzione
Peh-RO FAHT-cha aht-tents-YO-nay
But watch out

alla polizia stradale."
AHL-la po-leet-SEE-ah stra-DA-lay."
for the highway police."

Il signore lo ringrazia,
Eel see-NYO-re lo reen-GRAHTS-ya,
The gentleman thanks him,

e continua per due isolati ancora.
ay kohn-TEE-nwa pehr DOO-ay ee-zo-LA-tee ahn-KO-ra.
and continues for two blocks more.

Poi prende la sinistra
Poy PREN-day la see-NEE-stra
Then he takes a left

e continua fino al semaforo.
ay kohn-TEE-nwa FEE-no ahl seh-MA-fo-ro.
and continues up to the traffic light.

Infine volta a destra.
Een-FEE-nay VOHL-ta ah DESS-tra.
Finally he truns right.

Però un poliziotto in motocicletta
Peh-RO oon po-leets-YOHT-toh een mo-toh-chee-KLEHT-ta
But a policeman on a motorcycle

lo segue. Lo ferma.
lo say-gway. Lo FEHR-ma.
follows him. He stops him.

Gli dice: "Alt!
L'yee DEE-chay: "Ahlt!
He tells him: "Stop!

Mi mostri la Sua patente."
Mee MO-stree la SOO-ah pa-TEN-tay."
Show me your license."

Il signore gli mostra la patente.
Eel seen-YO-ray l'yee MO-stra la pa-TEN-tay.
The gentleman shows him the license.

Il poliziotto gli domanda:
Eel po-leets-YOHT-toh l'yee doh-MAHN-dah:
The policeman asks him then:

"Perchè tanta fretta?
"Pehr-KAY TAHN-ta FREHT-ta?
"Why so much hurry?

Mi dia anche il Suo libretto di circolazione."
Mee DEE-ah AHN-kay eel SOO-oh lee-BREHT-toh dee
        cheer-ko-lahts-YO-nay."
Give me also your registration."

Il signore glielo da.
Eel seen-YO-ray L'YAY-lo da.
The gentleman gives it to him.

Position of pronoun objects
When two object pronouns are used in front of a verb, they follow the order of the indirect object pronoun used first and the direct object pronoun following. The indirect object pronoun "to him" and "to her" are written together with the direct object pronoun — *glielo, gliela.*

He tells it to him — *Glielo dice*

Object pronouns ending in *-i* change the *-i* to *-e* or add an *-e* when used with another pronoun before the verb.

Tell me	— *Mi dica*
Tell it to me	— *Me lo dica*
Give him	— *Gli dia*
Give it to him	— *Glielo dia*

Il poliziotto scrive una contravvenzione
Eel po-leets-YOHT-toh SKREE-vay OO-na kohn-trahv-vents-YO-nay
The policeman writes a summons

e la da al signore.
ay la da ahl seen-YO-ray.
and gives it to the gentleman.

Gli ridà anche la patente
L'yee ree-DA AHN-kay la pa-TEN-tay
He gives him back also the license

e il libretto di circolazione,
ay eel lee-BRET-toh dee cheer-ko-lahts-YO-nay,
and the registration,

dicendogli: — "Ecco qui!
dee-CHEN-doll-yee: — "EK-ko kwee!
telling him: — "Here you are!

E faccia più attenzione
Ay FAHT-cha p'yoo aht-tents-YO-nay
And pay more attention

Uses of "fare"

Fare — "to do" or "to make" is often used in idiomatic expressions:

fare attenzione	— to pay attention, or to be careful
fare un bagno	— to take a bath
fare una domanda	— to ask a question
fare la barba	— to shave
fare una passeggiata	— to take a walk

la prossima volta."
la PROSS-see-ma VOHL-ta"
the next time."

INSTANT CONVERSATION: GIVING ORDERS

UNA SIGNORA:
OO-na Seen-YO-ra:
A LADY:

Maria, non sente?
Ma-REE-ah, nohn SEN-tay?
Maria, don't you hear?

C'è qualcuno alla porta.
Chay kwahl-KOO-no AHL-la POHR-ta.
There is someone at the door.

Apra, per favore. Chi è?
AH-pra, pehr fa-VO-ray. Kee ay?
Open it, please. Who is it?

MARIA:
Ma-REE-ah:
MARIA:

È il garzone del
Ay eel gahrd-ZO-nay del
It's the boy from

negozio di generi alimentari
nay-GOHTS-yo dee GAY-nay-ree ah-lee-men-TA-ree
the grocery store

che viene a consegnarci i viveri.
kay V'YAY-nay ah kohn-sehn-YAHR-chee ee VEE-vay-ree.
who is coming to deliver the groceries to us.

Pronouns attached to the infinitive
When used with infinitives, object pronouns are added directly to the infinitive, which, in turn, drops its final -e before the pronoun is added.

Viene a verderci — He is coming to see us.

LA SIGNORA:
Bene. Li metta nel frigorifero.
BAY-nay. Lee MET-ta nel free-go-REE-fay-ro.
Good. Put them in the refrigerator.

E dica al ragazzo di lasciare il conto
Ay DEE-ka ahl ra-GAHTS-so dee la-SHA-ray eel KOHN-toh
And tell the boy to leave the bill

sul tavolo della cucina.
sool TA-vo-lo DEL-la koo-CHEE-na.
on the kitchen table.

Ecco la lista per domani.
EK-ko la LEE-sta pehr doh-MA-nee.
Here is the list for tomorrow.

La prenda e gliela dia, per cortesia.
La PREN-da ay L'YAY-la DEE-ah, pehr kohr-tay-ZEE-ah.
Take it and give it to him, please.

MARIA:
Sì, signora. Subito.
See, seen-YO-ra. SOO-bee-toh.
Yes, madam. Right away.

LA SIGNORA:
E adesso esco.
Ay ah-DESS-so AY-sko.
And now I am going out.

Vado prima al salone di bellezza,
VA-doh PREE-ma ahl sa-LO-nay dee bel-LEHTS-sa,
I am going first to the beauty parlor,

Nel salone di bellezza
The following will be useful for ladies when they
go to the beauty parlor (*il salone di bellezza*):

wash and set — *lavaggio e messa in piega*
too hot — *troppo caldo*
lighter — *più chiaro*
darker — *più scuro*
manicure — *una manicure*

Dal barbiere
And for men when they visit the barber's (*il
barbiere*):

a haircut — *mi tagli i capelli* (cut my hair)
not too short — *non troppo corti*
a shave — *mi faccia la barba*
a massage — *un massaggio*

e dopo vado a fare delle spese.
ay DOH-po VA-doh ah FA-ray DEL-lay SPAY-zay.
and then I am going shopping.

Nel frattempo, pulisca la casa
Nel fraht-TEHM-po, poo-LEE-ska la KA-za
Meanwhile, clean the house

e prepari il pranzo.
ay pray-PA-ree eel PRAHND-zo.
and prepare the dinner.

Ecco due vestiti, un gonna e un abito.
EK-ko DOO-eh vay-STEE-tee, OO-na GOHN-na ay oo-NA-bee-toh.
Here are two dresses, a skirt and a suit.

Li porti alla lavanderia a secco.
Lee POHR-tee AHL-la la-vahn-day-REE-ah ah SEHK-ko.
Take them to the dry cleaner's.

Diamine! Ancora il telefono . . .
D'YA-mee-nay! Ahn-KO-ra eel tay-LAY-fo-no . . .
Heavens! The telephone again . . .

Diamine!
Several mild Italian expletives of annoyance,
surprise or frustration have no exact translation
in English but, since you will hear them constantly, you should be able to recognize them
and pronounce them.

Here are some other expletives with their literal
meanings:

> *perbacco!* — by Bacchus!
> *santo cielo!* — holy heaven!
> *santa Madonna!* — holy Madonna!

Risponda, per favore . . . Chi è?
Ree-SPOHN-da, pehr fa-VO-ray . . . Kee ay?
Answer it, please . . . Who is it?

MARIA:
È il mio amico Giulio.
Ay eel MEE-oh ah-MEE-ko JOOL-yo.
It's my friend Giulio.

Mi invita a ballare per questa sera.
Mee een-VEE-ta ah bahl-LA-ray pehr KWESS-ta SAY-ra.
He's inviting me to a dance for tonight.

LA SIGNORA:
Ma abbiamo degl'invitati!
Ma ahb-B'YA-mo dell-yeen-vee-TA-tee!
But we have guests!

Bene. Vada pure. Ma prima ci serva il pranzo.
**BAY-nay. VA-da POO-ray. Ma PREE-ma chee SEHR-va eel
　　　　　　　　　　　　　　　　　　　PRAHND-zo.**
Well. Go ahead. But first serve us dinner.

TEST YOUR ITALIAN

Translate these imperatives into Italian. Where pronouns are used, gender is indicated. Score 5 points for each correct answer. See answers below.

1. Come here!	11. Give it to me! (mas.)
2. Continue straight!	12. Open it (fem.)
3. Don't go!	13. Close it! (mas.)
4. Turn right!	14. Take it! (fem.)
5. Turn left!	15. Carry them! (mas.)
6. Tell me!	16. Clean them! (mas.)
7. Show me!	17. Give it to him! (fem.)
8. Wait!	18. Put it here! (fem.)
9. Answer!	19. Do it! (mas.)
10. Pay attention!	20. Don't do it!

Answers: 1. Venga qui! 2. Continui diritto! 3. Non vada! 4. Volti a destra! 5. Volti a sinistra! 6. Mi dica! 7. Mi mostri! 8. Aspetti! 9. Rispondi! 10. Faccia attenzione! 11. Me lo dia! 12. La apra! 13. Lo chiuda! 14. La prenda! 15. Li porti! 16. Li pulisca! 17. Gliela dia! 18. La metta qui! 19. Lo faccia! 20. Non lo faccia!

SCORE _____%

115

HOW TO SAY "WANT," "CAN," "MAY," "MUST," AND "WOULD LIKE TO"

Un giovane vuole vedere
Oon JO-va-nay VWO-lay vay-DAY-ray
A young man wants to see

la partita di calcio,
la pahr-TEE-ta dee KAHL-cho,
the soccer game,

ma non può entrare.
ma nohn pwo en-TRA-ray.
but he can't get in.

Perchè non può entrare?
Pehr-KAY nohn pwo en-TRA-ray?
Why can't he get in?

Perchè non ha il biglietto d'entrata.
Pehr-KAY no-NA eel beel-YEHT-toh den-TRA-ta.
Because he doesn't have a ticket.

Perchè non ne compra uno?
Pehr-KAY nohn nay KOHM-pra OO-no?
Why doesn't he buy one?

Perchè non ha abbastanza denaro.
Pehr-KAY no-NA ahb-ba-STAHNT-sa day-NA-ro.
Because he doesn't have enough money.

Senza denaro non può vedere la partita.
SENT-za day-NA-ro nohn pwo vay-DAY-ray la pahr-TEE-ta.
Without money he cannot see the game.

Se vuole vederla, deve pagare.
Say VWO-lay vay-DEHR-la, DAY-vay pa-GA-ray.
If he wants to see it, he must pay.

Volere, potere, dovere

Volere — "to want," *potere* — "can" or "to be able to," and *dovere* — "must" or "to owe" can be used alone or, when they are used in conjunction with another verb, are followed by the infinitive. These three verbs are irregular in the present tense.

volere	potere	dovere
voglio	*posso*	*devo*
vuole	*può*	*deve*
vogliamo	*possiamo*	*dobbiamo*
vogliono	*possono*	*devono*

Ma ecco uno dei suoi amici:
Ma EK-ko OO-no day SWO-ee ah-MEE-chee:
But here is a friend of his:

Gli domanda: — Ho bisogno di duemila lire
**L'yee doh-MAHN-da: — Oh bee-ZOHN-yo dee
DOO-way-mee-la-LEE-ray**
He asks him: — I need two thousand lira

To need

Aver bisogno di means "to need" —
Abbiamo bisogno di sapone e di asciuga-mani — "We need soap and towels."

The verb *bisognare* usually means "to be necessary" or "must," and it is always used in the third person.

Bisogna andare via — "It is necessary to leave," or "I (you, he, she etc.) must leave."

per vedere la partita.
pehr vay-DAY-ray la pahr-TEE-ta.
to see the game.

Può prestarmele?
Pwo pray-STAHR-may-lay?
Can you lend them to me?

— Dipende ... Quando può ridarmele?
Dee-PEN-day ... KWAHN-doh pwo ree-DAHR-may-lay?
It depends ... When can you give them back to me?

— Oh, domani, certamente. Parola d'onore!
Oh, doh-MA-nee, chehr-ta-MEN-tay. Pa-RO-la doh-NO-ray!
Oh, tomorrow, certainly. My word of honor!

— La mia auto non può andare avanti.
La MEE-ya OW-toh nohn pwo ahn-DA-ray ah-VAHN-tee.
My car cannot go.

Per il Suo automobile
While on the subject of automobiles note the following key expressions:

Fill it — *Faccia il pieno*
Check the oil — *Verifichi l'olio*
Check the air — *Verifichi l'aria*
Check the battery — *Verifichi la batteria*
This is not working well — *Questo non funziona bene.*
Can you fix it? — *Lo può riparare?*
This tire must be changed — *Bisogna cambiare questa ruota.*
How long must we wait? — *Quanto tempo bisogna aspettare?*

— Non sa perchè?
Nohn sa pehr-KAY?
Don't you know why?

— Perchè non c'è benzina nel serbatoio.
Pehr-KAY nohn chay bend-ZEE-na nel sehr-ba-TOH-yo.
Because there's no gas in the tank.

Quando non c'è benzina nel serbatoio,
KWAHN-doh nohn chay bend-ZEE-na nel sehr-ba-TOH-yo,
When there's no gas in the tank,

il motore non può funzionare.
eel mo-TOH-ray nohn pwo foonts-yo-NA-ray.
the motor cannot function.

Bisogna metterci della benzina.
Bee-ZOHN-ya MEHT-tehr-chee DEL-la bend-ZEE-na.
One must put gas in.

Ci — una parola importante
Ci means "us" or "to us," but there is also another *ci,* spelled the same way, but a completely different word, which can substitute for a variety of prepositional phrases, of which just a few are "in it," "on it," "to it," "at it," "here," "there," and "to that place." *Ci* cannot substitute, however, for the prepositional phrases such as "from there," "from it," etc., or partitive phrases such as "of them," "of it," which are expressed by *ne.*

Are you going there? — *Ci va?*
No, I'm coming from there. — *No, ne vengo.*

— Dove si può comprare della benzina?
DOH-vay see pwo kohm-PRA-ray DEL-la bend-ZEE-na?
Where can one buy gas?

— Se ne può comprare a una stazione di servizio.
**Say nay pwo kohm-PRA-ray ah OO-na stahts-YO-nay dee
                                    sair-VEETS-yo.**
One can buy some at a gas station.

Ce n'è una qui vicino?
Chay nay OO-na kwee vee-CHEE-na?
Is there one nearby?

Words you didn't know you knew
Stazione is easily recognizable in English when you change the *-zione* ending to "-tion." This is true of hundreds of other Italian words ending in *-zione.* Although they are feminine, they form the plural in *-i* because their singular form already ends in *-e.*
Here are a few others:

emozione	*attenzione*
operazione	*occupazione*
informazione	*sensazione*
presentazione	*posizione*
adorazione	*rivoluzione*
conversazione	*nazione*

Due ragazze
DOO-ay ra-GAHT-say
Two young girls

sono in difficoltà.
SO-no een dee-fee-kohl-TA.
are in difficulty.

Un pneumatico della loro macchina è forato.
Oon pnay-oo-MA-tee-ko DEL-la LO-ro MA-kee-na ay fo-RA-toh.
A tire of their car is flat.

Esse non possono cambiare la ruota
Ay-say nohn PO-so-no kahm-B'YA-ray la roo'OH-ta
They cannot change the wheel

perchè non hanno un cricco.
pehr-KAY nohn AHN-no oon KREEK-ko.
because they haven't a jack.

Ma ecco un giovane
Ma EK-ko oon JO-va-nay
But here's a young man

che arriva in una macchina sportiva.
kay ah-RREE-va een OO-na MA-kee-na spor-TEE-va.
who arrives in a sports car.

Domanda loro: "Posso aiutare loro?"
Doh-MAHN-da LO-ro: "PO-so ah-yoo-TA-ray LO-ro?"
He asks them: "May I help you?"

"Certamente! Può lei prestarci un cricco?"
"Chehr-ta-MEN-tay Pwo lay pres-TAR-chee oon KREEK-ko?"
"Certainly! Can you lend us a jack?"

"Ma posso fare ancora di più," dice lui.
"Ma POHS-so FA-ray ahn-KO-ra dee p'yoo," DEE-chay LOO-ee.
"But I can do even more," he says.

"Posso cambiare la ruota io stesso."
"POHS-so kahm-B'YA-ray la roo'OH-ta EE-oh STESS-so."
"I can change the wheel myself."

INSTANT CONVERSATION:
A TV PROGRAM

FRANCO:

Che peccato! Stasera danno
Kay pehk-KA-toh! Sta-SAY-ra DAHN-no
What a shame! Tonight they're giving

un programma così interessante
oon pro-GRAHM-ma ko-ZEE een-tay-ress-SAHN-tay
such an interesting program

alla televisione. Ma, sfortunatamente,
AHL-la tay-lay-veez-YO-nay. Ma, sfohr-too-na-ta-MEN-tay,
on television. But, unfortunately,

non posso vederlo, perchè
nohn POHS-so vay-DEHR-lo, pehr-KAY
I can't see it, because

il mio apparecchio non funziona.
eel MEE-oh ahp-pa-REHK-k'yo nohn foonts-YO-na.
my set is not working.

Bisogna farlo riparare.
Bee-ZOHN-ya FAHR-lo ree-pa-RA-ray.
I must have it repaired.

To have something done
To have something done is expressed by *fare*
with the next verb in the infinitive. For your travels, this is especially useful in hotels.

Vuole far stirare questo?
Will you have this pressed?
Vuole far portare la colazione?
Will you have breakfast sent up?

121

Both cases use *fare* because you do not expect the person you are talking to to do it personally — but to have it done. As you may have noticed in the examples above, when *fare* is followed by an infinitive, it drops its final -*e*.

ALBERTO:

Ma perchè non chiama il servizio di riparazioni?
Ma pehr-KAY nohn K'YA-ma eel sehr-VEETS-yo dee
          ree-pa-rahts-YO-nee?
But why don't you call the repair service?

FRANCO:

A quale scopo? Lei sa
Ah KWA-lay SKO-po? Lay sa
What for? You know

che non possono mai venire subito.
kay nohn POHS-so-no MA-ee vay-NEE-ray SOO-bee-toh.
that they can never come right away.

Again — the double negative
Constructions with "never" — *mai*, take a double negative, literally "not never," the same as *niente* — "nothing," and *nessuno* — "nobody," in Step 4.

ALBERTO:

Allora, se vuole vedere tanto
Ahl-LO-ra, say VWO-lay vay-DAY-ray TAHN-toh
Then, if you want to see this program

questo programma, venga da me.
KWESS-toh pro-GRAHM-ma, VEN-ga da may.
so much, come to my house.

FRANCO:

Questo è molto gentile da parte Sua.
KWESS-toh ay MOHL-toh jen-TEE-lay da PAHR-tay SOO-ah.
That is very kind of you.

Ma non vorrei disturbarLa.
Ma nohn vo-RRAY dee-stoor-BAHR-la.
But I wouldn't want to bother you.

Vorrei — I would like
Vorrei is the conditional form of *volere*, which
we will take up at a later Step. We want to give
you, however, the first person form now, *vorrei*,
which is equivalent to "I would like," as a separate expression, as it is naturally much more
polite, in making your request known, to say "I
would like," instead of "I want."

ALBERTO:

Ma che dice! Che disturbo?
Ma kay DEE-chay! Kay dee-STOOR-bo?
What are you saying! What bother?

Anzi! Possiamo vedere il programma insieme!
AHNT-see! Pohs-YA-mo vay-DAY-ray eel pro-GRAHM-ma
eens-YAY-may!
On the contrary! We can see the program together!

A proposito! Che tipo di programma è?
A pro-PO-zee-toh! Kay TEE-po dee pro-GRAHM-ma ay?
By the way! What kind of a program is it?

FRANCO:

Come! Non lo sa? È il Festival di San Remo,
KO-may! Nohn lo sa? Ay eel FAY-stee-vahl dee Sahn RAY-mo,
What! Don't you know? It's the San Remo Festival,

con tutte le nuove canzoni di quest'anno!
kohn TOOT-tay lay NWO-vay kahnt-SO-nee dee kwess-TAHN-no!
with all the new songs of this year!

ALBERTO:

A che ora comincia?
Ah kay OH-ra ko-MEEN-cha?
At what time does it start?

FRANCO:

Alle nove precise.
AHL-lay NO-vay pray-CHEE-zay.
At nine o'clock exactly.

123

ALBERTO:

Allora, possiamo mangiare qualche cosa prima.
Ahl-LO-ra, poss-YA-mo mahn-JA-ray KWAHL-kay KO-za PREE-ma.
Then, we can eat something first.

Vuole tenermi compagnia a pranzo?
VWO-lay tay-NEHR-mee kohm-pahn-YEE-ah ah PRAHND-zo?
Would you like to keep me company at dinner?

FRANCO:

Volentieri! Ma vorrei invitarLa io.
Vo-lent-YAY-ree! Ma vo-RRAY een-vee-TAHR-La EE-oh.
Gladly! But I would like to invite you.

ALBERTO:

Ma no, La prego!
Ma no, La PRAY-go!
But no, not at all!

FRANCO:

Ma sì, insisto.
Ma see, een-SEE-sto.
But yes, I insist.

ALBERTO:

In questo caso, se insiste,
Een KWESS-toh KA-zo, say een-SEE-stay,
In that case, if you insist,

non posso rifiutare.
nohn POHS-so reef-yoo-TA-ray.
I can't refuse.

FRANCO:

Allora siamo d'accordo.
Ahl-LO-ra S'YA-mo dahk-KOHR-doh.
Then we're agreed.

Entriamo in questa piccola trattoria.
Entr-YA-mo een KWESS-ta PEEK-ko-la traht-toh-REE-ya.
Let's go in this small restaurant.

Trattoria — Ristorante
The difference between *ristorante* and *trattoria*
is that a *trattoria* is smaller and usually run by a
family. The food tends to be more "home style"
(*fatto in casa*).

Non è molto cara
No-NAY MOHL-toh KA-ra
It's not very expensive

e si mangia benissimo.
ay see MAHN-ja bay-NEESS-see-mo.
and one eats very well.

ALBERTO:
Bisogna mangiare
Bee-ZOHN-ya mahn-JA-ray
We must eat

un po' alla svelta,
oon po AHL-la ZVEL-ta,
somewhat in a hurry,

se non vogliamo perdere
se nohn voll-YA-mo PEHR-day-ray
if we don't want to miss

l'inizio del programma.
lee-NEETS-yo del pro-GRAHM-ma.
the beginning of the program.

Attenzione alla eccezione
Although we have pointed out that most words
ending in -a are feminine, there are some
exceptions.

Il programma — the program

TEST YOUR ITALIAN

Translate these phrases into English. Score 10 points for each correct answer. See answers below.

1. Ho bisogno di soldi.

2. Bisogna pagare.

3. Siamo d'accordo.

4. Vuole tenermi compagnia a pranzo?

5. Può prestarmi duemila lire?

6. Non vorrei disturbarLa.

7. Vorrei vedere la partita.

8. Venga da me.

9. Perchè non compra un biglietto?

10. Perchè non ha abbastanza denaro.

SCORE _____%

126

step 12   HOW TO USE REFLEXIVE VERBS

Il signor Capobianco si alza di buon'ora.
Eel seen-YOHR Ka-po-B'YAHN-ko see AHLT-sa dee bwo-NO-ra.
Mr. Capobianco gets up early.

Reflexive verbs and pronouns
Si alza and *si lava* are examples of reflexive verbs (*alzarsi* and *lavarsi*). You have already seen an example of a reflexive verb in Step 7 with *chiamarsi* — "to be named" or "to be called." Reflexive verbs are so called because the subject of the verb acts on itself, such "to get oneself up," "to wash oneself," "to dress oneself," etc. Here are the verbs *alzarsi* and *lavarsi*, with the reflexive pronouns:

mi alzo	*mi lavo*
si alza	*si lava*
ci alziamo	*ci laviamo*
si alzano	*si lavano*

Although the subject pronoun is frequently dropped, the reflexive pronoun is not — in other words, *io mi alzo* or *mi alzo* are equally correct.

Si lava i denti e la faccia,
See LA-va ee DEN-tee ay la FAHT-cha,
He washes (cleans) his teeth and his face,

e si fa la barba.
ay see fa la BAHR-ba.
and he shaves.

If you do it to yourself, it's reflexive.
Fare la barba is "to shave," as indicates a barber shaving someone, but "to shave oneself" is reflexive — *farsi la barba.*

Italian Step by Step

Poi si veste.
Poy see VAY-stay.
Then he gets dressed.

Un po' più tardi si alzano i bambini.
Oon po p'yoo TAHR-dee see AHLD-za-no ee bahm-BEE-nee.
A little later the children get up.

Si lavano, si pettinano i capelli
See LA-va-no, see PEHT-tee-na-no ee ka-PEL-lee
They wash themselves, comb their hair

> **Use the article**
> The possessive pronoun is generally not used in speaking of the parts of the body, but the definite article is used instead.
>
> *Mi lavo la faccia* — I wash my face

e si vestono in fretta.
ay see VAY-sto-no een FREHT-ta.
and get dressed quickly.

Quindi, si mettono a travola
KWEEN-dee, see MEHT-toh-no ah TA-vo-la
Then, they sit down at the table

per fare colazione.
pehr FA-ray ko-lahts-YO-nay.
to eat breakfast.

Per la prima colazione,
Pehr la PREE-ma ko-lahts-YO-nay,
For breakfast,

> **La prima colazione — La segunda colazione**
> Both "lunch" and "breakfast" are each called *la colazione*, although "breakfast" is sometimes *la prima colazione* to differentiate it from "lunch," which is sometimes called *la seconda colazione*. The main meal of the day is *il pranzo* — "dinner," whether served in the evening, or at midday, as it frequently is in Italian homes. "Supper" is *la cena*.

128

prendono del succo d'arancia,
PREN-doh-no del SOOK-ko da-RAHN-cha,
they take some orange juice,

e dei biscotti con una
ay day bee-SKOHT-tee kohn OO-na
and some cookies with a

tazza di caffellatte.
TAHTS-sa dee kahf-fel-LAHT-tay.
cup of coffee with milk.

Dopo la colazione, il signor Capobianco
DOH-po la ko-lahts-YO-nay, eel seen-YOHR Ka-poB'YAHN-ko
After breakfast, Mr. Capobianco

si mette il cappotto e il cappello
see MEHT-tay eel kahp-POHT-toh ay eel kahp-PEL-lo
puts on his coat and his hat

e va in ufficio.
ay va ee-noof-FEE-cho.
and goes to his office.

I bambini si mettono
Ee bahm-BEE-nee see MEHT-toh-no
The children put on

i cappotti e i berretti,
ee kahp-POHT-tee ay ee bay-RRET-tee,
their coats and their berets,

prendono le cartelle
PREN-doh-no lay kahr-TEL-lay
take their book bags

e vanno a scuola.
ay VAHN-no ah SKWO-la.
and go to school.

Adesso, la signora Capobianco
Ah-DESS-so, la seen-YO-ra Ka-poB'YAHN-ko
Now, Mrs. Capobianco

si sente stanca; si ricorica
see SEN-tay STAHN-ka; see ree-KO-ree-ka
feels tired; she goes to bed again

> **To go to bed**
> *Coricarsi* is "to go to bed," while *ricoricarsi*
> means "to go to bed again."

e subito si addormenta di nuovo.
ay SOO-bee-toh see ahd-dohr-MEN-ta dee NWO-vo.
and soon she falls asleep again.

In Italia la seconda colazione
Ee-nee-TAHL-ya la say-KOHN-da ko-lahts-YO-nay
In Italy lunch

si fa generalmente
see fa jen-nay-rahl-MEN-tay
is eaten in general

fra l'una e le tre.
fra LOO-na ay lay tray.
between one and three o'clock.

La maggior parte della gente
La mahd-JOHR PAHR-tay DEL-la JEN-tay
The majority of people

> **"Gente" = "people"**
> *Gente* — "people," is singular in Italian, al-
> though plural in English. *Gente* is a feminine
> word, even though it includes males as well.

spesso ritorna a casa per mangiare,
SPESS-so ree-TOHR-na ah KA-za pehr mahn-JA-ray,
often return home to eat,

e poi ritorna in ufficio nel pomeriggio.
ay poy ree-TOHR-na ee-noof-FEE-cho nel po-may-REED-jo.
and then return to the office in the afternoon.

I negozi chiudono usualmente
Ee nay-GOHT-see K'YOO-doh-no oo-soo-ahl-MEN-tay
The stores usually close

dall'una alle quattro.
dahl-LOO-na AHL-lay KWAHT-tro.
from one to four o'clock.

E poi riaprono
Ay poy ree-AH-pro-no
They then reopen

e rimangono aperti fino alle otto.
ay ree-MAHN-go-no ah-PEHR-tee FEE-no AHL-lay OHT-toh.
and remain open until eight.

Poi la gente torna a casa o
Poy la JEN-tay TOHR-na ah KA-za oh
Then the people return home or

a qualche ristorante o trattoria
ah KWAHL-kay ree-sto-RAHN-tay oh traht-toh-REE-ya
to some restaurant or "trattoria"

Altri prendono un caffe
AHL-tree PREN-doh-no oon kahf-FAY
Others take coffee

o un aperitivo
oh oon ah-pay-ree-TEE-vo
or an aperitive

in un caffè all'aperto
een oon kahf-FAY ahl-la-pehr-toh
in an open air café

per conversare con gli amici
pehr kohn-vehr-SAY-ray KOHN-l'yee ah-MEE-chee
in order to converse with friends

e per vedere passare la gente
ay pehr vay-DAY-ray pahs-SA-ray la JEN-tay
and to watch the people pass by

per il corso di sera.
pehr eel KOR-so dee SAY-ra.
along the avenue in the evening.

INSTANT CONVERSATION:
GOING TO A BUSINESS MEETING

— Faccia presto.
FAHT-cha PRESS-toh.
Hurry up.

Dobbiamo andarcene adesso.
Dohb-B'YA-mo ahn-DAHR-chay-nay ah-DESS-so.
We must leave now.

> **One verb — two attached pronouns**
> The infinitive *andarsene* — "to leave" or "to be
> off," is formed by *andare* plus *si* plus *ne*, all
> written together. The *ce* in *andarcene* is the re-
> flexive form for "us" — *ci*, which, like the *si*,
> changes to *ce*, as it is followed by *ne*.

Non volgliamo arrivare tardi
Nohn voll-YA-mo ah-rree-VA-ray TAHR-dee
We don't want to arrive late

alla riunione.
AHL-la ree-oon-YO-nay.
at the meeting.

— Non si preoccupi.
Nohn see pray-OHK-koo-pee.
Don't worry.

Abbiamo ancora una mezz'ora.
Ahb-B'YA-mo ahn-KO-ra OO-na mehdz-ZO-ra.
We still have a half hour.

Non vogliamo arrivare troppo presto.
Nohn voll-YA-mo ah-rree-VA-ray TROHP-po PRESS-toh.
We don't want to arrive too early.

— Vediamo — Lei s'incarica
Vehd-YA-mo — Lay s'een-KA-ree-ka
Let's see — You are taking charge

di portare i documenti, vero?
dee pohr-TA-ray ee doh-koo-MEN-tee, VAY-ro?
of bringing the documents, right?

— Sì; ecco la corrispondenza
See; EK-ko la ko-ree-spohn-DENT-sa
Yes; here's the correspondence

concernente il contratto.
kohn-chehr-NEN-tay eel kon-TRAHT-toh.
concerning the contract.

— Ma il contratto stesso?
Ma eel kohn-TRAHT-toh STESS-so?
But the contract itself?

Dio mio! Dov'è?
DEE-oh MEE-oh! Doh-VAY?
My God! Where is it?

— È Lei che ce l'ha.
Ay Lay kay chay la.
You're the one who has it (with you).

It sounds better
The *ce* in this sentence is the *ci* of location, generally used as a substitute for a prepositional phrase. As it is used before another pronoun, in this case *l'*, it becomes *ce*, which is easier to say and which sounds better, an outstanding characteristic of Italian.

— Ah, sì; ora mi ricordo.
Ah, see; OH-ra mee ree-KOHR-doh.
Ah, yes; now I remember.

Mi aspetti qui.
Mee ah-SPEHT-tee kwee.
Wait here for me.

Vado a cercare un tassì.
VA-doh ah chehr-KA-ray oon tass-SEE.
I'm going to get a taxi.

A short cut to the future
You can express plans in the future by the use of *andare a* plus the infinitive. "Tomorrow we are going to visit the vatican Museum" — *Domani andiamo a visitare il Museo del Vaticano.*

Although the regular future will not be presented until Step 17, this use of *andare a* will serve, in the meantime, as a good short cut to express the future actions.

— Non si disturbi.
Nohn see dee-STOOR-bee.
Don't bother.

Emotional states and reflexive verbs
Many of the reflexive verbs denote an emotional state one is undergoing. *Disturbarsi* — "to be bothered" or "to bother oneself with"; *preoccuparsi* — "to worry"; *calmarsi* — "to calm down"; *arrabbiarsi* — "to get angry"; *agitarsi* — "to become upset" or "nervous."

Me ne occupo io.
May nay OHK-koo-po EE-oh.
I'll take care of it.

Ecco: ce n'è uno che aspetta
EK-ko: chay nay OO-no kay ah-SPEHT-ta
Here you are: there is one waiting

giù, davanti all'entrata.
joo, da-VAHN-tee ahl-len-TRA-ta.
downstairs, in front of the entrance.

— Benone — Andiamo via dunque,
Bay-NO-nay — Ahnd-YA-mo VEE-ah DOON-kway,
Very good — Let's go then,

e subito.
ay SOO-bee-toh.
and quickly.

— Ma si calmi, caro amico!
Ma see KAHL-mee, KA-ro ah-MEE-ko!
But calm yourself, dear friend!

E soprattutto,
Ay so-praht-TOOT-toh,
and above all,

non si agiti
nohn see AH-jee-tee
don't get nervous

durante la riunione.
doo-RAHN-tay la ree-oon-YO-nay.
during the meeting.

TEST YOUR ITALIAN

Translate into Italian, using reflexive verbs. Score 10 points for each correct answer. See answers below.

1. They get up early.

2. He shaves (himself).

3. He washes his face.

4. She feels tired.

5. She falls asleep.

6. Don't worry.

7. Hurry up.

8. Don't get nervous.

9. Don't bother.

10. Calm yourself.

SCORE _____%

step 13

EXPRESSING PREFERENCES AND OPINIONS

Siamo alla spiaggia.
S'YA-mo AHL-la SP'YAHD-ja.
We are at the beach.

Tre ragazze
Tray ra-GAHTS-say
Three girls

sono sedute sulla spiaggia.
SO-no say-DOO-tay SOOL-la SP'YAHD-ja.
are sitting on the beach.

> **Seduto**
> There is no difference between ''sitting'' and
> ''seated.'' The word is *seduto*, modified by
> number and gender. ''Standing'' is translated
> by the phrase *in piedi*.

Non vogliono nuotare.
Nohn VOLL-yo-no nwo-TA-ray.
They do not want to swim.

L'acqua è fredda.
LAHK-kwa ay FREHD-da.
The water is cold.

Il sole è caldo.
Eel SO-lay ay KAHL-doh.
The sun is hot.

E preferiscono stare al sole.
Ay pray-fay-REE-sko-no STA-ray ahl SO-lay.
And they prefer to stay in the sun.

Una di loro porta
OO-na dee LO-ro POHR-ta
One of them is wearing

un costume da bagno rosso.
oon ko-STOO-may da BAHN-yo ROHS-so.
a red bathing suit.

Il costume dell'altra è verde.
Eel ko-STOO-may del-LAHL-tra ay VEHR-day.
The other's suit is green.

Masculine & feminine
Not all adjectives change for masculine and feminine. If an adjective ends in -e, like *verde*, it stays the same for the feminine, and the plural for masculine and feminine is -i, in such cases, — *verdi*. In like manner, a feminine noun ending in -e such as *canzone*, makes its plural with -i — *canzoni*. Although it has the masculine form, it is still feminine as far as the modifying adjectives are concerned.

Il bikini della terza è bianco.
Eel bee-kee-nee DEL-la TEHRT-sa ay B'YAHN-ko.
The bikini of the third one is white.

Il cielo è azzurro chiaro
Eel chay-lo ay ahdz-ZOO-rro K'YA-ro
The sky is light blue

con nuvole bianche.
kohn NOO-vo-lay B'YAHN-kay.
with white clouds.

Il mare è azzurro scuro.
Eel MA-ray ay ahdz-ZOO-rro SKOO-ro.
The sea is dark blue.

Davanti alle ragazze
Da-VAHN-tee AHL-lay ra-GAHTS-say
In front of the girls

alcuni giovanotti stanno suonando
ahl-KOO-nee jo-va-NOHT-tee STAHN-no swo-NAHN-doh
some young men are playing

la chitarra e cantando canzoni.
la kee-TA-rra ay kahn-TAHN-doh kahnd-ZO-nee.
the guitar and singing songs.

Le ragazze stanno ascoltando la musica.
Lay ra-GAHTS-say STAHN-no ah-skohl-TAHN-doh la MOO-see-ka.
The girls are listening to the music.

A loro piace sentire la musica,
Ah LO-ro P'YA-chay sen-TEE-ray la MOO-see-ka,
They like to listen to music,

Le piace? — Do you like it?
Piacere a — "to like" is a verb used with the indirect object. Here, the literal translation of "they like" is "it pleases them" — *piace loro* or *a loro piace.* The other forms are:

I like	*mi piace*	or	*piace a me*
he likes	*gli piace*	or	*piace a lui*
she likes	*le piace*	or	*piace a lei*
you like	*Le piace*	or	*piace a Lei*
we like	*ci piace*	or	*piace a noi*

As you can see, *piace* doesn't change, but, if what you like is plural, then *piace* becomes *piacciono.*

Do you like Italian women? —
Le piacciono le donne italiane?

When *di più* is added to this construction it means "to like more" or "to prefer":

Quale Le piace di più? —
Which do you like more? (or) Which do you prefer?

ed ai giovanotti piace suonare.
ay-DA-ee jo-va-NOHT-tee P'YA-chay swo-NA-ray.
and the young men like to play.

La ragazza bionda dice alla bruna:
La ra-GAHTS-sa B'YOHN-da DEE-chay AHL-la BROO-na:
The blonde girl says to the brunette:

"Cantano bene, non crede?"
"KAHN-ta-no BAY-nay, nohn KRAY-day?"
"They sing well, don't you think?"

"Certo," risponde la bruna.
"CHEHR-toh," ree-SPOHN-day la BROO-na.
"Certainly," answers the brunette.

"Cantano bene tutti quanti,
"KAHN-ta-no BAY-nay TOOT-tee KWAHN-tee,
"They all sing well,

però quello nel mezzo canta meglio di tutti."
pay-RO KWEL-lo nel MEHTS-so KAHN-ta MELL-yo dee
TOOT-tee."
but the one in the middle sings best of all."

Comparison of adverbs
Adverbs are compared by the use of *più*:
  piano — "slowly"
  più piano — "more slowly"
  più piano di tutti — "(the) most slowly of all"

Bene and male are irregular adverbs:
  bene — "well"
  meglio — "better"
  meglio di tutti — "(the) best of all"

  male — "badly"
  peggio — "worse"
  peggio di tutti — "(the) worst of all"

the ending *-issimo* can also be applied to adjectives and adverbs to mean "very" or "extremely":
  E bellissima — "she is very beautiful"
  interessantissimo! — "extremely interesting!"

"Si sbaglia," dice la bionda.
"See SBALL'ya," DEE-chay la B'YOHN-da.
"You are wrong," says the blonde.

"Quello a destra canta meglio."
"KWEL-lo ah DAY-stra KAHN-ta MELL-yo."
"The one on the right sings better."

Dopo un poco i giovanotti smettono di cantare.
DOH-po oon PO-ko ee jo-va-NOHT-tee SMEHT-toh-no dee
kahn-TA-ray.
After a while the young men stop singing.

Uno dice all'altro:
OO-no DEE-chay ahl-LAHL-tro:
One says to the other:

"Sono carine quelle ragazze, no?
"SO-no ka-REE-nay KWEL-lay ra-GAHTS-say, no?
"They are pretty, those girls, aren't they?

Mi piace di più la bruna."
Mee P'YA-chay dee p'yoo la BROO-na."
I like the dark one best."

"Macchè!" dice l'altro.
"Ma-KAY!" DEE-chay LAHL-tro.
"Don't be silly," says the other.

> **Macchè!**
> *Macchè!* is the equivalent of any of several idiomatic expressions, such as "don't be silly," "go on," "come off it," etc.

"la bionda è più carina della bruna."
"la B'YOHN-da ay p'yoo ka-REE-na DEL-la BROO-na."
"The blonde is prettier than the brunette."

> **Comparison of adjectives**
> Adjectives are compared by prefixing *più* for the comparative and *il più* or *la più* for the superlative.
>
> | big | bigger | the biggest |
> |---|---|---|
> | *grande* | *più grande* | *il più grande* |
> | small | smaller | the smallest |
> | *piccolo* | *più piccolo* | *il più piccolo* |

The two irregular comparisons are

good	better	the best
buono	*migliore*	*l'ottimo*
bad	worse	the worst
cattivo	*peggiore*	*il peggiore*

Paolo è più alto di Mario.—
Paul is taller than Mario.
Paolo è il più alto della classe.—
Paul is the tallest of the class.

Il terzo dice: "Non è vero!
Eel TEHRT-so DEE-chay: "No-NAY VAY-ro!
The third one says: "It is not true!

La rossa è la più carina di tutte."
La ROHS-sa ay la p'yoo ka-REE-na dee TOOT-tay."
The red-headed one is the prettiest of all.''

INSTANT CONVERSATION: SHOPPING

UNA SIGNORA:
OO-na Seen-YO-ra:
A LADY:

Dobbiamo comprare alcuni regali
Dohn-B'YA-mo kohm-PRA-ray ahl-KOO-nee ray-GA-lee
We have to buy some gifts

per gli amici e la famiglia.
pehr ll'ya-MEE-chee ay la fa-MEELL-ya.
for our friends and family.

Ecco un buon negozio. Entriamo?
EHK-ko oon bwohn nay-GOHTS-yo. Entr-YA-mo?
Here is a good store. Shall we go in?

LA COMMESSA:
La kohm-MESS-sa:
THE salesgirl:

Desidera, signora?
Day-SEE-day-ra, seen-YO-ra?
You wish, madam?

LA SIGNORA:

Per favore, ci mostri
Pehr fa-VO-ray, chee MO-stree
Please, show us

alcune sciarpe di seta.
ahl-KOO-nee SHAR-pay dee SAY-ta.
some silk scarves.

LA COMMESSA:

Eccone due, signora,
EK-ko-nay DOO-ay, seen-YO-ra,
Here are two, madam,

The partative "ne"
When the article is not mentioned, it is customary with numbers to use the partitive *ne*. The clerk could either say: *Ecco due.* — or *Eccone due.*

una nera e bianca
OO-na NAY-ra ay B'YAHN-ka
one black and white

e l'altra verde e blù.
ay LAHL-tra VEHR-day ay bloo.
and the other green and blue.

The adjective *blù* is not inflected. It is the same form for masculine and feminine singular and plural.

Le piacciono?
Lay p'YAHT-cho-no?
Do you like them?

LA SIGNORA:
Mi piace questa qui.
Mee P'YA-chay KWESS-ta kwee.
I like this one here.

I colori sono più vivaci,
Ee ko-LO-ree SO-no p'yoo vee-VA-chee,
The colors are more vivacious,

e il disegno è più bello.
ay eel dee-SEHN-yo ay p'yoo BEL-lo.
and the design is prettier.

Quanto costa?
KWAHN-toh KO-sta?
How much is it?

LA COMMESSA:
Duemila e novecentocinquanta lire, signora.
DOO-ay-MEE-la eh NO-vay-CHEN-toh cheen-KWAHN-ta LEE-ray,
                                  seen-YO-ra.
Two thousand and nine hundred fifty lire, madam.

LA SIGNORA:

Cielo! È abbastanza caro!
CHAY-lo! Ay ahb-ba-STAHNT-sa KA-ro!
Heavens! It is quite expensive!

Non ha qualcosa di meno caro?
No-NA kwahl-KO-za dee MAY-no KA-ro?
Don't you have something less expensive?

LA COMMESSA:

Sì, signora. Però non è di seta pura.
See, seen-YO-ra. Pay-RO no-NAY dee SAY-ta POO-ra.
Yes, madam. But it is not pure silk.

Come trova queste?
KO-may TRO-va KWESS-tay?
How do you find these?

Vengono in giallo, in rosa,
VEN-go-no een JAHL-lo, een RO-za,
They come in yellow, pink,

violetto e altri colori.
v'yo-LEHT-toh ay AHL-tree ko-LO-ree.
violet and other colors.

Ed in più, sono meno care,
Ed een p'yoo, SO-no MAY-no KA-ray,
And besides, they are less expensive,

duemila e mille e cinquecento lire.
DOO-way-MEE-la ay MEEL-ay ay cheen-kway-CHEN-toh LEE-ray.
two thousand and one thousand five hundred liras.

LA SIGNORA:

Non sono tanto belle
Nohn SO-no TAHN-toh BEL-lee
They are not as beautiful

> **Tanto**
> *Tanto* meaning "so" is used in negative comparisons.
>
> *non tanto caro* — not so expensive
> *non tanto buono* — not so good

145

quanto le altre.
KWAHN-toh lay AHL-tray.
as the others.

Comunque, compriamo questa violetta
Ko-MOON-kway, kohmpr-YA-mo KWESS-ta v'yo-LEHT-tah
However, let's buy this violet one

per la zia Isabella.
pehr la DZEE-ah Ee-sa-BEL-la.
for Aunt Isabel.

IL SIGNORE:
Il seen-YO-ray:
THE GENTLEMAN:
D'accordo. E adesso,
Dahk-KOHR-doh. Ay ah-DESS-so,
All right. And now,

> **D'accordo**
> *D'accordo*, literally "in accord," is a colloquial
> way of saying "all right," "agreed," or "okay."

che compriamo per la mamma?
kay kohmpr-YA-mo pehr la MAHM-ma?
what shall we buy for mother?

LA COMMESSA:
Guardi questa bella collana, signore.
GWAHR-dee KWESS-ta BEL-la kohl-LA-na, seen-YO-ray.
Look at this beautiful necklace, sir.

Costa solo dieci mila lire.
KO-sta SO-lo D'YAY-chee MEE-la LEE-ray.
It costs only ten thousand lire.

È molto bella, non Le pare?
Ay MOHL-toh BEL-la, nohn lay PA-ray?
It is very beautiful, don't you think so?

> **Non Le pare?**
> Other verbs, including *parere* — "to appear,"
> *sembrare* — "to seem," take the indirect object
> the same as *piacere*.

It seems to me that (or) I think that — *mi sembra che* (or) *mi pare che*

IL SIGNORE:
Sì, è vero.
See, ay VAY-ro.
Yes, that is true.

LA SIGNORA:
La compriamo, caro?
La kohmpr-YA-mo, KA-ro?
Shall we buy it, dear?

IL SIGNORE:
Sì, perchè no?
See, pehr-KAY no?
Yes, why not?

LA SIGNORA:
La prendiamo.
La prend-YA-mo.
We'll take it.

IL SIGNORE:
Ed ora, vorrei comprare
Ay-DOH-ra, vo-RRAY kohm-PRA-ray
And now, I would like to buy

e = ed
When followed by a vowel, *e* can be written as *ed* for purposes of euphony.

qualche cosa per la mia segretaria.
KWAHL-kay KO-za pehr la MEE-ah say-gray-TAHR-ya.
something for my secretary.

Quei grandi orecchini —
Kway GRAHN-dee oh-rehk-KEE-nee —
Those big earrings —

me li può mostrare?
may lee pwo mo-STRA-ray?
can you show them to me?

147

LA COMMESSA:

Certamente, signore.
Chehr-ta-MEN-tay, seen-YO-ray.
Certainly, sir.

Sono d'oro e sono molto belli.
SO-no DOH-ro ay SO-no MOHL-toh BEL-lee.
They are made of gold and are very beautiful.

LA SIGNORA:

Alfredo, per l'amor del cielo!
Ahl-FRAY-doh, pehr la-MOHR del CHAY-lo!
Alfred, for Heaven's sake! (lit: "for the love of heaven!")

Dropping the "e" for harmony
Italian has a tendency to drop the final -e of some words as well as verb infinitives to make the sentence more harmonious, as in this case, where *amore* is shortened to *amor*.

Non possiamo spendere
Nohn poss-YA-mo SPEN-day-ray
We cannot spend

tanto denaro in regali.
TAHN-toh day-NA-ro een ray-GA-lee.
so much money on presents.

In ogni caso, quegli orecchini
Ee-NOHN-yee KA-zo, KWELL-yee oh-rehk-KEE-nee
In any case, those earrings

non si possono portare nell'ufficio.
nohn see POHS-so-no pohr-TA-ray nel-loof-FEE-cho.
cannot be worn in the office.

La traduzione = "translation"
Literally translated, *non si possono portare* means "they cannot wear themselves," although the meaning is "they cannot be worn."

Perchè non comprare
Pehr-KAY nohn kohm-PRA-ray
Why not buy

quella spilla d'argento
KWEL-la SPEEL-la dahr-JEN-toh
that silver pin

nella forma della lupa romana?
NEL-la FOHR-ma DEL-la LOO-pa ro-MA-na?
in the shape of the Roman Wolf?

> **La lupa romana**
> The she wolf who was a foster mother to Rom-
> ulus and Remus, the legendary founders of
> Rome. A male wolf would be *lupo*.

È un bel ricordo di Roma,
Ay oon bel ree-KOHR-doh dee RO-ma,
It is a pretty souvenir of Rome,

ed è pratico ed originale.
ay-DAY PRA-tee-ko ehd oh-ree-jee-NA-lay.
and it is practical and original.

IL SIGNORE:
Va bene. Prendo la spilla.
Va BAY-nay. PREN-doh la SPEEL-la.
All right. I'll take the pin.

LA COMMESSA:
Signora, non vuole vedere gli orecchini?
Seen-YO-ra, nohn VWO-lay vay-DAY-ray l'yo-rehk-KEE-nee?
Madam, don't you want to see the earrings?

Sono molto belli, no?
SO-no MOHL-toh BEL-lee, no?
They are very lovely, no?

LA SIGNORA:
Sì, sono magnifici!
See, SO-no mahn-YEE-fee-chee!
Yes, they are magnificent!

Però suppongo che sono molto cari.
Peh-RO soop-POHN-go kay SO-no MOHL-toh KA-ree.
But I suppose that they are very expensive.

To suppose
Suppongo is from *supporre* and is conjugated the same as *porre*, another word for "to put." The forms of *porre* are *pongo, pone, poniamo, pongono*, while those of *supporre* are *suppongo, suppone, supponiamo, suppongono*. Related verbs, such as these, are easily recognizable, as only the prefix is different.

LA COMMESSA:

Abbastanza, però sono fra i migliori.
Ahb-ba-STAHNT-sa, peh-RO SO-no fra ee meell-YO-ree.
Quite, but they are among the best.

Valgono ventotto mila lire.
VAHL-go-no ven-TOHT-toh MEE-la LEE-ray.
They are worth twenty-eight thousand lire.

IL SIGNORE:

Non importa.
No-neem-POHR-ta.
It doesn't matter.

Li compro per mia moglie.
Lee KOHM-pro pehr MEE-ah MOLL-yay.
I will buy them for my wife.

LA SIGNORA:

Oh, che delizia!
Oh, kay de-LEETS-ya!
Oh, what a delight!

Grazie mille,
GRAHTS-yay MEEL-lay,
A thousand thanks,

amore mio.
ah-MO-ray MEE-oh.
my love.

Possessives after a noun
A possessive adjective can be used before or after the noun, when used after the noun, it has a more intensive meaning, as indicated here.

TEST YOUR ITALIAN

Fill in the verb forms. Score 10 points for each correct answer. See answers below.

1. Shall we go in?

   _____?

2. You wish, madam?

   _____, signora?

3. Do you like them?

   Le _____?

4. I like this one.

   Mi _____ questo.

5. Shall we buy it?

   Lo _____?

6. We'll take it.

   Lo _____.

7. Can you show them to me?

   Me li _____ _____?

8. I like the blonde one best.

   Mi _____ di più la bionda.

9. I would like to buy something.

   _____ _____ qualche cosa.

10. We have to buy some gifts.

    _____ _____ alcuni regali.

SCORE _____%

151

Una signora va al mercato.
OO-na seen-YO-ra va ahl mehr-KA-toh.
A lady is going to the market.

Va a comprare della carne,
Va ah kohm-PRA-ray DEL-la KAHR-nay,
She is going to buy meat,

dei legumi e della frutta,
day lay-GOO-mee ay DEL-la FROOT-ta,
vegetables and fruit,

> **Ricordi! — The use of the partitive**
> Remember that when you name lists of food or other things, you must always use the partitive, that is, *di* combined with the definite articles, whether "some" would be said in English or not:
> *del, dello, della, dell', dei, degli, delle.*

degli spaghetti, del pesce e del pane.
DELL-yee spa-GEHT-tee, del PAY-shay ay del PA-nay.
spaghetti, fish and bread.

Va prima dal macellaio.
Va PREE-ma dahl ma-chel-LA-yo.
She goes first to the butcher.

> **Da me**
> *Da* is used to express "at the house of" or "at the establishment of":
> *da me* — to (at) my house
> *da Roberto* — at (to) Robert's
> *dal verdumaio* — at (to) the greengrocers

Domanda al macellaio:
Doh-MAHN-da ahl ma-chel-LA-yo:
She asks the butcher:

"Ha del vitello ben tenero?"
"Ah del vee-TEL-lo ben TAY-nay-ro?"
"Have you some very tender veal?"

Il macellaio le risponde: "Certamente, signora.
Eel ma-chel-LA-yo lay ree-SPOHN-day: "Chehr-ta-MEN-tay,
seen-YO-ra.
The butcher replies: "Certainly, madam.

Quanti chili vuole?"
KWAHN-tee KEE-lee VWO-lay?"
How many kilos do you want?"

"Uno solo, per favore," dice la signora.
"OO-no SO-lo, pehr fa-VO-ray," DEE-chay la seen-YO-ra.
"Only one, please," says the lady.

Compra anche un pollo e delle bistecche.
KOHM-pra AHN-kay oon POHL-lo ay DEL-lay bee-STEHK-kay.
She also buys a chicken and some steaks.

Alla salumeria, compra del prosciutto.
AHL-la sa-loo-may-REE-ah, KOHM-pra del pro-SHOOHT-toh.
At the pork and sausage shop, she buys some ham.

An important suffix "-ia"
When a noun ends in -ia, it usually indicates a place where something is sold or where something is done.

> macelleria — butcher's
> pasticceria — pastry and cake shop
> latteria — shop for dairy products
> pescheria — fish market
> farmacia — pharmacy
> gioielleria — jewelry store
> lavanderia — laundry
> lavanderia a secco — dry cleaning
> trattoria — small restaurant

Poi va in un negozio di verdure
Poy va ee-NOON ne-GOHTS-yo dee vehr-DOO-reh
Then she goes into a vegetable store

per comprare delle patate,
pehr kohm-PRA-ray DEL-lay pa-TA-tay,
to buy some potatoes,

dei fagiolini verdi,
day fa-jo-LEE-nee VEHR-dee,
some green beans,

una lattuga e due chili di pomodori.
OO-na laht-TOO-ga ay DOO-ay KEE-lee dee po-mo-DOH-ree.
a lettuce and two kilos of tomatoes.

"Quant'è al chilo l'uva oggi?"
"Kwahn-TAY ahl KEE-lo LOO-va OHDJ-jee?"
"How much a kilo are grapes today?"

domanda al venditore.
doh-MAHN-da ahl ven-dee-TOH-ray.
she asks the vendor.

Compra anche delle pere,
KOHM-pra AHN-kay DEL-lay PAY-ray,
She also buys pears,

delle mele e delle pesche.
DEL-lay MAY-lay ay DEL-lay PAY-skay.
apples and peaches.

Nel negozio di generi alimentari,
Nel nay-GOHTS-yo dee JAY-nay-ree ah-lee-men-TA-ree,
At the grocery store,

compra degli spaghetti
KOHM-pra DELL-yee spa-GEHT-tee
she buys spaghetti

e dell'olio d'oliva.
ay del-LOHL-yo doh-LEE-va.
and olive oil.

Alla latteria, compra del latte,
AHL-la laht-tay-REE-ah, KOHM-pra del LAHT-tay,
At the dairy store, she buys milk,

del burro e una dozzina d'uova.
del BOO-rro ay OO-na dohdz-ZEE-na DWO-va.
butter and one dozen eggs.

Poi passa dal pescivendolo
Poy PAHS-sa dahl pay-shee-VEN-doh-lo
Then she goes to the fish vendor's

per comprare del baccalà
pehr kohm-PRA-ray del bahk-ka-LA
to buy codfish

e dei calamari.
ay day ka-la-MA-ree.
and small squids.

Infine, dal panettiere, domanda:
Een-FEE-nay, dahl pa-neht-T'YAY-ray, doh-MAHN-da:
Finally, at the baker's, she asks:

"Ha dei filoni ben freschi?"
"Ah day fee-LO-nee ben FRAY-skee?"
"Do you have very fresh loaves?"

Il panettiere risponde: "Come no, signora!
Eel pa-neht-T'YAY-ray ree-SPOHN-day: "KO-may no, seen-YO-ra!
The baker answers: "Certainly, madam!

Il nostro pane è sempre fresco."
Eel NO-stro PA-nay ay SEHM-pray FRAY-sko."
Our bread is always fresh."

Dopo la spesa, la signora ritorna a casa
DOH-po la SPAY-sa, la seen-YO-ra ree-TOHR-na ah KA-za
After shopping, the lady goes back home

con la macchina piena di pacchetti
kohn la MAHK-kee-na P'YAY-na dee pahk-KET-tee
with the car full of packages

e con cibo sufficente
ay kohn CEE-bo soof-fee-CHEN-tay
and with enough food

per una settimana.
pehr OO-na set-tee-MA-na.
for a week.

INSTANT CONVERSATION: IN A RESTAURANT

UN CLIENTE:
Oon klee-YEN-tay:
A CUSTOMER:
È libero questo tavolo?
Ay LEE-bay-ro KWESS-toh TA-vo-lo?
Is this table free?

UNA CAMERIERE:
OO-na ka-mehr-YAY-ray:
A WAITER:
Sissignore! Si accomodi, prego.
Sees-seen-YO-ray! See ahk-KO-mo-dee, PRAY-go.
Yes, sir! Sit down, please.

Ecco il menù.
EK-ko eel meh-NOO.
Here is the menu.

IL CLIENTE:
Grazie. Per cominciare vorrei
GRAHTS-yay. Pehr ko-meen-CHA-ray vo-RRAY
Thank you. To begin I would like

degli antipasti vari.
dell-yahn-tee-PA-stee VA-ree.
some assorted appetizers.

IL CAMERIERE:
Niente zuppa?
N'YEN-tay DZOOP-pa?
No soup?

157

Niente

Niente — "nothing," can be used for "no" in the partitive, as if it were, "nothing for soup?" And, in the unlikely case that you would not want any delicious Italian desserts (*dolci*) you can use *niente affatto* — "nothing at all"

Abbiamo un eccellente minestrone.
Ahb-B'YA-mo oo-neht-chel-LEN-tay mee-nay-STRO-nay.
We have an excellent minestrone soup.

IL CLIENTE:

Grazie, niente zuppa. Invece,
GRAHTS-yay, N'YEN-tay DZOOP-pa. Een-VAY-chay,
Thank you, no soup. Instead,

prendo un piatto
PREN-doh oon P'YAHT-toh
I will take a plate

di spaghetti alle vongole.
dee spa-GEHT-tee AHL-lay VOHN-go-lay.
of spaghetti with mussels.

E come secondo, che cos'hanno?
Ay KO-may say-KOHN-doh, kay ko-ZAHN-no?
And as a second (course) what do you have?

IL CAMERIERE:

Oggi raccomandiamo
OHDJ-jee rahk-ko-mahnd-YA-mo
Today we recommend

pollo alla cacciatora,
POHL-lo AHL-la kaht-cha-TOH-ra,
"Hunters" chicken,

o cotoletta alla milanese.
oh ko-toh-LET-ta AHL-la mee-la-NAY-zay.
or (a) cutlet "Milanese."

IL CLIENTE:

Che cosa sono i cannelloni alla romana?
Kay KO-za SO-no ee kahn-nel-LO-nee AHL-la ro-MA-na?
What are cannelloni Roman style?

Come viene preparato?
As Italy has such a variety of special dishes, it
is not unusual even for Italians to ask explanations about the menu, such as:

What is it? — *Che cos'è?,*
Che cosa sono?
How is it prepared? — *Come viene preparato?*

IL CAMERIERE:

Sono dei cannelloni
SO-no day kahn-nel-LO-nee
They are cannelloni

ripieni di carne
reep-YAY-nee dee KAHR-nay
filled with meat

invece di ricotta.
een-VAY-chay dee ree-KOHT-ta.
instead of cheese.

IL CLIENTE:

Credo che preferisco
KRAY-doh kay pray-fay-REE-sko
I think that I prefer

delle scaloppine al Marsala.
DEL-lay ska-lohp-PEE-nay AHL mar-SA-la.
veal cooked with Marsala wine sauce.

IL CAMERIERE:

E come contorno, che cosa desidera?
Ay KO-may kohn-TOHR-no, kay KO-za day-ZEE-day-ra?
And as a side dish, what would you like?

IL CLIENTE:
Che legumi hanno?
Kay lay-GOO-mee AHN-no?
What vegetables do you have?

IL CAMERIERE:
Abbiamo carote, piselli, zucchine,
Ahb-B'YA-mo ka-RO-tay, pee-SEL-lee, dzook-KEE-nay,
We have carrots, peas, squash,

asparagi e fagiolini verdi.
ah-SPA-ra-jee ay fa-jo-LEE-nee VEHR-dee.
asparagus and green beans.

IL CLIENTE:
Piselli, per favore.
Pee-ZEL-lee, pehr fa-VO-ray.
Peas, please.

Mi porti anche un'insalata verde
Mee POHR-tee AHN-kay oo-neen-sa-LA-ta VEHR-day
Bring me also a green salad

condita con olio e aceto
kohn-DEE-ta kohn OHL-yo ay ah-CHAY-toh
seasoned with oil and vinegar

ma senza sale.
ma SENT-sa SA-lay.
but without salt.

IL CAMERIERE:
E come vino?
Ay KO-may VEE-no?
And as for wine?

IL CLIENTE:
Del vino rosso —
Del VEE-no ROHS-so —
Some red wine —

un mezzo litro di Valpolicella.
oon MEHDZ-zo LEE-tro dee Vahl-po-lee-CHEL-la.
half a liter of Valpolicella.

IL CAMERIERE:
Perfetto, signore.
Pehr-FEHT-toh, seen-YO-ray.
Perfect, Sir.

IL CAMERIERE:
Vuole dei dolci o del formaggio?
VWO-lay day DOHL-chee oh del fohr-MAHDJ-jo?
Would you like some sweets or cheese?

IL CLIENTE:
Che tipo di gelato hanno?
Keh TEE-po dee jeh-LA-toh AHN-no?
What type of ice cream do you have?

IL CAMERIERE:
Abbiamo spumone, tortone ed altri.
Ahb-B'YA-mo spoo-MO-nay, tohr-TOH-nay ay-DAHL-tree.
We have spumone, tortone and others.

Ma raccomandiamo specialmente
Ma rahk-ko-mahnd-YA-mo spay-chahl-MEN-tay
But we recommend above all

il gelato di zabaione. È squisito.
eel jay-LA-toh dee dza-ba-YO-nay. Ay skwee-ZEE-toh.
zabaione ice cream. It is exquisite.

IL CLIENTE:
Non ne dubito. Ma è troppo —
Nohn nay DO-bee-toh. Ma ay TROHP-po —
I don't doubt it. But it is too much —

prendo solo una tazza di caffè.
PREN-doh SO-lo OO-na TAHTS-sa dee kahf-FAY.
I will take only a cup of coffee.

IL CAMERIERE:
Abbiamo caffè espresso e cappuccino.
Ahb-B'YA-mo kahf-FAY ay-SPREHS-so ay kahp-poot-CHEE-no.
We have espresso coffee or "cappuccino."

> **Cappuccino**
> *Cappuccino* is coffee pressurized with foamy
> hot milk. (*È buono!*)

Quale preferisce?
KWA-lay pray-fay-REE-shay?
Which do you prefer?

IL CLIENTE:
Caffè espresso, per favore.
Kahf-FAY ay-SPREHS-so, pehr fa-VO-ray.
Espresso coffee, please.

IL CAMERIERE:
Subito, signore.
SOO-bee-toh, seen-YO-ray.
Right away, sir.

_____

IL CLIENTE:
Camariere, il conto, prego.
Ka-mar-YAY-ray, eel KOHN-toh, PRAY-go.
Waiter, the check, please.

IL CAMERIERE:
Eccolo, signore.
EK-ko-lo, seen-YO-ray.
Here it is, sir.

IL CLIENTE:
Il servizio è incluso?
Eel sehr-VEETS-yo ay ink-LOO-zo?
Is the service charge included?

IL CAMERIERE:
Nossignore.
Nohs-seen-YO-ray.
No, sir.

È soddisfatto del suo pranzo?
Ay sohd-dees-FAHT-toh del SOO-oh PRAHND-zo?
Are you satisfied with your dinner?

IL CLIENTE:
Oh, sì, un pranzo squisito. Ecco.
Oh, see, oon PRAHND-zo skwee-ZEE-toh. EK-ko.
Oh, yes, an exquisite dinner. Here.

IL CAMERIERE:
Le riporto il resto in un momento.
Lay ree-POHR-toh eel RAY-sto ee-NOON mo-MEN-toh.
I will bring you back the change in a moment.

IL CLIENTE:
Non c'è bisogno. Lo tenga.
Nohn chay bee-ZOHN-yo. Lo TEHN-ga.
It isn't necessary. Keep it.

IL CAMERIERE:
Grazie mille, signore.
GRAHTS-yay MEEL-lay, seen-YO-ray.
Thank you very much, sir.

Ritorni ancora, prego.
Ree-TOHR-nee ahn-KO-ra, PRAY-go.
Come again, please.

TEST YOUR ITALIAN

Match these foods. Score 5 points for each correct answer. See answers on following page.

1. fagiolini verdi   vegetables

2. prosciutto   fish

3. uva   meat

4. pesce   veal

5. pesche   bread

6. latte   ham

7. baccalà   chicken

8. pere   potatoes

9. lattuga   green beans

10. carne   lettuce

11. pollo   tomatoes

12. legumi   grapes

13. pane   pears

14. pomodori   apples

15. vitello   peaches

16. mele   olive oil

17. olio d'oliva   milk

18. burro   butter

19. calamari   codfish

20. patate.   squids

19.

Answers: 12, 4, 10, 15, 13, 2, 11, 20, 1, 9, 14, 3, 8, 16, 5, 17, 6, 18, 7,

SCORE _____%

HOW AND WHEN TO USE THE FAMILIAR FORM

Ecco alcuni esempi
EK-ko ahl-KOO-nee ay-ZEM-pee
Here are some examples

dell'uso del *tu.*
del-LOO-zo del *too.*
of the use of tu (the familiar for "you").

Tu si usa fra membri
***Tu* see OO-za fra MEM-bree**
Tu is used between members

di una famiglia
dee OO-na fa-MEELL-ya.
of a family.

UNA MADRE:
OO-na MA-dray:
A MOTHER:

Sentimi! Finisci di mangiare!
SEN-tee-mee! Fee-NEE-shee dee mahn-JA-ray!
Listen to me! Finish eating!

The familiar form for "Lei" — "tu"
Tu, the familiar form for "you," consists of the pronoun and the verb form used informally, instead of the more formal *Lei.* The present tense of the verb used with *tu* always ends in -*i,* and is therefore quite easily recognizable.

parlare — tu parli; scrivere — tu scrivi; partire — tu parti; finire — tu finisci

The affirmative imperative ends in -*a* for the first conjugation, but remains the same as the indicative form for the 2nd and 3rd conjugations.

parla! — speak; *scrivi!* — write!

But the negative imperative for *tu* is expressed simply by *non* plus the infinitive of the verb.

Non essere in ritardo! — Don't be late!

SUA FIGLIA:
SOO-wa FEEL-ya:
HER DAUGHTER:
Non ho fame, mammina
Nohn oh FA-may, mahm-MEE-na.
I'm not hungry, mother. (Mammina is the familiar for Madre.)

LA MADRE:
E finisci anche
Ay fee-NEE-shee AHN-kay
And also finish

di bere il tuo latte!
dee BAY-ray eel TOO-oh LAHT-tay!
drinking your milk!

Pronoun forms of "tu"
The pronoun forms of *tu* and *tuo* for the possessive, and *ti* for the direct object: *Ti amo* —"I love you." The indirect object is *ti* or *te*, depending on the position.

Ti do le chiavi — I give you the keys.
Te le do — I give them to you.

The reflexive pronoun is also *ti:*

Come ti senti? — How do you feel?

LA FIGLIA:
Non ho sete nemmeno.
Nohn oh SAY-tay nehm-MAY-no.
I'm not thirsty either.

LA MADRE:
Se non finisci tutto,
Say nohn fee-NEE-shee TOOT-toh,
If you don't finish everything,

glielo dico a tuo padre.
LL'YAY-lo DEE-ko ah TOO-oh PA-dray.
I am going to tell your father.

LA FIGLIA:

Ma mammina, perchè
Ma mahm-MEE-nah, pehr-KAY
But mother, why

mi fai mangiare tanto?
mee FAH-ee mahn-JA-ray TAHN-toh?
do you make me eat so much?

Non voglio diventare grassa.
Nohn VOLL-yo dee-ven-TA-ray GRAHS-sa.
I don't want to become fat.

To have something done
"To make somebody do something" or "to have something done" is expressed by the verb *fare* with another infinitive

His father makes him study very hard.
Suo padre lo fa studiare molto.

When two infinitives are used, the final *-e* of *fare* is dropped.

I want to have the car repaired.
Voglio far riparare l'auto.

Tu si usa fra buoni amici.
Tu **see OO-za fra BWO-nee ah-MEE-chee.**
Tu is used between good friends.

— Ciao, Peppino. Come stai?
Chow, Pep-PEE-no. KO-may STA-ee?
Hi, Joe. How are you?

Ciao!
The use of *ciao* as a greeting is quite infomal and should be used by people who are on informal terms with each other. *Ciao!* can mean either "hello," "goodbye," "hi there" and "so long."

— Così, così, Giulio. E tu?
Ko-ZEE, ko-ZEE, JOOL-yo. Ay too?
So-so, Julius. And you?

— Non c'è male. Senti,
Nohn chay MA-lay. SEN-tee,
Not bad. Listen,

sai che c'è una festa
SA-ee kay chay OO-na FAY-sta
do you know that there is a party

in casa di Domenico questa sera?
een KA-za dee Doh-MAY-nee-ko KWESS-ta SAY-ra?
at Dominick's tonight?

Non ci vai?
Nohn chee vye?
Aren't you going?

— Non sono invitato.
Nohn SO-no een-vee-TA-toh.
I am not invited.

Eppoi, ho un appuntamento con Lucia.
Ehp-POY, oh oo-nahp-poon-ta-MEN-toh kohn Loo-CHEE-ah.
Anyway, I have a date with Lucy.

— Ma non importa.
Ma no-neem-POHR-ta.
But it doesn't matter.

Venite voi due.
Vay-NEE-tay voy DOO-ay.
The two of you come.

"Voi" — the plural of "tu"
The plural of *tu* is *voi*, that is, when you are
speaking to two or more people, each of which
you are in the habit of addressing informally.
For example, an elementary school teacher
would address the young students as *voi*, while
a child would always use *Lei* and *Loro*. The *voi*
ending for the first conjugation is *-ate*, for the

169

second conjugation it is -*ete*, and for the third it is -*ite*. For example, the present tense form of *voi* in the verbs *mangiare, scrivere,* and *finire* is *voi mangiate, voi scrivete,* and *voi finite.* The imperative for *voi* is exactly the same as the indicative. The object form is *vi* and the possessive form is *vostro.*

Here is where they give you your passports.
Qui è dove vi danno i vostri passaporti.

The reflexive pronoun is also *vi:*

At what time do you want to get up tomorrow morning?
A che ora vi volete alzare domani mattina?

Veramente, dovete venire.
Vay-ra-MEN-tay, doh-VAY-tay vay-NEE-ray.
Really, you must come.

Venite verso le otto.
Vay-NEE-tay VEHR-so lay OHT-toh.
Come around eight o'clock.

E porta una bottiglia di vino.
Ay POHR-ta OO-na boht-TEELL-ya dee VEE-no.
And bring a bottle of wine.

Plural and singular
Giulio has been just talking to Peppino with the *voi* form, as he was addressing his invitation to both Peppino and Lucia, even though Lucia isn't there. However, when he mentions bringing wine to the party, he goes back to the singular form of the familiar *tu* in that he is addressing his conversation to just one person, Peppino.

Non dimenticare.
Nohn dee-men-tee-KA-ray.
Don't forget.

Tu si usa fra innamorati.
Tu see OO-za fra een-na-mo-RA-tee.
Tu is used between lovers.

LEI:
Lay:
SHE:

> Dimmi, mi ami?
> **DEEM-mee, mee AH-mee?**
> Tell me, do you love me?

LUI:
LOO-ee:
HE:

> Sì, cara. Ti voglio molto bene.
> **See, KA-ra. Tee VOLL-yo MOHL-toh BAY-nay.**
> Yes, dear. I love you very much.

To love

There are two interchangeable expressions for "to love" — *voler bene* (or *volere bene*), and *amare*. Literally, *voler bene* means "to wish someone well," an interesting concept for "to love."

Note that the final "e" of the infinitive is sometimes dropped, as in *voler* instead of *volere*. Examples of this occur in two other Italian expressions you probably already know: *Arrivaderla* — "to seeing you again" or "good bye", and *dolce far niente* — *"(it is) sweet to do nothing"*.

LEI:
> Per sempre?
> **Pehr SEHM-pray?**
> For ever?

LUI:

Chissà?
Kees-SA?
Who knows?

LEI:

Perchè dici — "Chissà?"
Pehr-KAY DEE-chee — "Kees-SA?"
Why do you say — "Who knows?"

Sei un bruto. Ti odio.
Say oon BROO-toh. Tee OHD-yo.
You are a brute. I hate you.

Tu si usa quando si parla con i bambini.
Tu **see OO-za KWAHN-doh see PAHR-la kohn ee bahm-BEE-nee.**
Tu is used when speaking to children.

— Vieni qui, piccolina.
V'YAY-nee kwee, peek-ko-LEE-na.
Come here, little one.

Diminutives

The diminutive of adjectives or nouns is formed by adding *-ino* or *-etto* for the masculine, and *-ina* or *-etta* for the feminine. These endings serve to make the nouns either smaller or more endearing.

brother	— *fratello*
little brother	— *fratellino*
sister	— *sorella*
little sister	— *sorellina*
cat	— *gatto*
kitten	— *gattino*
house	— *casa*
little house	— *casetta*
shoe	— *scarpa*
little (delicate) shoe	— *scarpina* or *scarpetta*

Come ti chiami?
KO-may tee K'YA-mee?
What is your name?

— Mi chiamo Giuseppina.
Mee K'YA-mo Joo-sehp-PEE-na.
My name is Josephine.

— E questo bambino è tuo fratello?
Ay KWESS-toh bahm-BEE-no ay TOO-oh fra-TEL-lo?
And this baby is your brother?

— Sì. È ancora molto piccolo.
See. Ay ahn-KO-ra MOHL-toh PEEK-ko-lo.
Yes. He is still very small.

Non sa parlare.
Nohn sa pahr-LA-ray.
He doesn't know how to talk.

— Però tu sai parlare bene, no?
Pay-RO too SA-ee pahr-LA-ray BAY-nay, no?
But you know how to speak well, don't you?

Ecco una caramella per te
EK-ko OO-na ka-ra-MEL-la pehr tay
Here is a candy for you

ed un'altra per il tuo fratellino.
ed oo-NAHL-tra pehr eel TOO-oh fra-tel-LEE-no.
and another for your little brother.

Fatevi più là.
FA-tay-vee p'yoo la.
Move over there.

Voglio farvi una fotografia.
VOLL-yo FAHR-vee OO-na fo-toh-gra-FEE-ah.
I want to take a picture of you.

Sorridete!
So-rree-DAY-tay!
Smile!

Tu si usa quando si parla ad animali.
Tu see **OO-za KWAHN-doh see PAHR-la ah-da-nee-MA-lee.**
Tu is used when speaking to animals.

When speaking to animals
As we recommend using *tu* when speaking to animals, the question might be asked whether animals would notice whether you were using the right form in speaking to them, — *tu* instead of *Lei* for the singular, and *voi* instead of *Loro* for the plural. Although animals don't care about your grammar, onlookers would certainly find the use of *Lei* to an animal rather curious.

This question really summarizes the whole concept of *Tu* — which is that it is informal, and that you are on familiar and informal terms with them.

Fido, scendi dal sofà!
FEE-doh, SHEN-dee dahl so-FA!
Fido, get off the sofa!

Lascia in pace il gatto!
LA-sha een PA-chay eel GAHT-toh!
Leave the cat alone!

Stai zitto!
STA-ee DZEET-toh!
Keep quiet!

Non fare tanto rumore!
Nohn FA-ray TAHN-toh roo-MO-ray!
Don't make so much noise!

Esci di qui, cattivo!
ES-shee dee kwee, kaht-TEE-vo!
Get out of here, bad one!

INSTANT CONVERSATION: AT A SIDEWALK CAFÉ

LUI:
LOO-ee:
HE:
Ho sete. Vuoi prendere
Oh SAY-tay. VWO-ee PREN-day-ray
I am thirsty. Do you want to take (have)

qualcosa da bere in questo caffè?
kwahl-KO-za da BAY-ray een KWESS-toh kahf-FAY?
something to drink in this café?

LEI:
Lay:
SHE:
Che buona idea! Andiamo.
Kay BWO-na ee-DAY-ah! Ahn-DYA-mo.
What a good idea! Let's go.

LUI:
Ecco un tavolo libero.
EK-ko oon TA-vo-lo LEE-bay-ro.
Here is a free table.

Sediamoci qui all'aperto
Sehd-YA-mo-chee kwee ahl-la-PEHR-toh
Let's sit here in the open air

dove possiamo guardare la gente.
DOH-vay poss-YA-mo gwahr-DA-ray la JEN-tay.
where we can watch the people.

LEI:
Benone! Vuoi guardare
Bay-NO-nay! VWO-ee gwahr-DA-ray
Very good! You want to watch

passare le belle ragazze.
pahs-SA-ray lay BEL-lay ra-GAHTS-say.
the beautiful girls go by.

Two infinitives together
Two infinitives can be used together after a verb.

I want to hear her sing.
Voglio sentirla cantare.

LUI:

Ma che dici! Lo sai
Ma kay DEE-chee! Lo SA-ee
But what are you saying! You know

che non guardo che te.
kay nohn GWAHR-doh kay tay.
that I only look at you.

Cameriere!
Ka-mehr-YAY-ray!
Waiter!

CAMERIERE:
Ka-mehr-YAY-ray:
WAITER:

I signori desiderano?
Ee seen-YO-ree day-ZEE-day-ra-no?
What do you (gentlemen) wish?

I signori
I signori, literally "the gentlemen," is used here correctly by the waiter in speaking to a lady and gentleman together, although if he were speaking to two ladies together, he would say *le signore.*

LUI:

Che prendi, cara?
Kay PREN-dee, KA-ra?
What will you take, darling?

LEI:

Non so ... un'aranciata, forse.
Nohn so ... oo-na-rahn-CHA-ta, FOHR-say.
I don't know ... an orangeade, maybe.

SUI:

Bene. Ci porti un'aranciata
BAY-nay. Chee POHR-tee oo-na-rahn-CHA-ta
Good. Bring us an orangeade

per la signora e per me
pehr la seen-YO-ra ay pehr may
for the lady and for me

un Cinzano con ghiaccio.
oon Cheend-ZA-no kohn G'YAHT-cho.
a Cinzano on the rocks.

LEI:

Caro, puoi cambiare l'ordinazione?
KA-ro, PWO-ee kahmb-YA-ray lohr-dee-nahts-YO-nay?
Dear, can you change the order?

Vorrei provare un Campari,
Vo-RRAY pro-VA-ray oon kahm-PA-ree,
I would like to try a Campari,

invece dell'aranciata.
een-VAY-che del-la-rahn-CHA-ta.
instead of the orangeade.

LUI:

Va bene. Così sono le donne.
Va BAY-nay. Ko-ZEE SO-no lay DOHN-nay.
All right. That's how women are.

Cambiano sempre di parere.
KAHMB-ya-no SEHM-pray dee pa-RAY-ray.
They always change their minds.

Cameriere! Cambiamo l'ordinazione.
Ka-mehr-YAY-ray! Kahmb-YA-mo lohr-dee-nahts-YO-nay.
Waiter! We are changing the order.

Un Campari per la signora
Oon Kahm-PA-ree pehr la seen-YO-ra
A Campari for the lady

e dell'acqua minerale, per favore.
ay del-LAHK-wa mee-nay-RA-lay, pehr fa-VO-ray.
and some mineral water, please.

LEI:

Non sei arrabbiato con me?
Nohn say ah-rrahb-B'YA-toh kohn may?
You're not angry with me?

LUI:

Sai bene che non sono mai
SA-ee BAY-nay kay nohn SO-no my
You know well that I am never

arrabbiato con te.
ah-rrahb-B'YA-toh kohn tay.
angry with you.

Ecco le bevande. Alla tua salute.
EHK-ko lay bay-VAHN-day. AHL-la TOO-ah sa-LOO-tay.
Here are the drinks. To your health.

LEI:

E alla tua, amore.
Ay AHL-la TOO-ah, ah-MO-ray.
And to yours, my love.

Amore
Besides *amore,* some other current terms of endearment, applicable to either sex are: *tesoro mio* — "my treasure," *vita mia* — "my life," *gioia mia* — "my jewel," as well as "dear" — *caro* (to a man) and *cara* (to a woman).

And now that you have learned some words of endearment, it might bo of intereast for you, for purposes of comparison, to note some current Italian not-too-violent insults. These are not, of course, recommended for use, but only for purposes of *recognition:*

Pazzo! — Crazy!
Imbecille! — Imbecile!
Cretino! — Utter fool!
Maledetto! — Accursed one!

Tu + voi in the verb plan

As we have now presented the verb form for *tu*
and the plural form for *tu* — *voi*, all verb forms
given in future tenses will show the forms for *tu*
and *voi* in their regular conjugational positions,
which are number 2 and 5 in the six-form pattern as follows, taking *parlare* as an example:

(io)	parlo	(noi)	parliamo
(tu)	parli	(voi)	parlate
(Lei, egli or ella)	parla	(Loro, loro)	parlano

Note that *lui* and *lei* are used as alternates for
egli and *ella*.

TEST YOUR ITALIAN

Translate the following phrases into Italian, using the familiar singular form (*tu*). Score 5 points for each correct answer. See answers on following page.

1. What is your name? _____

2. How are you? _____

3. Aren't you going there? _____

4. Do you love me? _____

5. You are a brute. _____

6. I love you very much. _____

7. I hate you. _____

8. Listen to me! _____

9. Keep quiet! _____

10. Don't make so much noise! _____

Translate the following phrases into Italian, using the familiar plural form (*voi*). Score 5 points for each correct answer. See answers below.

1. You have to come. _____

2. Finish eating! _____

3. Do you know that there is a party? _____

4. Don't forget! _____

5. The two of you come. _____

6. Move over there. _____

7. Smile! _____

8. Do you want something to drink? _____

9. What will you take? _____

10. Can you change the order? _____

SCORE _____%

step 16 DAYS, MONTHS, DATES, SEASONS, THE WEATHER

I giorni della settimana sono:
Ee JOHR-nee DEL-la seht-tee-MA-na SO-no:
The days of the week are:

lunedì, martedì, mercoledì,
loo-nay-DEE, mahr-tay-DEE, mehr-ko-lay-DEE,
Monday, Tuesday, Wednesday,

giovedì, venerdì, sabato e domenica.
jo-vay-DEE, vay-nehr-DEE, SA-ba-toh ay doh-MAY-nee-ka.
Thursday, Friday, Saturday and Sunday.

I mesi dell'anno si chiamano:
Ee MAY-zee del-LAHN-no see K'YA-ma-no:
The months of the year are called:

gennaio, febbraio, marzo,
jen-NA-yo, fehb-BRA-yo, MAHRT-so,
January, February, March,

aprile, maggio, giugno,
ah-PREE-lay, MAHDJ-jo, JOON-yo,
April, May, June,

luglio, agosto, settembre,
LOOLL-yo, ah-GO-sto, seht-TEM-bray,
July, August, September,

ottobre, novembre e dicembre.
oht-TOH-bray, no-VEM-bray ay dee-CHEM-bray.
October, November and December.

Gennaio è il primo mese dell'anno.
Jen-NA-yo ay eel PREE-mo MAY-zay del-LAHN-no.
January is the first month of the year.

Il primo gennaio è l'Anno Nuovo.
Eel PREE-mo jen-NA-yo ay LAHN-no NWO-vo.
The first of January is New Year's Day.

Quanti ne abbiamo del mese?
The first of the month is the only date given an
ordinal number; the other dates use the cardinal
numbers.

February 1st. — *il primo febbraio*
February 2nd. — *il due febbraio*
February 26th — *il ventisei febbraio*

An idiomatic way of asking the date is: *Quanti
ne abbiamo del mese?* literally, "How many
have we of the month?"

Allora diciamo ai nostri amici:
Ahl-LO-ra dee-CHA-mo AH-ee NO-stree ah-MEE-chee:
Then we say to our friends:

"Buon Anno!," o "Buon Capo d'Anno!"
"Bwo-NAHN-no!," oh "Bwohn Ka-po-DAHN-no!"
"Happy New Year!," or "Happy Beginning of the Year!"

Il venticinque dicembre
Eel ven-tee-CHEEN-kway dee-CHEM-bray
The twenty-fifth of December

è il giorno di Natale.
ay eel JOHR-no dee Na-TA-lay.
is Christmas Day.

La gente dice: "Buon Natale!"
La JEN-tay DEE-chay: "Bwohn Na-TA-lay!
People say: "Merry Christmas!"

In Italia, il quindici agosto
Ee-nee-TAHL-ya, eel KWEEN-dee-chee ah-GO-sto
In Italy, the fifteenth of August

comincia il ferragosto,
ko-MEEN-cha eel feh-rra-GO-sto,
starts the August holiday,

Ferragosto

Ferragosto, (August 15), is the day when most Italians begin their yearly vacations, as it is considered the hottest day of the year, a signal of mass exodus from Italian cities.

The expression itself comes from *ferro* (iron) and *agosto* (August) meaning that August, after the 15th, becomes as hot as a red hot iron. *È vero, no?*

quando la maggior parte della gente
KWAHN-doh la mahdj-JOHR PAHR-tay DEL-la JEN-tay
when most people

va in vacanza.
va een va-KAHND-za.
go on vacation.

Allora, si dice:
Ahl-LO-ra, see DEE-chay:
Then, one says:

"Buone vacanze!"
"BWO-nay va-KAHND-zay!"
"(Have a) good vacation!"

L'anno è diviso in quattro stagioni:
LAHN-no ay dee-VEE-so een KWAHT-tro sta-JO-nee:
The year is divided into four seasons:

la primavera, l'estate, l'autunno e l'inverno.
la pree-ma-VAY-ra, lay-STA-tay, la-oo-TOON-no ay leen-VEHR-no.
spring, summer, autumn and winter.

D'inverno fa freddo
Deen-VEHR-no fa FREHD-doh
In winter it is cold

e d'estate fa caldo.
ay day-STA-tay fa KAHL-doh.
and in summer it is hot.

In primavera e in autunno
Een pree-ma-VAY-ra ay ee-na-oo-TOON-no
In spring and in autumn

generalmente fa bel tempo,
jay-nay-rahl-MEN-tay fa bel TEM-po,
it is generally good weather,

> **Che tempo fa?**
> The third person form of *fare* is used to describe various aspects of the weather and the temperature.
>
> | | |
> |---|---|
> | fa freddo | — it is cold |
> | fa caldo | — it is hot |
> | fa bel tempo | — it is nice weather |
> | fa brutto tempo | — it is bad weather |
> | fa fresco | — it is cool |
> | Che tempo fa? | — How is the weather? |
>
> But remember that when a person is hot, cold, hungry, or thirsty, *avere* — not *fare* — is used.

ma piove spesso.
ma P'YO-vay SPEHS-so.
but it rains often.

In autunno le foglie cambiano colore
Ee-na-oo-TOON-no lay FOLL-yay KAHMB-ya-no ko-LO-ray
In autumn the leaves change color

e cadono dagli alberi.
ay KA-doh-no DALL-yee AHL-bay-ree.
and fall from the trees.

Il clima d'Italia è generalmente
Eel KLEE-ma dee-TAHL-ya ay jay-nay-rahl-MEN-tay
The climate of Italy is generally

molto più gradevole di quello
MOHL-toh p'yoo gra-DAY-vo-lay dee KWEL-lo
much more agreeable than that

del Nord America.
Del Nohr-da-MAY-ree-ka.
of North America.

Non fa nè così freddo nè così caldo.
Nohn fa nay ko-ZEE FREHD-doh nay ko-ZEE KAHL-doh.
It is neither as cold nor as hot.

Però il clima del Settentrione
Peh-RO eel KLEE-ma del seht-ten-tree-YO-nay
But the climate of the North

Settentrione and Mezzogiorno

Settentrione and Mezzogiorno are two special words for north and south relating to Italy. The *mezzogiorno*, also meaning "midday," refers to the sun being to the south at noon over the Italian penninsula, while *settentrione* refers to the Latin name for the Big Dipper in the northern sky, which the ancient Romans called the "Seven Oxen."

è più simile a quello
ay p'yoo SEE-mee-lay ah KWEL-lo
is more similar to that

del Nord degli Stati Uniti,
del Nohrd DELL-yee STA-tee Oo-NEE-tee,
of the North of the United States,

mentre il Mezzogiorno è simile
MEN-tray eel medz-zo-JOHR-no ay SEE-mee-lay
while the South is similar

alla parte meridionale della California.
AHL-la PAHR-tay may-reed-yo-NA-lay DEL-la KA-lee-FOHRN-ya.
to the southern part of California.

Per di più, la vicinanza
Pehr dee p'yoo, la vee-chee-NAHNT-sa
Moreover, the nearness

delle montagne al mare —
DEL-lay mohn-TAHN-yay ahl MA-ray —
of the mountains to the sea —

le Alpi, gli Appennini,
lay AHL-pee, ll'yahp-pen-NEE-nee,
the Alps, the Apennines,

e d i cinque mari che circondano
ayd ee CHEEN-kway MA-ree kay cheer-KOHN-da-no
and the five seas that surround

> **Italia fra i cinque mari**
> From an Italian point of view, the Mediterranean
> Sea is one of these five seas, although the
> other four are part of it. The Italian names for
> these five seas are *il Mar Mediterraneo, il Mar
> Adriatico, il Mar Ionio, il Mar Tirreno* and *il Mar
> Ligure.*

la penisola — e soprattutto
la pay-NEE-so-la — ay so-praht-TOOT-toh
the peninsula — and above all

il cielo così azzurro
eel CHAY-lo ko-ZEE ahdz-ZOO-rro
the sky so blue

fanno dell'Italia un posto ideale
FAHN-no del-lee-TAHL-ya oon PO-sto ee-day-AH-lay
make of Italy an ideal place

per passare le vacanze
pehr pahs-SA-ray lay va-KAHNT-say
to spend vacations

o, anche meglio, per viverci.
oh, AHN-kay MELL-yo, pehr VEE-vehr-chee.
or, even better, to live there.

INSTANT CONVERSATION:
TALKING ABOUT THE WEATHER

Tutti fanno osservazioni
TOOT-tee FAHN-no ohs-sehr-vahts-YO-nee
Everyone makes observations

sul tempo che fa.
sool TEM-po kay fa.
on what sort of weather it is.

In primavera, quando brilla il sole
Een pree-ma-VAY-ra, KWAHN-doh BREEL-la eel SO-lay
In spring, when the sun shines

e soffia una brezza piacevole
ay SOHF-f'ya OO-na BREHTS-sa p'ya-CHAY-vo-lay
and a pleasant breeze blows

e l'aria odora di fiori,
ay LAHR-ya oh-DOH-ra dee F'YO-ree,
and the air smells of flowers,

si dice: "Che bella giornata!"
see DEE-chay: "Kay bel-la jor-NA-ta!"
one says: "What a beautiful day!"

E, quando la notte è chiara
Ay, KWAHN-doh la NOHT-tay ay K'YA-ra
And, when the night is clear

e vediamo la luna e le stelle,
ay vehd-YA-mo la LOO-na ay lay STEL-lay,
and we see the moon and the stars,

diciamo: "Che notte meravigliosa!"
dee-CHA-mo: "Kay NOHT-tay may-ra-veell-YO-za!"
we say: "What a marvelous night!"

188

D'estate, quando il sole è più forte,
Day-STA-tay, KWAHN-doh eel SO-lay ay p'yoo FOHR-tay,
In summer, when the sun is stronger,

diciamo: "Fa un caldo tremendo, no?"
dee-CHA-mo: "Fa oon KAHL-doh, tray-MEN-doh, no?"
we say: "It is tremendously hot, isn't it?"

Quando piove, si dice spesso:
KWAHN-doh P'YO-vay, see DEE-chay SPEHS-so:
When it rains, one often says:

"Fa brutto tempo oggi.
"Fa BROOT-toh TEM-po OHDJ-jee.
"The weather is bad today.

Piove a dirotto."
P'YO-vay ah dee-ROHT-toh."
It is pouring rain."

Nel tardi autunno, quando comincia il freddo,
Nel TAHR-dee ah-oo-TOON-no, KWAHN-doh ko-MEEN-cha eel
FREHD-doh,
In the late autumn, when the cold weather starts,

si dice: "Fa abbastanza fresco, no?"
see DEE-chay: "Fa ahb-ba-STAHNT-sa FREHS-ko, no?"
one says: "It is quite cool, isn't it?"

D'inverno, quando nevica, spesso si dice:
Deen-VEHR-no, KWAHN-doh NAY-vee-ka, SPEHS-so see DEE-chay:
In winter, when it snows, one often says:

"Sta nevicando molto.
"Sta nay-vee-KAHN-doh MOHL-toh.
"It is snowing a lot.

Che freddo fa! Le strade
Kay FREHD-doh FA! Lay STRA-day
How cold it is! The roads

devono essere molto brutte,
DAY-vo-no EHS-say-ray MOHL-toh BROOT-tay,
must be very bad,

con tutta questa neve."
kohn TOOT-ta KWESS-ta NAY-vay."
with all this snow.''

Quando c'è molto vento
KWAHN-doh chay MOHL-toh VEN-toh
When it is very windy

con tuoni e lampi
kohn T'WO-nee ay LAHM-pee
with thunder and lightening

e con molta pioggia,
ay kohn MOHL-ta P'YOHDJ-ja,
and much rain,

si dice: "Che temporale!"
see DEE-chay: "Kay tem-poh-RA-lay!"
one says: "What a storm!''

E quando c'è la nebbia, a volte
Ay KWAHN-doh chay la NEHB-b'ya, ah VOHL-tay
And when there is fog, sometimes

diciamo: "Quanta nebbia c'è!
dee-CHA-mo: "KWAHN-ta NEHB-b'ya chay!
we say: "How much fog there is!

Quasi non si può vedere niente.
KWA-zee nohn see PWO vay-DAY-ray N'YEN-tay.
One can hardly see anything.

È molto pericoloso guidare.
Ay MOHL-toh pay-ree-ko-LO-zo gwee-DA-ray.
It is very dangerous to drive.

Invece di uscire,
Een-VAY-chay dee oo-SHEE-ray,
Instead of going out,

restiamo qui a casa
rest-YA-mo kwee ah KA-za
let's remain here at home

e guardiamo la televisione."
ay gwahrd-YA-mo la tay-lay-vees-YO-nay."
and let's watch television.''

Let's
The first person plural of a verb can be used by itself without the *noi,* as a way of saying ''let's.''

let's talk — parliamo

If a verb is reflexive, *ci* comes after the verb.

let's sit down — sediamoci
let's go to bed — corichiamoci

TEST YOUR ITALIAN

Translate these comments on the weather into English. Score 10 points for each correct answer. See answers below.

1. Che bella giornata! _____

2. Che notte meravigliosa! _____

3. Fa un caldo tremendo, no? _____

4. Fa brutto tempo oggi. _____

5. Piove a dirotto. _____

6. Fa abbastanza fresco, no? _____

7. Sta nevicando molto. _____

8. Che freddo fa! _____

9. Che temporale! _____

10. Quanta nebbia c'è! _____

Answers: 1. What a beautiful day! 2. What a marvelous night! 3. It is tremendously hot, isn't it? 4. It is bad weather today. 5. It is pouring. 6. It is quite cool, isn't it? 7. It is snowing a lot. 8. How cold it is! 9. What a storm! 10. How much fog there is!

SCORE _____%

HOW TO FORM
THE FUTURE TENSE

Il tempo futuro
Eel TEM-po foo-TOO-ro
The future tense

è molto facile.
eh MOHL-toh FA-chee-lay.
is very easy.

La forma del futuro per *io* finisce in *-ò.*
La FOHR-ma del foo-TOO-ro pehr *io* fee-NEE-shay een *-ò.*
The form of the future for "i" ends in *-ò.*

The future tense
The future tense for the first person *io* ends in
-ò. To form the stem, the final *-e* of the infinitive
is dropped in all three conjugations and *-ò* is
added. In the case of the first conjugation, however, the *-a-* of the *-are* ending is changed to
-e-.

INFINITIVE	FUTURE
parlare	*parlerò*
scrivere	*scriverò*
finire	*finirò*

For the negative future, we simply preface the
future with *non.*
    I will not write — *non scriverò*

Certain future forms are somewhat irregular in
that they make slight changes in their stem, before adding the regular endings. The first persons of the future tense of some of the most
important of these verbs are as follows:

INFINITIVE	FUTURE
avere	avrò
essere	sarò
venire	verrò
andare	andrò
dovere	dovrò
vedere	vedrò
mangiare	mangerò
volere	vorrò
sapere	saprò
potere	potrò

There are no words for the auxiliaries "shall," "will," "won't," "will not," "shall not" in Italian, as the endings of the verb themselves indicate the future.

Domani mattina mi alzerò molto presto.
Doh-MA-nee maht-TEE-na mee ahld-zay-RO MOHL-toh PRAY-sto.
Tomorrow morning I will get up very early.

Dovrò andare dal dottore.
Dohv-RO ahn-DA-ray dahl doht-TOH-ray.
I will have to go to the doctor.

Dal dottore
When visiting or being visited by a doctor, you will find the following phrases very useful, for indicating where you feel discomfort:

I have a headache.	— *Ho mal di testa.*
I have a sore throat.	— *Ho male alla gola.*
I have a stomach-ache.	— *Ho mal di stomaco.*
I am dizzy.	— *Ho le vertigini.*
It hurts here.	— *Mi fa male qui.*

"A prescription" is *una ricetta*, and things the doctor will say to you will include:

You must stay in bed.	— *Deve rimanere a letto.*
Take this three times a day.	— *Prenda questo tre volte al giorno.*
You will feel better.	— *Si sentirà meglio.*

Come back in two days. — *Ritorni frà due giorni.*

Gli domanderò qualche cosa per la mia tosse.
Ll-yee doh-mahn-day-RO KWAHL-kay KO-za pehr la MEE-ah TOHS-say.
I shall ask him for something for my cough.

La chiamerò dal suo ufficio,
La k'ya-may-RO dahl SOO-oh oof-FEE-cho,
I will call you from his office,

e Le dirò a che ora sarò di ritorno.
ay Lay dee-RO ah kay OH-ra sa-RO dee ree-TOHR-no.
and I will tell at what time I will be back.

La forma per *Lei* finisce in *-à.*
La FOHR-ma pehr *Lay* fee-NEE-shay een à.
The form for "you" (and "he," "she" and "it") ends in -à.

— Quando arriverà Raimondo?
KWAHN-doh ah-rre-vay-RA Ra-ee-MOHN-doh?
When will Raimondo arrive?

You add to the stem
The future stem that you have learned for the first person *io*, is constant for the other future endings as well. The future endings for the six persons are as follows:

-ò, -ai, -à, -emo, -ete, -anno,

and are attached directly to the future stem, as in the following example for *sentire:*

(io)	sentirò
(tu)	sentirai
(egli, ella, Lei)	sentirà
(noi)	sentiremo
(voi)	sentirete
(loro, Loro)	sentiranno

— Verrà domani.
Vay-RRA doh-MA-nee.
He will come tomorrow.

— Sarà possibile parlargli del contratto?
Sa-RA pohs-SEE-bee-lay pahr-LAHRLL-yee del kohn-TRAHT-toh?
Will it be possible to speak to him about the contract?

— Non credo che potrà. Partirà alle due.
Nohn KRAY-doh kay po-TRA. Pahr-tee-RA AHL-lay DOO-ay.
I don't think that you will be able to. He will leave at two.

Prenderà l'aereo per la Libia, dove visiterà
Pren-day-RA la-AY-ray-o pehr la LEEB-ya, DOH-vay vee-zee-tay-RA
He will fly to Libya, where he will visit

i nuovi campi di petrolio.
ee NWO-vee KAHM-pee dee pay-TRO-l'yo.
the new oil fields.

Non verrà all'aeroporto?
Nohn vay-RRA ahl-la-ay-ro-POHR-toh?
Won't you come to the airport?

Così avrà tempo di parlargli.
Ko-ZEE ahv-RA TEM-po dee pahr-LAHRL-yee.
In this way you will have time to speak to him.

La forma per *tu* finisce in -*ai*.
La FOHR-ma pehr *too* fee-NEE-shay een *ai*.
The form for "you" (familiar) ends in -*ai*.

LEI:
Mi telefonerai domani?
Mee tay-lay-fo-nay-RYE doh-MA-nee?
Will you telephone me tomorrow?

LUI:
Certo. Ma non sarai a casa.
CHEHR-toh. Ma nohn sa-RYE ah KA-za.
Certainly. But you will not be home.

Uscirai presto, no? Quando ritornerai?
Oo-shee-RYE PRAY-sto, no? KWAHN-doh ree-tohr-nay-RYE?
You will go out early, won't you? When will you be back?

LEI:

Alle cinque del pomeriggio.
AHL-lay CHEEN-kway del po-may-REEDJ-jo.
At five in the afternoon.

Potrai chiamarmi dopo le cinque.
Po-TRY k'ya-MAHR-mee DOH-po le CHEEN-kway.
You can call me after five.

La forma per *voi* finisce in *-ete.*
La FOHR-ma pehr *voi* fee-NEE-shay een *-ete.*
The form for "you" (fam. pl.) ends in -*ete.*

"Bevete Fernet-Branca
"Bay-VAY-tay Fehr-NEHT-BRAHN-ka
"Drink Fernet-Branca

e vi sentirete forti come un leone."
ay vee sen-tee-RAY-tay FOHR-tee KO-may oon lay-OH-nay."
and you will feel as strong as a lion."

> **Uses of "voi"**
> The form *voi*, the plural of the familiar form *tu*, is often used in advertising, as if the manufacturer were already on rather familiar terms with the reading public. *Voi* is also sometimes used in conversation for speaking to one person, instead of using *Lei*.

"Quando sarete al volante di una Ferrari
"KWAHN-doh sa-RAY-tay ahl vo-LAHN-tay dee OO-na Fay-RRA-ree
"When you will be at the wheel of a Ferrari

volerete come il vento."
vo-lay-RAY-tay KO-may eel VEN-toh."
you will fly like the wind."

La forma per *noi* finisce in *-emo.*
La FOHR-ma pehr *noi* fee-NEE-shay een *-emo.*
The form for "we" ends in -*emo.*

Sabato prossimo andremo tutti in campagna.
**SA-ba-toh PROHS-see-mo ahn-DRAY-mo TOOT-tee een
 kahm-PAHN-ya.**
Next Saturday we shall all go to the country.

Prenderemo il treno e scenderemo a Benevento.
**Pren-day-RAY-mo eel TRAY-no ay shen-day-RAY-mo ah
 Bay-nay-VEN-toh.**
We will take the train and get off at Benevento.

Poi andremo in automobile
Poy ahn-DRAY-mo ee-na-oo-toh-MO-bee-lay
Then we will go by car

fino alla fattoria di Don Antonio.
FEE-no AHL-la faht-toh-REE-ya dee Doh-nahn-TOHN-yo.
to Don Antonio's farm.

Lì, andremo a cavallo,
Lee, ahn-DRAY-mo ah ka-VAHL-lo,
There, we will go horseback riding,

vedremo i dintorni,
vay-DRAY-mo ee deen-TOHR-nee,
we will see the surroundings,

e poi nuoteremo nella piscina.
ay poy nwo-tay-RAY-mo NEL-la pee-SHEE-na.
and then we will swim in the pool.

La sera, se il tempo lo permetterà,
La SAY-ra, say eel TEM-po lo pehr-meht-tay-RA,
In the evening, if the weather will permit it,

pranzeremo all'aperto.
prahnt-say-RAY-mo ahl-la-PEHR-toh.
we will have dinner outdoors.

Ascolteremo canzoni
Ah-skohl-tay-RAY-mo kahnt-SO-nee
We will listen to

e musiche tipiche regionali.
ay MOO-zee-kay TEE-pee-kay ray-jo-NA-lee.
typical regional songs and music.

Credo che ci divertiremo molto.
KRAY-doh kay chee dee-vehr-tee-RAY-mo MOHL-toh.
I think that we will enjoy ourselves very much.

La forma per *Loro* (loro), finisce in *-anno*.
La FOHR-ma pehr *Loro* (*loro*), fee-NEE-shay een
                                                    -anno.
The form for "you" (formal pl.), (and "they" —
                    masc. and fem. pl.) ends in *-anno.*

UN GIOVANE:
Oon jo-VA-nay:
A YOUNG MAN:
Crede che gli uomini vivranno
KRAY-day kay LL'WO-mee-nee veev-RAHN-no
Do you think that men will live

sulla luna un giorno?
sool-la LOO-na oon JOHR-no?
on the moon someday?

UN VECCHIO:
Oon VEK-yo:
AN OLD MAN:
Senza dubbio. Fra poco,
SENT-sa DOOB-b'yo. Fra PO-ko,
Without a doubt. Soon,

ci saranno delle basi
chee SA-rahn-no DEHL-lee BA-zee
there will be bases there

e probabilmente
ay pro-ba-beel-MEN-tay
and probably

vi saranno dei voli giornalieri.
vee sahr-RAHN-no day vo-lee jor-nahl-YAY-ree.
there will be daily flights there.

IL GIOVANE:
Crede che andranno anche fino ai pianeti?
KRAY-day kay ahnd-RAHN-no AHN-kay FEE-no eye
                                  p'ya-NAY-tee?
Do you think that they will go to the planets too?

IL VECCHIO:
Sicuro. Una volta sulla luna,
See-KOO-ro. OO-na VOHL-ta SOOL-la LOO-na,
Sure. Once on the moon,

i viaggi futuri saranno molto più facili,
ee V'YAHDJ-jee foo-TOO-ree sa-RAHN-no MOHL-toh p'yoo
                                           FA-chee-lee,
future trips will be much easier,

e continueranno fino ai pianeti.
ay kohn-tee-nway-RAHN-no FEE-no eye p'ya-NAY-tee.
and they will continue to the planets.

Però credo che gli astronauti
Pay-RO KRAY-doh kay l'ya-stro-NA-oo-tee
But I think that the astronauts

non arriveranno fino alle stelle
no-na-rree-vay-RAHN-no FEE-no AHL-lay STEL-lay
will not get to the stars

nel vicino futuro.
nel vee-CHEE-no foo-TOO-ro.
in the near future.

Forse voialtri giovani
FOHR-say vo-YAHL-tree JO-va-nee
Maybe you young people

"Noialtri" and "voialtri"
Voialtri is composed of two words: *voi* —
"you," and *altri* — "others," an inclusive

pronominal plural. Another example is *noialtri*, as in:

Noialtri italiani non sappiamo parlare senza gesticolare. —

We Italians don't know how to speak without gesturing.

lo vedrete un giorno.
lo vay-DRAY-tay oon JOHR-no.
will see it one day.

INSTANT CONVERSATION:
PLANNING A TRIP TO ITALY

ANNAMARIA:

Il mese entrante Loro partiranno
Eel MAY-say en-TRAHN-te LO-ro pahr-tee-RAHN-no
Next month you will be leaving

per l'Italia, non è vero?
pehr lee-TAHL-ya, no-NAY VAY-ro?
for Italy, right?

MARCELLA:

Sì, per mio marito sarà un viaggio d'affari
See, pehr MEE-ya ma-REE-toh sa-RA oon V'YA-jo d'ahf-FA-ree
Yes, for my husband it will be a business trip

Dropping the article
The possessive pronoun before a noun is preceded by the definite article, except in the case
of members of one's family.

mia moglie — my wife
la mia automobile — my automobile
il mio dottore — my doctor

ma per me sarà un viaggio di piacere.
ma pehr may sa-RA oon V'YA-jo dee p'ya-CHAY-ray.
but for me it will be a pleasure trip.

Luigi andrà
Lwee-jee ahn-DRA
Luigi will go

direttamente a Milano,
dee-reht-ta-MEN-tay ah Mee-LA-no,
directly to Milan,

lì si occuperà dei suoi affari.
lee see ohk-koo-pay-RA day SWO-ee ahf-FA-ree.
there he will take care of his business.

Io cambierò aereo a Milano
EE-yo kahm-bee-ya-RO ah-AY-ree-yo ah Mee-LA-no
I'll change planes at Milan

e proseguirò per Napoli.
ay pro-say-gwee-RO pair NA-po-lee.
and will continue to Naples.

ANNAMARIA:
Suo marito l'incontrerà a Napoli?
SOO-wo ma-REE-toh leen-kohn-tray-RA ah NA-po-lee?
Your husband will meet you in Naples?

MARCELLA:
No, credo che non potrà venire.
No, KRAY-doh kay nohn po-TRA vay-NEE-ray.
No, I think that he will not be able to come.

Mi aspetterà a Roma invece.
Mee ah-speht-tay-RA ah RO-ma een-VAY-chay.
He will wait for me in Rome instead.

Ma prima di continuare
Ma pree-ma dee kohn-tee-NWA-ray
But before continuing

verso Roma, farò certamente
VEHR-so RO-ma, fa-RO chehr-ta-MEN-tay
on to Rome, I will certainly make

una visita a Capri.
OO-na VEE-zee-ta ah KA-pree.
a visit to Capri.

— Quando sarà a Capri,
KWAHN-doh sa-RA ah KA-pree,
When you will be in Capri,

non si dimentichi
nohn see dee-MEN-tee-kee
do not forget

> Spelling changes frequently occur to keep the sound of the verb. The hard -c- in *dimenticare* would change to the sound *ci* (chee) in the polite imperative, if the -h- were not added here to keep the "k" sound. The -h- is also added to keep the hard sound when the -a- of *dimenticare* has to change to -e-, as in the future — *dimenticherò*. Without the inserted -h-, it would be pronounced "cheh." This is true of any verb ending in -care or -gare.

di andare in barca
dee ahn-DA-ray een BAHR-ka
to go by boat

a visitare la Grotta Azzurra.
ah vee-zee-TA-ray la GROHT-ta ahdz-ZOO-rra.
to visit the Blue Grotto.

La troverà così bella!
La tro-vay-RA ko-ZEE BEHL-la!
You will find it so beautiful!

— Va bene. Non dimenticherò.
Va BAY-nay. Nohn dee-men-tee-kay-RO.
All right. I will not forget.

— E a Roma, quanto tempo resteranno?
Ay ah RO-ma, KWAHN-toh TEM-po ray-stay-RAHN-no?
And in Rome, how long will you remain?

— Ci saremo soltanto una settimana,
Chee sa-RAY-mo sohl-TAHN-toh OO-na seht-tee-MA-na,
We will be there only a week,

ma faremo come tutti i turisti.
ma fa-RAY-mo KO-may TOOT-tee ee too-REE-stee.
but we will do like all the tourists.

Vedremo le rovine, le chiese,
Vay-DRAY-mo lay ro-VEE-nay, lay K'YAY-zay,
We will see the ruins, the churches,

i giardini, i musei, il Vaticano,
ee jahr-DEE-nee, ee moo-ZAY-ee, eel Va-tee-KA-no,
the gardens, the museums, the Vatican,

i monumenti, le catacombe . . .
ee mo-noo-MEN-tee, lay ka-ta-KOHM-bay . . .
the monuments, the Catacombs . . .

— E dopo Roma, per dove partiranno?
Ay DOH-po RO-ma, pehr DOH-vay pahr-tee-RAHN-no?
And after Rome, where will you head for?

— Andremo a Milano,
Ahn-DRAY-mo ah Mee-LA-no,
We will go to Milan,

dove Alberto dovrà andare
DOH-vay Ahl-BEHR-toh dohv-RA ahn-DA-ray
where Albert will have to go

ad un'altra riunione d'affari.
ahd oon-AHL-tra ree-oon-YO-nay dahf-FA-ree.
to another business meeting.

Euphony
For purposes of euphony, a characteristic of
Italian, *a* often becomes *ad* when the following
word begins with a vowel.

Ma dopo, affitteremo un'auto
Ma DOH-po, ahf-feet-tay-RAY-mo oo-NA-oo-toh
But afterwards, we will rent a car

e faremo un giro — visiteremo
ay fa-RAY-mo oon JEE-ro — vee-zee-tay-RAY-mo
and we will make a tour — we will visit

Pisa, Siena, Firenze,
PEE-za, S'YAY-na, Fee-RENT-say,
Pisa, Siena, Florence,

Bologna e altre città.
Bo-LOHN-ya ay AHL-tray cheet-TA.
Bologna and other cities.

— Sono sicura che Alberto
SO-no see-KOO-ro kay Ahl-BEHR-toh
I am sure that Albert

sarà una guida espertissima.
sa-RA OO-na GWEE-da ay-spehr-TEES-see-ma.
will be a very expert guide.

Conosce molto bene quella parte d'Italia.
Ko-NO-shay MOHL-toh BAY-nay KWEL-la PAHR-tay dee-TAHL-ya.
He knows that part of Italy very well.

— Sì, forse, se potrà dimenticare
See, FOHR-say, say po-TRA dee-men-tee-KA-ray
Yes, maybe, if he will be able to forget

gli affari per qualche giorno.
ll'yahf-FA-ree pehr KWAHL-kay JOHR-no.
business for a day or so.

— Senta, perchè non vanno a Venezia —
SEN-ta, pehr-KAY nohn VAHN-no ah Vay-NEHTS-ya —
Listen, why don't you go to Venice —

si troveranno giusto in tempo
see tro-vay-RAHN-no JOO-sto een TEM-po
you will be just in time

per la Regata, la storica
pehr la Ray-GA-ta, la STO-ree-ka
for the Regata, the historic

sfilata di gondole lungo
sfee-LA-ta dee GOHN-doh-lay LOON-go
parade of gondolas along

il Canal Grande.
eel Ka-NAHL GRAHN-day.
the Grand Canal.

Quando Suo marito si troverà
Kwan-doh SOO-oh ma-REE-toh see tro-vay-RA
When your husband will find himself

fra tanta allegria e tanta baldoria,
fra TAHN-ta ahl-lay-GREE-ah ay TAHN-ta bahl-DOHR-ya,
in the midst of so much gaiety and excitement,

con feste, balli, sfilate,
kohn FAY-stay, BAHL-lee, sfee-LA-tay,
with parties, dances, parades,

fuochi artificiali sopra i canali e tutto il resto,
FWO-kee ahr-tee-fee-CHAL-lee SO-pra ee ka-NA-lee eh toot-toh eel
                                                          RAY-sto,
fireworks over the canals, and everything else,

mi dica, come farà
mee DEE-ka, KO-may fa-RA
tell me, how will he manage

a pensare agli affari?
ah pen-SA-ray ahll'yahf-FA-ree?
to think about business?

TEST YOUR ITALIAN

Translate into Italian, using the future tense. Score 10 points for each correct answer. See answers below.

1. Tomorrow morning I shall get up early.

2. I will have to go to the office.

3. Will you telephone me tonight? (familiar "you" in the singular)

4. On Monday we will all go to the country.

5. When will he come back?

6. We will go by car.

7. We will have dinner at eight o'clock.

8. What will you do when you will be in Rome?

9. We will be there a month.

10. He will be a very expert guide.

Answers: 1. Domani mattina mi alzerò presto. 2. Dovrò andare in ufficio. 3. Mi telefonerai stasera? 4. Lunedì andremo tutti in campagna. 5. Quando ritornerà? 6. Andremo in macchina. 7. Pranzeremo alle otto. 8. Che cosa farà quando sarà a Roma? 9. Ci saremo un mese. 10. Sarà una guida espertissima.

SCORE ____%

step 18

HOW TO FORM THE PAST PARTICIPLE

Quando passeggiamo per una città italiana,
KWAHN-doh pahs-sehj-JA-mo pehr OO-na cheet-TA ee-tahl-YA-na,
When we take a walk about an Italian city,

spesso vediamo scritto:
SPEHS-so vehd-YA-mo SKREET-toh:
we often see written:

CHIUSO LA DOMENICA.
K'YOO-zo la doh-MAY-nee-ka.
CLOSED ON SUNDAYS.

CHIUSO PER RIPARAZIONI.
K'YOO-zo pehr ree-pa-rahts-YO-nee.
CLOSED FOR REPAIRS.

APERTO FINO ALLE 22.
Ah-PEHR-toh FEE-no AHL-lay ven-tee-DOO-ay.
OPEN UNTIL 10 P.M.

24 hour system
Note the frequent use of the 24 hour system in Italian.

INTERDETTO AI PEDONI.
Een-tehr-DEHT-toh eye pay-DOH-nee.
FORBIDDEN TO PEDESTRIANS.

VIETATO IL PARCHEGGIO.
V'yay-TA-toh eel pahr-KAY-jo.
NO PARKING.

PARCHEGGIO AUTORIZZATO.
Pahr-KEHJ-jo ow-toh-reedz-ZA-toh.
PARKING PERMITTED.

209

PASSAGGIO INTERDETTO.
Pahs-SAHJ-jo een-tehr-DET-toh.
PASSAGE CLOSED.

STRADA CHIUSA AL TRAFFICO.
STRA-da K'YOO-za ahl TRAHF-fee-ko.
STREET CLOSED TO TRAFFIC.

È PROIBITO CALPESTARE L'ERBA.
Ay pro-ee-BEE-toh kahl-pay-STA-ray LEHR-ba.
IT IS FORBIDDEN TO WALK ON THE GRASS.

Le parole *chiuso, vietato, aperto,*
Lay pa-RO-lay *K'YOO-zo, v-yay-TA-toh, ah-PEHR-toh,*
The words, "closed," "forbidden," "open,"

permesso, autorizzato e *proibito*
pehr-mess-so, ah-oo-toh-reedz-ZA-toh,* ay *pro-ee-BEE-toh
"permitted," "allowed," and "prohibited"

sono i participi passati dei verbi
SO-no ee pahr-tee-CHEE-pee pahs-SA-tee day VEHR-bee
are the past participles of the verbs

chiudere, vietare, aprire,
K'YOO-day-ray, v'yay-TA-ray, ah-PREE-ray,
"to close," "to forbid," "to open,"

permettere, autorizzare e *proibire.*
pehr-MET-tay-ray, ow-toh-reedz-ZA-ray* ay *pro-ee-BEE-ray.
"to allow," "to permit" and "to prohibit."

Il participio passato

The past participle corresponds generally to the English past participle of the verb, such as "taken," "given," "included," "closed," "opened," "begun," "finished," etc. The past participles of Italian verbs are formed as follows:

The infinitive endings for the three conjugations: *-are, -ere,* and *-ire* are dropped and the ending *-ato, -uto* and *-ito* are added.

chiamare	— to call	chiamato	— called
vendere	— to sell	venduto	— sold
finire	— to finish	finito	— finished

There are certain verbs that form their past participles in an abbreviated or different way. Some of these irregular past participles are as follows:

chiudere	— to close	chiuso	— closed
aprire	— to open	aperto	— open
dire	— to say	detto	— said
fare	— to do	fatto	— done
essere	— to be	stato	— been
scrivere	— to write	scritto	— written
leggere	— to read	letto	— read
mettere	— to put	messo	— put
permettere	— to permit	permesso	— permitted (allowed)
vedere	— to see	veduto (or) visto	— seen
prendere	— to take	preso	— taken
morire	— to die	morto	— dead
nascere	— to be born	nato	— born

E dopo, quando entriamo in un negozio,
Ay DOH-po, KWAHN-doh entr-YA-mo ee-NOON nay-GOHTS-yo,
And then, when we enter a shop,

vediamo o sentiamo delle espressioni come:
vehd-YA-mo oh sent-YA-mo DEL-lay ay-sprehs-S'YO-nee KO-may:
we see or hear expressions such as:

PREZZI RIDOTTI
PREHTS-see ree-DOHT-tee
PRICES REDUCED

Prezzi ridotti
The past participle of *ridurre* — "to reduce" is *ridotto* — "reduced." When the past participle is used as an adjective, as here, in "reduced prices," the *ridotto* agrees in number and gender with the noun — *prezzi* — and therefore becomes *ridotti*, the masculine plural form.

211

TUTTI I NOSTRI PREZZI SONO MARCATI.
TOOT-tee ee NO-stree PREHTS-see SO-no mahr-KA-tee.
ALL OUR PRICES ARE MARKED.

"È pagato. Ecco la sua ricevuta."
"Ay pa-GA-toh. EK-ko la SOO-ah ree-chay-VOO-ta."
"It is paid. Here is your receipt."

E qualche volta:
Ay KWAHL-kay VOHL-ta:
And sometimes:

"Mi dispiace. È venduto."
"Mee deesp-YA-chay. Ay ven-DOO-toh."
"I regret. It is sold."

Questi sono i participi passati di
KWESS-tee SO-no ee pahr-tee-CHEE-pee pahs-SA-tee dee
These are the past participles of

ridurre, marcare, pagare,
ree-DOO-rray, mahr-KA-ray, pa-GA-ray,
"to reduce," "to mark," "to pay,"

ricevere e *vendere.*
ree-CHAY-vay-ray ay VEN-day-ray.
"to receive" and "to sell."

I participi passati sono impiegati dappertutto:
Ee pahr-tee-CHEE-pee pahs-SA-tee SO-no eemp-yay-GA-tee
           dahp-pehr-TOOT-toh:
The past participles are used everywhere:

Al cinema:
Ahl CHEE-nay-ma:
At the movies:

CONSIGLIATO AGLI ADULTI.
Kohn-see-L'YA-toh AHLL-yee ah-DOOL-tee.
RECOMMENDED TO ADULTS.

PROIBITO AI MINORI DI 16 ANNI.
Pro-ee-BEE-toh eye mee-NO-ree dee SAY-dee-chee AHN-nee.
FORBIDDEN TO MINORS UNDER SIXTEEN.

"È cominciato?"
"Ay ko-meen-CHA-toh?"
"Is it started?"

"No, è appena finito cinque minuti fa."
"No, ay ahp-PAY-na fee-NEE-toh CHEEN-kway mee-NOO-tee fa."
"No, it hardly finished five minutes ago."

All'Ufficio Postale:
Ahl-loof-FEE-cho Po-STA-lay:
At the Post Office:

LETTERE E PACCHI RACCOMANDATI.
LEHT-tay-ray ay PAHK-kee rahk-ko-mahn-DA-tee.
REGISTERED LETTERS AND PACKAGES.

"È assicurato?"
"Ay ahs-see-koo-RA-toh?"
"Is it insured?"

Nelle stazioni e nei treni:
NEL-lay stahts-YO-nee ay nay TRAY-nee:
In railroad stations and trains:

L'INGRESSO VIETATO AI NON ADDETTI
leen-GREHS-so v'yay-TA-toh AH-ee no-nahd-DEHT-tee
EMPLOYEES ONLY (ENTRANCE FORBIDDEN TO NON-EMPLOYEES)

UFFICIO OGGETTI SMARRITI
Oof-FEE-cho ohdj-JEHT-tee sma-RREE-tee
LOST AND FOUND (LOST OBJECTS OFFICE)

POSTO PRENOTATO.
PO-sto pray-no-TA-toh.
RESERVED SEAT.

— È occupato questo posto?
Ay ohk-koo-PA-toh KWESS-toh PO-sto?
Is this seat occupied?

— Sì, è occupato.
See, ay oh-koo-PA-toh.
Yes, it is occupied.

— È permesso fumare?
Ay pehr-MEHS-so foo-MA-ray?
Is smoking allowed?

— No, è vietato.
No, ay v'yay-TA-toh.
No, it is forbidden.

Guardi, È scritto là.
GWAHR-dee. Ay SKREET-toh la.
Look. It is written there.

E nel vagone-ristorante:
Ay nel va-GO-nay-ree-sto-RAHN-tay:
And in the dining-car:

— Primo turno — Il pranzo è servito.
PREE-mo TOOR-no — Eel PRAHNT-so ay sehr-VEE-toh.
First call — Dinner is served.

— Il servizio è compreso?
Eel sehr-VEETS-yo ay kohm-PRAY-zo?
Is the service charge included?

> **Il servizio e la mancia**
> *Servizio* is a service charge — a general tip to
> the personnel — that is calculated as a per-
> centage of the total bill and added to the check.
> An extra tip is also customary, usually from 5%
> to 10%. The word for "tip" is *mancia*.

In campagna a volte vediamo:
Een kahm-PAHN-ya ah VOHL-tay vehd-YA-mo:
In the country at times we see:

VIETATA LA CACCIA — VIETATA LA PESCA
V'yay-TA-tah la KAHT-cha — V'yay-TA-ta la PAY-ska
NO HUNTING — NO FISHING

ACCESSO INTERDETTO
Aht-CHEHS-so een-tehr-DEHT-toh
ACCESS FORBIDDEN

Gli avvisi
Step 18 has dealt principally with past participles as you may see them on signs or may hear them used as adjectives. However, as all signs do not always include past participles, here are some other signs whose meaning you should know, especially if you travel through Italy:

vietato entrare	— no admittance
cautela	— caution
senso unico	— one way
passaggio a livello	— railroad crossing
rallentare	— slow down
deviare a destra	— detour (to the right)
incrocio pericoloso	— dangerous crossroads
passaggio pedonale	— passage for pedestrians
strada senza uscita	— dead-end street
consegna bagagli	— baggage checked
biglietteria	— ticket window
ufficio informazioni	— information
toletta	— toilet
signore	— ladies
signori	— gentlemen
uscita	— exit
entrata	— entrance

Ecco ancora degli esempi
EHK-ko ahn-KO-ra dell-yay-ZEHM-pee
Here are some more examples

del participio passato
del pahr-tee-CHEEP-yo pahs-SA-toh
of the past participle

questa volta impiegato al passivo:
KWESS-ta VOHL-ta eemp-yay-GA-toh ahl pahs-SEE-vo:
this time used in the passive:

L'italiano è parlato in Italia,
Lee-tahl-YA-no ay pahr-LA-toh ee-nee-TAHL-ya,
Italian is spoken in Italy,

> **Two ways of saying it**
> You can say — *L'italiano si parla* or *l'italiano è parlato.* The former is more frequently used.

ed anche in vari paesi del Mediterraneo.
ayd AHN-kay een VA-ree pa-AY-zee del may-dee-tay-RRA-nay-oh.
and also in various countries of the Mediterranean.

È usato inoltre in differenti parti
Ay oo-ZA-toh ee-NOHL-tray een deef-fay-REHN-tee PAHR-tee
It is used moreover in different parts

del mondo, dovunque si trovano
del MOHN-doh, doh-VOON-kway see TRO-va-no
of the world, wherever are found

grandi gruppi di immigranti italiani,
GRAHN-dee GROOP-pee dee eem-mee-GRAHN-tee ee-tahl-YA-nee,
large groups of Italian immigrants,

come negli Stati Uniti, in Argentina,
KO-may NELL-yee STA-tee oo-NEE-tee, ee-nahr-jen-TEE-na,
like in the United States, in Argentina,

nel Brasile, nel Canadà
nel Bra-SEE-lay, nel KA-na-DA
in Brazil, in Canada

ed in Australia.
ayd ee-na-oo-STRAHL-ya.
and in Australia.

> **"In" or "to" a country**
> The majority of countries are feminine in Italian. To say "in Italy," "in France," "to Italy," "to France," therefore, you say *in Italia, in Francia.* When the country is masculine *in* combines with the definite article — *nel* — *nel Canadà, nel Messico, nel Portogallo* or when the name of a country is plural, as

negli Stati Uniti (U.S.), nei Paesi Bassi (The Netherlands).

Sometimes, however, if the feminine country begins with s- followed by another consonant, an i- is prefaced to the name of that country to make it easier to say, as in the case of

in (or) to Spain   — in Ispagna
in (or) to
Switzerland   — in Isvizzera
in (or) to
Sweden   — in Isvezia
in (or) to Scotland — in Iscozia

The definite article is never used with names of continents, since all of them are also feminine: in Europa, in America, in Africa, in Asia.

La lingua italiana è conosciuta
La LEEN-gwa ee-tahl-YA-na ay ko-no-SHOO-ta
The Italian language is known

per la dolcezza e la bellezza
pehr la dohl-CHEHTS-sa ay la behl-LEHTS-sa
for the sweetness and beauty

dei suoi suoni, e per questo
day SWO-ee SWO-nee, ay pehr KWESS-toh
of its sounds, and for this

è molto usata nel canto,
ay MOHL-toh oo-SA-ta nel KAHN-toh,
it is very much used in singing,

dall'opera fino alle canzoni popolari.
dahl-LO-pay-ra FEE-no AHL-lay kahnt-SO-nee po-po-LA-ree.
from opera to popular songs.

TEST YOUR ITALIAN

Match these signs. Score 5 points for each correct answer. See answers on following page.

1. CHIUSO LA DOMENICA	RECOMMENDED TO ADULTS
2. VIETATO ENTRARE	PRICES REDUCED
3. APERTO FINO ALLE 22	ONE WAY
4. USCITA	CLOSED FOR REPAIRS
5. CHIUSO PER RIPARAZIONI	CLOSED ON SUNDAYS
6. PASSAGGIO A LIVELLO	LADIES
7. UFFICIO INFORMAZIONI	NO PARKING
8. VIETATO IL PARCHEGGIO	RESERVED SEAT
9. SIGNORI	OPEN TILL 10 P.M.
10. VIETATO FUMARE	NO ADMITTANCE
11. INCROCIO PERICOLOSO	GENTLEMEN
12. PREZZI RIDOTTI	LOST AND FOUND
13. TOLETTA	DETOUR (TO THE LEFT)
14. OGGETTI SMARRITI	RAILROAD CROSSING
15. SENSO UNICO	DANGEROUS CROSSROADS
16. POSTO PRENOTATO	TOILET
17. CONSIGLIATO AGLI ADULTI	INFORMATION

218

18. DEVIARE A SINISTRA   EXIT

19. BIGLIETTERIA   NO SMOKING

20. SIGNORE   TICKET WINDOW

SCORE _____%

step 19

HOW TO FORM THE PAST TENSE WITH *AVERE*

Il participio passato è impiegato
Eel pahr-tee-CHEEP-yo pahs-SA-toh ay eemp-yay-GA-toh
The past participle is used

per formare il passato dei verbi.
pehr fohr-MA-ray eel pahs-SA-toh day VEHR-bee.
to form the past tense of verbs.

Per essempio:
Pair es-*SEMP*-yo:
For example:

Si prende il presente di *avere*
See PREN-day eel pray-ZEN-tay dee *ah-VAY-ray*
You take the present of "to have"

e si mette col participio passato del verbo.
ay see MEHT-tay kohl pahr-tee-CHEEP-yo pahs-SA-toh del VEHR-bo.
and you put it with the past participle of the verb.

Ed ecco! Il passato è formato.
Ay-DEHK-ko! Eel pahs-SA-toh ay fohr-MA-toh.
And there you are! The past is formed.

Ecco degli esempi con verbi che formano
EK-ko dell-yay-ZEM-pee kohn VEHR-bee kay FOHR-ma-no
Here are some examples with verbs that form

il participio passato in -*ato*.
eel pahr-tee-CHEEP-yo pahs-SA-toh een -*ato*.
The past participle in -*ato*.

Il passato prossimo
The most important use of the past participle, which you just studied in Step 18, is its use in forming the ordinary past tense, called in Italian

il passato prossimo. This tense is formed by using the present of *avere* or *essere*, combined with the past participle of the verb. In Step 19, we are considering only the verbs that form their past with *avere*, while in Step 20, we will consider verbs that form their *passato prossimo* with the present of *essere*. Here is the *passato prossimo* of *trovare*, a verb of the first conjugation:

(io)	*ho trovato* — I have found (or) I found
(tu)	*hai trovato* — you have found (or) you found
(egli, ella, Lei)	*ha trovato* — he, she, you have found (or) he, etc. found
(noi)	*abbiamo trovato* — we have found (or) we found
(voi)	*avete trovato* — you have found (or) you found
(loro, Loro)	*hanno trovato* — they, you have found (or) they, you found

We have translated *ho trovato*, etc. both ways to show that there is no difference in Italian between "I have found" and "I found," as they are both expressed by the *passato prossimo*.

IO

Ieri, ho visitato il Museo del Vaticano.
YAY-ree, oh vee-zee-TA-toh eel Moo-ZAY-oh del Va-tee-KA-no.
Yesterday, I visited the Vatican Museum.

Ho guardato le statue ed i quadri.
Oh gwahr-DA-toh lay STA-tway ayd ee KWA-dree.
I looked at the statues and paintings.

Ho parlato a lungo con la guida.
Oh pahr-LA-toh ah LOON-go kohn la GWEE-da.
I spoke a long time with the guide.

Ho ascoltato le sue spiegazioni
Oh ah-skohl-TA-toh lay SOO-ay sp'yay-gahts-YO-nee
I listened to his explanations

con grande interesse.
kohn GRAHN-day een-tay-REHS-say.
with great interest.

L'ho ringraziato e gli ho dato una buona mancia.
Lo reen-grahts-YA-toh ay ll'yo DA-toh OO-na BWO-na MAHN-cha.
I thanked him and I gave him a good tip.

EGLI, ELLA

Ha telefonato qualcuno?
Ah tay-lay-fo-NA-toh kwahl-KOO-no?
Did anyone phone?

Sì, la signora Alberti ha chiamato.
See, la seen-YO-ra Ahl-BEHR-tee ah k'ya-MA-toh.
Yes, Mrs. Alberti called.

Ha lasciato un messaggio?
Ah la-SHA-toh oon mehs-SAHJ-jo?
Did she leave a message?

No, non ne ha lasciato.
No, nohn nay ah la-SHA-toh.
No, she didn't leave any.

Italian, as you will remember, has no special word for "do" or "don't" in asking questions or making negations and, in like manner, has no special word for "did" or "did not." The negative past is expressed the same as the present, by *non*, while the past is indicated by the form of the verb itself.

NOI

Abbiamo cercato un appartamento dappertutto.
**Ahb-B'YA-mo chehr-KA-toh oo-nahp-pahr-ta-MEN-toh
                                    dahp-pehr-TOOT-toh.**
We have looked for an apartment everywhere.

Abbiamo parlato con molta gente.
Ahb-B'YA-mo pahr-LA-toh kohn MOHL-ta JEN-tay.
We have spoken to many people.

Ma non abbiamo trovato niente.
Ma nohn ahb-B'YA-mo tro-VA-toh N'YEN-tay.
But we haven't found anything.

VOI

Che cosa avete studiato oggi a scuola?
Kay KO-za ah-VAY-tay stood-YA-toh OHDJ-jee ah SKWO-la?
What have you studied today at school?

Avete ascoltato bene il maestro?
Ah-VAY-tay ah-skohl-TA-toh BAY-nay eel ma-AY-stro?
Did you listen well to the teacher?

Avete giocato con i vostri piccoli amici?
Ah-VAY-tay jo-KA-toh kohn ee VO-stree PEE-ko-lee ah-MEE-chee?
Did you play with your little friends?

Avete mangiato i vostri panini?
Ah-VAY-tay mahn-JA-toh ee VO-stree pa-NEE-nee?
Did you eat your sandwiches?

LORO

Hanno passato una buon'estate?
AHN-no pahs-SA-toh OO-na bwo-nay-STA-tay?
Did you have a good summer?

Dicono che Loro hanno viaggiato molto.
DEE-ko-no kay LO-ro AHN-no v'yahdj-JA-toh MOHL-toh.
They say that you have travelled a lot.

> **"Loro" or "loro"**
> *Loro*, the form for "you" (plural), and *loro*, the
> form for "they," are the same; the only differ-
> ence being in the writing, in that a capital *L* indi-
> cates "you," while a small *l* indicates "they."

Quale città hanno trovato la più bella?
KWA-lay cheet-TA AHN-no tro-VA-toh la p'yoo BEL-la?
Which city did you find the most beautiful?

I Bernardi non hanno ancora accettato
Ee Behr-NAHR-dee no-NAHN-no ahn-KO-ra aht-cheht-TA-toh
The Bernards haven't yet accepted

il nostro invito per sabato.
eel NO-stro een-VEE-toh pehr SA-ba-toh.
our invitation for Saturday.

Spero che non lo hanno dimenticato.
SPEH-ro kay nohn lo AHN-no dee-men-tee-KA-toh.
I hope that they did not forget it.

Ecco alcuni esempi di verbi
EK-ko ahl-KOO-nee ay-ZEM-pee dee VEHR-bee
Here are some examples of verbs

che formano il participio passato in -*uto*.
kay FOHR-ma-no eel pahr-tee-CHEEP-yo pahs-SA-toh een -*uto*.
that form the past participle in -*uto*.

Ci scusi! Non abbiamo potuto
Chee SKOO-zee! No-nahb-B'YA-mo po-TOO-toh
Excuse us! We have not been able

venire più presto, perchè
vay-NEE-ray p'yoo PRAY-sto, pehr-KAY
to come earlier, because

ho dovuto aspettare mia moglie.
oh doh-VOO-toh ah-speht-TA-ray MEE-ah MOHL-yay.
I have had to wait for my wife.

Ha perduto più di un'ora
Ah pehr-DOO-toh p'yoo dee oo-NO-ra
She wasted more than an hour

> **Perdere**
> *Perdere* means "to lose," but in this case, the apologetic husband uses it to mean "spending," or "wasting time."

solamente per vestirsi.
so-la-MEN-tay pehr vay-STEER-see.
just to get dressed.

Ed ecco alcuni esempi di verbi
Ay-DEHK-ko ahl-KOO-nee ay-ZEM-pee dee VEHR-bee
And here are some examples of verbs

che formano il participio passato in -*ito.*
kay FOHR-ma-no eel pahr-tee-CHEEP-yo pahs-SA-toh een -*ito.*
that form the past participle in -*ito.*

— Hai finito di scrivere ad Elena?
Eye fee-NEE-toh dee SKREE-vay-ray ahd AY-lay-na?
Did you finish writing to Helen?

— Sì, ho finito di scriverle
See, oh fee-NEE-toh dee SKREE-vehr-lay
Yes, I finished writing to her

due ore fa, e ho già
DOO-ay OH-ray fa, ay oh ja
two hours ago, and I have already

> **Molto tempo fa**
> The third person singular of *fare* — *fa* — is
> used to express "ago."
>
> > *due anni fa* — two years ago
> > *un'ora fa* — an hour ago

spedito la lettera.
spay-DEE-toh la LET-tay-ra.
mailed the letter.

Alcuni verbi hanno
Ahl-KOO-nee VEHR-bee AHN-no
Some verbs have

dei participi passati irregolari:
day pahr-tee-CHEE-pee pahs-SA-tee ee-rray-go-LA-ree:
irregular past participles:

Avviso
Refer to Step 18, for a review of other irregular
past participles.

— Ha letto l'articolo su Enrico Lamore?
Ah LEHT-toh lahr-TEE-ko-lo soo En-REE-ko La-MO-ray?
Did you read the article on Enrico Lamore?

— Sì, l'ho visto.
See, lo VEE-sto.
Yes, I have seen it.

È scritto nel giornale di stamane.
Ay SKREET-toh nel johr-NA-lay dee sta-MA-nay.
It is written up in this morning's newspaper.

Ma non l'ho ancora letto.
Ma nohn lo ahn-KO-ra LEHT-toh.
But I have not read it yet.

Chi è? Che cosa ha fatto?
Kee ay? Kay KO-za ah FAHT-toh?
Who is he? What did he do?

— È un grande don Giovanni.
Ay oon GRAHN-day dohn Jo-VAHN-nee.
He is a great Don Juan.

Si figuri. L'articolo ha detto
See fee-GOO-ree. Lahr-TEE-ko-lo ah DEHT-toh
Imagine. The article said

che ha avuto cinque mogli.
kay ah ah-VOO-toh CHEEN-kway MOLL-yee.
that he has had five wives.

Avere
Avere, whose past participle is *avuto*, uses itself
to form the *passato prossimo:*

She has had a cold (or)
She had a cold
Ha avuto un raffreddore.

— Formidabile! Si può dire
Fohr-mee-DA-bee-lay! See pwo DEE-ray
Formidable! One can say

che ha vissuto molto, non crede?
kay ah vees-SOO-toh MOHL-toh, nohn KRAY-day?
that he has lived a lot, don't you think?

INSTANT CONVERSATION:
WHAT HAPPENED AT THE OFFICE

LA SEGRETARIA
La say-gray-TAHR-ya
THE SECRETARY

Buon giorno, signor Direttore.
Bwohn JOHR-no, seen-YOHR Dee-reht-TOH-ray.
Good morning, Mr. Director.

Ha fatto un buon viaggio?
Ah FAHT-toh oon bwohn V'YAHDJ-jo?
Did you have a good trip?

As you will hear them
In the following office dialogue, the various past participles are used not in isolated groups, but mixed as you will hear them in conversation.

IL DIRETTORE
Eel dee-reht-TOH-ray
THE DIRECTOR

Abbastanza buono, grazie.
Ahb-ba-STAHNT-sa BWO-no, GRAHTS-yay.
Rather good, thank you.

LA SEGRETARIA
Lei ci è mancato molto.
Lay chee ay mahn-KA-toh MOHL-toh.
We missed you very much.

To miss — to be lacking to
Mancare — "to miss" — has a different construction in Italian. Instead of saying "we miss someone," it is inverted to someone is "missing," or "lacking" to a person.

IL DIRETTORE
Davvero? C'è qualcosa di nuovo?
Dahv-VAY-ro? Chay kwahl-KO-za dee NWO-vo?
Really? Is there something new?

LA SEGRETARIA
Sì, il signor Marino ha venduto
See, eel seen-YOHR Ma-REE-no ah ven-DOO-toh
Yes, Mr. Marino has sold

sei automobili durante la Sua assenza.
say ah-oo-toh-MO-bee-lee doo-RAHN-tay la SOO-ah ahs-SENT-sa.
six automobiles during your absence.

IL DIRETTORE
Molto bene. E gli altri
MOHL-toh BAY-nay. Ay L'YAHL-tree
Very good. And the other

venditori, che cosa hanno fatto?
ven-dee-TOH-ree, kay KO-za AHN-no FAHT-toh?
salesmen, what did they do?

LA SEGRETARIA
Hanno venduto quattro dei nostri
AHN-no ven-DOO-toh KWAHT-tro day NO-stree
They sold four of our

nuovi modelli, due camion,
NWO-vee mo-DEL-lee, DOO-ay KAHM-yohn,
new models, two trucks,

No plural form
Words ending in a consonant, usually of foreign importation, and those ending with an accented vowel, do not change their form for the plural.

lo sport	*gli sport*
la città	*le città*

e dieci motociclette.
ay D'YAY-chee mo-toh-cheek-LEHT-tay.
and ten motorcycles.

IL DIRETTORE
Eccellente, benone.
Eht-chel-LEN-tay, bay-NO-nay.
Excellent, very good.

Ed i depositi alla banca,
Ayd ee day-PO-zee-tee AHL-la BAHN-ka,
And the deposits at the bank,

chi li ha fatti?
kee lee ah FAHT-tee?
who made them?

Agreement depending on position
Whenever the direct object precedes the verb,
the past participle agrees with it.

Ieri ho visto una bellissima ragazza.
Yesterday I saw a beautiful girl.
Oggi l'ho vista di nuovo.
Today I saw her again.

LA SEGRETARIA
Io stessa.
Ee-oh STEHS-sa.
I myself.

Li ho portati tutti i giorni
Lee oh pohr-TA-tee TOOT-tee ee JOHR-nee
I took them every day

prima di mezzogiorno.
PREE-ma dee mehts-so-JOHR-no.
before noon.

IL DIRETTORE
Bene! Vedo che non avete perduto tempo
BAY-nay! VAY-doh kay no-na-VAY-tay pehr-DOO-toh TEM-po
Well! I see that no time has been lost

durante la mia assenza.
doo-RAHN-tay la MEE-ah ahs-SENT-sa.
during my absence.

LA SEGRETARIA
Non ho mai lasciato l'ufficio
No-NO MA-ee la-SHA-toh loof-FEE-cho
I never left the office

prima delle sette o delle otte
PREE-ma DEL-lay SEHT-tay oh DEL-lay OHT-tay
before seven or eight

durante tutta la settimana.
doo-RAHN-tay TOOT-ta la seht-tee-MA-na.
during the whole week.

Ho dovuto restare tardi
Oh doh-VOO-toh ray-STA-ray TAHR-dee
I have had to stay late

per finire la posta.
pehr fee-NEE-ray la PO-sta.
to finish the mail.

IL DIRETTORE
E Michelina, La ha aiutata?
Ay Mee-kay-LEE-na, La ah ah-yoo-TA-ta?
And Michelina, did she help you?

LA SEGRETARIA
Non ha potuto venire per tre giorni,
No-NA po-TOO-toh vay-NEE-ray pehr tray JOHR-nee,
She has not been able to come in for three days,

a causa di un raffreddore,
ah KA-oo-sa dee oon rahf-frehd-DOH-ray,
because of a cold,

niente di grave.
N'YEN-tay dee GRA-vay.
nothing serious.

IL DIRETTORE
E la nuova dattilografa,
Ay la NWO-va daht-tee-LO-gra-fa,
And the new typist,

ha lavorato bene?
ah la-vo-RA-toh BAY-nay?
did she work well?

LA SEGRETARIA
Per dire la verità,
Pehr DEE-ray la vay-ree-TA,
To tell the truth,

non ha fatto un gran che.
no-NA FAHT-toh oon grahn kay.
she did not do much.

> **La traduzione (translation)**
> *Un gran che*, an idiom used here for ''much,'' is
> based on the interrogative *che*, meaning
> ''what''; in other words the new typist didn't do
> a big what.

Ha passato più parte del tempo
Ah pahs-SA-toh p'yoo PAHR-tay del TEM-po
She spent most of the time

a parlare al telefono.
ah pahr-LA-ray ahl tay-LAY-fo-no.
talking on the phone.

> **The infinitive instead of the participle**
> Italian often uses the infinitive where English
> would use the present participle.
>
> I heard her singing — *L'ho sentita contare.*
> I saw him coming — *L'ho visto venire.*

IL DIRETTORE
A proposito. Ha ricevuto
Ah pro-PO-zee-toh. Ah ree-chay-VOO-toh
By the way, did you receive

messaggi per me?
mehs-SAHJ-jee pehr may?
any messages for me?

LA SEGRETARIA

Sì, e abbiamo conservato un elenco
See, ay ahb-B'YA-mo kohn-sehr-VA-toh oon ay-LEHN-ko
Yes, and we have kept a list

delle telefonate che abbiamo ricevute.
DEL-lay tay-lay-fo-NA-tay kay ahb-B'YA-mo ree-chay-VOO-tay.
of the telephone calls that we received.

Una signora, una certa Lucrezia,
OO-na seen-YO-ra, OO-na CHEHR-ta Loo-KREHTS-ya,
A lady, a certain Lucrezia,

ha telefonato parecchie volte.
ah tay-lay-fo-NA-toh pa-REHK-k'yay VOHL-tay.
has telephoned several times.

Ma non ha voluto lasciare nè il suo cognome
Ma no-NA vo-LOO-toh la-SHA-ray nay eel SOO-oh kohn-YO-may
But she did not want to leave neither her last name

nè il suo numero telefonico.
nay eel SOO-oh NOO-may-ro tay-lay-FO-nee-ko.
nor her telephone number.

IL DIRETTORE

Vediamo . . . Ah sì, credo
Vehd-YA-mo . . . Ah see, KRAY-doh
Let's see . . . Ah yes, I think

di sapere chi è.
dee sa-PAY-ray kee ay.
I know who she is.

Dove ha messo i miei messaggi?
DOH-vay ah mehs-so ee m'yay mehs-SAHJ-jee?
Where did you put my messages?

LA SEGRETARIA

Nel tiretto della Sua scrivania.
Nel tee-REHT-toh DEL-la SOO-ah skree-va-NEE-ah.
In your desk drawer.

L'ho chiuso a chiave. Eccola qui.
Lo K'YOO-zo ah K'YA-vay. EK-ko-la kwee.
I locked it with a key. Here it is.

IL DIRETTORE
I miei complimenti, signorina;
Ee m'yay kohm-plee-MEN-tee, seen-yo-REE-na;
My congratulations, signorina;

Lei ha dimostrato molta discrezione.
Lay ah dee-mo-STRA-toh MOHL-ta dee-skrehts-YO-nay.
you have shown much discretion.

E giacchè ha lavorato molto,
Ay jahk-KAY ah la-vo-RA-toh MOHL-toh,
And since you worked a lot,

ho deciso di darle l'aumento
oh day-CHEE-zo dee DAHR-lay la-oo-MEN-toh
I have decided to give you the raise

del quale abbiamo già parlato.
del KWA-lay ahb-B'YA-mo ja pahr-LA-toh.
about which we have already spoken.

LA SEGRETARIA
Veramente? La ringrazio, signor Direttore.
**Vay-ra-MEN-tay? Lay reen-GRAHTS-yo, seen-YOHR
Dee-reht-TOH-ray.**
Really? I thank you (Mr. Director).

TEST YOUR ITALIAN

Translate these sentences into Italian, using the past tense with *avere*. Score 10 points for each correct answer. See answers below.

1. Yesterday I visited the Museum.

2. I looked at the paintings.

3. Did anyone phone?

4. Renata called.

5. Did she leave a message?

6. Did you have a good trip?

7. What did he do?

8. They did not forget.

9. What did she tell you?

10. We could not come earlier.

Answers: 1. Ieri ho visitato il Museo. 2. Ho guardato i quadri. 3. Ha telefonato qualcuno? 4. Renata ha chiamato. 5. Ha lasciato un messaggio? 6. Ha fatto un buon viaggio? 7. Che cosa ha fatto? 8. Non hanno dimenticato. 9. Che cosa le ha detto? 10. Non abbiamo potuto venire più presto.

SCORE _____%

step 20

HOW TO FORM THE PAST TENSE WITH *ESSERE*

Ecco alcuni verbi che formano
EHK-ko ahl-KOO-nee VEHR-bee kay FOHR-ma-no
Here are some verbs that form

il loro passato col verbo *essere;*
eel LO-ro pahs-SA-toh kohl VEHR-bo *EHS-say-ray;*
their past with the verb "to be";

alcuni di questi verbi
ahl-KOO-nee dee KWESS-tee VEHR-bee
some of these verbs

esprimono movimenti
es-SPREE-mo-no mo-vee-MEN-tee
express motions

> **Coming or going**
> An important group of verbs which forms the past by combining their past participle with *essere,* including those of motion, expressing the ideas of "going to," "coming from," "entering," "leaving," "staying," etc.

d'arrivo o di partenza, come:
da-RREE-vo oh dee pahr-TENT-sa, KO-may:
of arrival or departure, such as:

andare, venire, entrare,
ahn-DA-ray, vay-NEE-ray, en-TRA-ray,
"to go," "to come," "to enter,"

uscire, arrivare, partire,
oo-SHEE-ray, ah-rree-VA-ray, pahr-TEE-ray,
"to go out," "to arrive," "to leave,"

236

salire, scendere, restare, ecc.
sa-LEE-ray, SHEN-day-ray, ray-STA-ray, **eht-CHAY-tay-ra.**
"to go up," "to go down," "to stay," etc.

Ecco degli esempi:
EK-ko DAY-l'yee es-SEM-pee:
Here are some examples:

Siamo arrivati in ritardo perchè
S'YA-mo ah-rree-VA-tee een ree-TAHR-doh pehr-KAY
We have arrived late because

Agreement with past participle
Verbs that form the *passato prossimo* with *essere* agree with the subject in number and gender. This is why *arrivati* is in the masculine plural. If it were the feminine plural, the past participle would be *arrivate* in this case, but when the masculine and feminine are mixed in the plural, the masculine predominates.

siamo stati bloccati dal traffico.
S'YA-mo STA-tee blohk-KA-tee dahl TRAHF-fee-ko.
we were blocked by the traffic.

Siamo partiti da casa molto in anticipo.
S'YA-mo pahr-TEE-tee da KA-za MOHL-toh een ahn-TEE-chee-po.
We left home much ahead of time.

Siamo entrati in un tassì,
S'YA-mo en-TRA-tee ee-NOON tahs-SEE,
We got into a taxi,

vicino a Piazza San Pietro;
vee-CHEE-no ah P'YAHTS-sa Sahn P'YAY-tro;
near Saint Peter's Square;

e lì, il tassì non si è mosso di un centimetro
ay lee, eel tahs-SEE nohn see ay MO-so dee oon chen-TEE-may-tro
and there, the taxi didn't move one centimeter

per una mezz'ora.
pehr OO-na mehd-ZO-ra.
for half an hour.

Allora siamo scesi dal tassì,
Ahl-LO-ra S'YA-mo SHAY-zee dahl tahs-SEE,
Then we got out of the taxi,

e siamo venuti con la metropolitana!
ay S'YA-mo vay-NOO-tee kohn la may-tro-po-lee-TA-na!
and we came by subway!

Ci sono due altri verbi —
Chee SO-no DOO-ay AHL-tree VEHR-bee —
There are two other verbs —

molto importanti —
MOHL-toh eem-pohr-TAHN-tee —
very important ones —

nascere e *morire,* che prendono
NA-*shay-ray* ay *mo-REE-ray,* kay PREN-doh-no
"to be born" and "to die," which take

anche il verbo *essere.*
AHN-kay eel VEHR-bo *EHS-say-ray.*
also the verb "to be."

> **Motion?**
> *Nascere* and *morire* can also be considered
> verbs of arriving and leaving a place, for obvi-
> ous reasons.

Papa Giovanni XXIII è nato
PA-pa Jo-VAHN-nee ven-tee-tray-AY-zee-mo ay NA-toh
Pope John XXIII was born

nel 1881,
nel MEEL-lay oht-toh-CHEN-toh oht-tahn-TOO-no,
in 1881,

ed è morto a Roma
ay-DAY MOHR-toh ah RO-ma
and died in Rome

nel 1963,
nel MEEL-lay no-vay-CHEN-toh sehs-sahn-ta-TRAY,
in 1963,

all'età di 82 anni.
ahl-lay-TA dee oht-tahn-ta-DOO-ay AHN-nee.
at the age of 82.

Tutti i verbi riflessivi, come
TOOT-tee ee VEHR-bee ree-flehs-SEE-vee, KO-may
All the reflexive verbs, like

alzarsi, lavarsi, vestirsi,
ahld-ZAHR-see, la-VAHR-see, vay-STEER-see,
"to get (oneself) up," "to wash (oneself)," "to dress (oneself),"

divertirsi, ecc.,
dee-vehr-TEER-see, **eht-CHAY-tay-ra,**
"to enjoy oneself," etc.,

formano anche il loro passato
FOHR-ma-no AHN-kay eel LO-ro pahs-SA-toh
form their past also

con *essere.*
kohn *EHS-say-ray.*
with "to be."

Questa mattina mi sono alzato di buon'ora.
KWESS-ta maht-TEE-na mee SO-no ahld-ZA-toh dee bwo-NO-ra.
This morning I got up early.

Mi sono vestito in fretta.
Mee SO-no vay-STEE-toh een FREHT-ta.
I got dressed quickly.

"Essere" with reflexive verbs

The reflexive verbs inasmuch as they form the
passato prossimo with *essere,* also agree in
number and gender with the subject. If a woman
said "I got dressed," she would say *mi sono
vestita,* instead of *mi sono vestito.*

Mi sono detto:
Mee SO-no DEHT-toh:
I told myself:

239

"Per una volta, non sarò in ritardo."
"Pehr OO-na VOHL-ta, nohn sa-RO een ree-TAHR-doh."
"For once, I won't be late."

E mi sono sbrigato in fretta
Ay mee SO-no z'bree-GA-toh een FREHT-ta
And I hurried in (great) haste

per andare via in tempo.
pehr ahn-DA-ray VEE-ah een TEM-po.
in order to leave on time.

Non appena mi sono seduto
No-nahp-PAY-na mee SO-no say-DOO-toh
As soon as I sat down

per fare colazione, Maria
pehr FA-ray ko-lahts-YO-nay, Ma-REE-ah
to eat breakfast, Maria

> **More on "fare"**
> *Fare* — "to make" — is frequently used in certain idioms, to translate what in English would be "to have" or "to take" or other verbs.
>
> | | |
> |---|---|
> | *fare colazione* | — to have breakfast (or) lunch |
> | *fare vedere* | — to show |
> | *fare sapere* | — to inform |
> | *fare una visita* | — to visit |
> | *fare ritorno* | — to return |
> | *fare a tempo* | — to be in time |
> | *fare tardi* | — to be late |

si è tagliata tagliando il pane.
see ay tahl-l'YA-ta tahl-*l'yahn*-doh eel PA nay.
cut herself (while) cutting the bread.

Mi sono preso cura di lei,
Mee SO-no PRAY-zo KOO-ra dee lay,
I took care of her,

e per questo ho fatto tardi di nuovo.
ay pehr KWESS-toh oh FAHT-toh TAHR-dee dee NWO-vo.
and for this I was late again.

Fortunatamente, quando sono arrivato in ufficio,
**Fohr-too-na-ta-MEN-tay, KWAHN-doh SO-no ah-rree-VA-toh
ee-noof-FEE-cho,**
Fortunately, when I arrived at the office,

il padrone non se n'è accorto.
eel pa-DRO-nay nohn say nay ahk-KOHR-toh.
the boss did not notice it.

A spelling change for sound
The verb "to notice" is *accorgersi di* "to take note of." *Ne* is used here for "of it" with the past participle of *accorgersi*, which is *accorto*. The *se* is used instead of *si* for the reflexive because of the rule that when two pronouns come in front of a verb, the first one, even if it ordinarily ends in *-i*, changes to *-e*.

Il participio passato con *essere*
Eel pahr-tee-CHEEP-yo pahs-SA-toh kohn *EHS-say-ray*
The past participle with "to be"

si accorda col soggetto:
see ahk-KOHR-da kohl sohdj-JEHT-toh:
agrees with the subject:

Il signore è uscito.
Eel seen-YO-ray ay oo-SHEE-toh.
The gentleman has gone out.

Anche la signora è uscita.
AHN-kay la seen-YO-ra ay oo-SHEE-ta.
The lady has gone out also.

Non sono ancora ritornati.
Nohn SO-no ahn-KO-ra ree-tohr-NA-tee.
They have not come back yet.

Il participio passato con *avere*
Eel pahr-tee-CHEEP-yo pahs-SA-toh kohn *ay-VAY-ray*
The past participle with "to have"

si accorda col complemento diretto,
see ahk-KOHR-da kohl kohm-play-MEN-toh dee-REHT-toh,
agrees with the direct object,

quando questo viene *prima* del verbo.
KWAHN-doh KWESS-toh V'YAY-nay *PREE-ma* del VEHR-bo.
when this comes *before* the verb.

— Chi ha preso la lettera
  Kee ah PRAY-zo la LEHT-tay-ra
  Who took the letter

  che ho messa sulla tavola?
  kay oh MEHS-sa SOOL-la TA-vo-la?
  that I put on the table?

— Non l'ha presa nessuno.
  Nohn la PRAY-za nehs-SOO-no.
  Nobody took it.

  L'ha messa nella Sua tasca.
  La MEHS-sa NEL-la SOO-ah TA-ska.
  You put it into your pocket.

— E le altre lettere, le ha scritte?
  Ay lay AHL-tray LEHT-tay-ray, lay ah SKREET-tay?
  And the other letters, did you write them?

— Sì, e le ho già spedite.
  See, ay lay oh ja spay-DEE-tay.
  Yes, and I already mailed them.

INSTANT CONVERSATION: WHAT HAPPENED AT THE PARTY

As you will hear them

In the instant conversation for this lesson, examples of the *passato prossimo* are mixed, some being the verbs which form the past with *avere* and some with *essere*, so that you can become accustomed to hearing them used together.

PIETRO:
PYAY-tro:
PETER:
Ti sei divertito, ieri sera?
Tee say dee-vehr-TEE-toh, YAY-ree SAY-ra?
Did you have a good time last night?

CARLO:
KAR-lo:
CHARLES:
Più o meno. Sono uscito con Felicita.
P'YOO oh MAY-no. SO-no oo-SHEE-toh kohn Fay-LEE-chee-ta.
More or less. I went out with Felicita.

PIETRO:
E che è successo?
Ay kay ay soot-CHEHS-so?
And what happened?

CARLO:
Si è incollerita, e non vuole più parlarmi.
See ay een-kohl-lay-REE-ta, ay nohn VWO-lay p'yoo pahr-LAHR-mee.
She became angry, and she does not want to talk to me any more.

PIETRO:

Come mai? Che è avvenuto?
KO-may mye? Kay ay ahv-vay-NOO-toh?
How come? What happened?

CARLO:

Siamo andati da Marcello.
S'YA-mo ahn-DA-tee da Mahr-CHEL-lo.
We went to Marcel's.

Abbiamo ballato, cantato,
Ahb-B'YA-mo bahl-LA-toh, kahn-TA-toh,
We danced, sang,

e ci siamo divertiti molto.
ay chee S'YA-mo dee-vehr-TEE-tee MOHL-toh.
and we enjoyed ourselves very much.

Tutto è andato bene
TOOT-toh ay ahn-DA-toh BAY-nay
Everything went fine

fino all'arrivo di Beatrice.
FEE-no ahl-la-RREE-vo dee Bay-ah-TREE-chay.
until the arrival of Beatrice.

Mi ha fatto gli occhi dolci.
Mee ah FAHT-toh LL'YOHK-kee DOHL-chee.
She made eyes at me.

La traduzione
Colloquial expressions can be approximated, although not translated exactly, as here, in the case of *fare gli occhi dolci a qualcuno* — literally, "to make sweet eyes at someone" — in English, the idiom would be "to make eyes at someone."

Ho ballato un poco con lei.
Oh bahl-LA-toh oon PO-ko kohn lay.
I danced a little with her.

E abbiamo anche parlato un poco.
Ay ahb-B'YA-mo AHN-kay pahr-LA-toh oon PO-ko.
And we also talked for a while.

PIETRO:

Ora vedo! E Felicita
OH-ra VAY-doh! Ay Fay-LEE-chee-ta
Now I see! And Felicita

si è incollerita.
see ay een-kohl-lay-REE-ta.
got angry.

CARLO:

Esattamente. E ha voluto
Ay-zaht-ta-MEN-tay. Ay ah vo-LOO-toh
Exactly. And she wanted

rincasare immediatamente.
reen-ka-SA-ray eem-mehd-ya-ta-MEN-tay.
to go home immediately.

Non ho potuto calmarla.
No-NO po-TOO-toh kahl-MAHR-la.
I was not able to calm her down.

Ho dovuto chiamare un tassì
Oh doh-VOO-toh k'ya-MA-ray oon tahs-SEE
I had to call a taxi

per portarla a casa.
pehr pohr-TAHR-la ah KA-za.
to take her home.

Quando l'ho lasciata, non mi ha detto
KWAHN-doh LO la-SHA-ta, nohn mee ah DEHT-toh
When I left her, she did not tell me

nè grazie nè arrivederci.
nay GRAHTS-yay nay ah-rree-vay-DEHR-chee.
either thank you or good-bye.

245

PIETRO:

E stamattina, le hai parlato?
Ay sta-maht-TEE-na, lay AH-ee pahr-LA-toh?
And this morning, did you talk to her?

CARLO:

Sicuro. Le ho telefonato.
See-KOO-ro. Lay oh tay-lay-fo-NA-toh.
Sure. I called her on the phone.

Ho cercato di parlarle.
Oh chehr-KA-toh dee pahr-LAHR-lay.
I tried to talk to her.

Where to use "di" with infinitives
Some verbs that combine with infinitives, combine directly, such as *potere, dovere, volere, sapere.*
I want to go out — *Voglio uscire*

Other verbs take *di* before the following infinitive. This group includes, among others:

dire di	— to tell (to)
promettere di	— to promise (to)
dimenticare di	— to forget (to)
finire di	— to finish . . .
ringraziare di	— to thank (for)
permettere di	— to permit (to)
rifiutare di	— to refuse (to)
cercare di	— to try (to)

Ma ha interrotto la comunicazione
Ma ah een-tay-RROHT-toh la ko-moo-nee-kahts-YO-nay
But she hung up

non appena ha riconosciuto la mia voce.
no-nahp-PAY-na ah ree-ko-no-SHOO-toh la MEE-ah VO-chay.
as soon as she recognized my voice.

Appena — non appena
Appena means "hardly" or "just," while *non appena* means "as soon as."

She just left — *È appena uscita.*
As soon as he comes — *Non appena arriva.*

PIETRO:

Allora, non ti ha lasciato
Ahl-LO-ra, nohn tee ah la-SHA-toh
Then, she did not even leave you

nemmeno il tempo di spiegarti.
nehm-MAY-no eel TEM-po dee sp'yay-GAHR-tee.
the time to explain yourself.

Cosa vuoi?
KO-za VWO-ee?
What can you do?

> **Cosa vuole?**
> *Cosa vuoi?*, or for the formal *cosa vuole?*, is lit-
> erally the familiar form of "what do you want?,"
> but idiomatically, it means "what can you do?"
> or "that is how it is!"

Felicita è sempre stata gelosa.
Fay-LEE-chee-ta ay SEM-pray STA-ta jay-LO-za.
Felicita has always been jealous.

CARLO:

È possibile . . .
Ay pohs-SEE-bee-lay . . .
That is possible . . .

ma non ho mai avuto problemi
ma no-NO MA-ee ah-VOO-toh prohb-LAY-mee
but I have never had problems

con lei . . . prima, cioè.
kohn lay . . . PREE-ma, cho-AY.
with her . . . before, that is.

PIETRO:

C'è sempre una prima volta.
Chay SEM-pray OO-na PREE-ma VOHL-ta.
There is always a first time.

Vuoi un consiglio?
VWO-ee oon kohn-SEELL-yo?
Do you want some advice?

Informal speech
You will have noticed that Pietro and Carlo have been using the verb forms corresponding to *tu* to each other, as natural to young people on informal terms.

Mandale dei fiori,
MAHN-da-lay day F'YO-ree,
Send her some flowers,

se non l'hai fatto ancora.
say nohn LA-ee FAHT-toh ahn-KO-ra.
if you have not yet done it.

Un tale gesto metterà tutto a posto.
Oon ta-lay JAY-sto met-tay-RA TOOT-toh ah PO-sto.
Such a gesture will arrange everything.

TEST YOUR ITALIAN

Fill in the past participles for the following constructions with *essere*. Score 10 points for each correct answer. See answers below.

1. Siamo _____ in ritardo. (fem.)
   (arrived)

2. Siamo _____ dal tassì. (masc.)
   (got out)

3. Siamo _____ con la metropolitana. (masc.)
   (came)

4. Mi sono _____ di buon'ora. (masc.)
   (got up)

5. Mi sono _____ in fretta. (fem.)
   (got dressed)

6. Paola non è ancora _____.
   (arrived)

7. Che cosa è _____?
   (happened)

8. Siamo _____ da Marcello. (masc.)
   (went)

9. Il signor Durante è _____.
   (left)

10. Quando è _____ Papa Giovanni XXIII?
    (died)

SCORE _____%

249

step 21

HOW TO USE THE CONDITIONAL FOR REQUESTS, INVITATIONS, AND REPORTED SPEECH

L'espressione *vorrei* è un esempio
Lay-spress-YO-nay vo-RRAY ay oo-nay-ZEMP-yo
The expression "I would like" is an example

del condizionale usato in termini educati.
del kohn-deets-yo-NA-lay oo-ZA-toh een TEHR-mee-nee ay-doo-KA-tee.
of the conditional used in polite terms.

> **The polite "would"**
> The conditional is not a tense but a mood, corresponding to several uses of the English "would," *Vorrei* — "I would like," which you have noted as a special expression in some previous Steps, is the conditional of "to want," meaning "I would want," or "I would like," a more polite and less blunt way of expressing yourself than simply to say "I want."

Il condizionale si usa spesso
Eel kohn-deets-yo-NA-lay see OO-za SPEHS-so
The conditional is often used

in inviti, in suggerimenti,
ee-neen-VEE-tee, een sooj-jay-ree-MEN-tee,
in invitations, suggestions,

in offerte o in domande, come:
ee-nohf-FEHR-tay oh een doh-MAHN-day, KO-may:
offers or requests, like:

Vorrebbe qualche cosa da bere?
Vo-RREHB-bay KWAHL-kay KO-za da BAY-ray?
Would you like something to drink?

Portrebbe venire con noi?
Po-TREHB-bay vay-NEE-ray kohn noy?
Could you come with us?

Per formare il condizionale,
Pehr fohr-MA-ray eel kohn-deets-yo-NA-lay,
To form the conditional,

si aggiungono le terminazioni
see ahj-JOO-go-no lay tehr-mee-nahts-YO-nee
one adds the endings

-ei, -esti, -ebbe, -emmo, -este, -ebbero

all'infinito,
ahl-leen-fee-NEE-toh,
to the infinitive,

The conditional endings

The conditional is formed in exactly the same way as the future tense, except that the endings are different. Here are the forms of *parlare*, in the conditional, equivalent to "would speak":

(io)	*parlerei* — I would speak
(tu)	*parleresti* — you would speak
(egli, ella, Lei)	*parlerebbe* — he, she, you would speak
(noi)	*parleremmo* — we would speak
(voi)	*parlereste* — you would speak
(loro, Loro)	*parlerebbero* — they, you would speak

And remember *lui* and *lei* are alternate forms of *egli* and *ella*.

The verbs that have irregular stems in the future, which we have noted in Step 17, retain the same stems for the conditional, with, of course, the conditional endings.

251

Degli esempi:
DAYL-yee es-sem-pee:
Some examples:

— Potrei farle una fotografia?
Po-TRAY FAR-lay OO-na fo-toh-gra-FEE-ah?
Could I take a picture of you?

> **Could I?**
> When *potere* meaning "can" or "may" is used
> in the conditional, it means "could" or "might."

— Me ne farebbe una anche a me?
May nay fa-REHB-bay OO-na AHN-kay ah may?
Would you take one of me too?

— Con questo bel tempo, non vi piacerebbe
Kohn KWESS-toh bel TEM-po, nohn vee p'ya-chay-REHB-bay
With this fine weather, wouldn't you like

fare una passeggiata in automobile?
FA-ray OO-na pahs-sehj-JA-ta ee-na-oo-toh-MO-bee-lay?
to take a ride in the car?

Potremmo andare al Ristorante
Po-TREM-mo ahn-DA-ray ahl Ree-sto-RAHN-tay
We could go to the Restaurant

Villa dei Cesari per fare colazione.
VEEL-la day CHAY-za-ree pehr FA-ray ko-lahts-YO-nay.
Villa of the Ceasars to have lunch.

Vi piacerebbe?
Vee p'ya-chay-REHB-bay?
Would you like that?

— Tanto. Ma non oggi.
TAHN-toh. Ma no-NOHDJ-jee.
Very much. But not today.

— Sarebbe possibile domani?
Sa-REHB-bay pohs-SEE-bee-lay doh-MA-nee?
Would it be possible tomorrow?

— Sì, credo che domani potrei.
See, KRAY-doh kay doh-MA-nee po-TRAY.
Yes, I think that tomorrow I might.

Ecco come si usa il condizionale
EK-ko KO-may see OO-za eel kohn-deets-yo-NA-lay
Here is how the conditional is used

per domandare qualche cosa
pehr doh-mahn-DA-ray KWAHL-kay KO-za
to request something

con educazione e cortesia.
kohn ay-doo-kahts-YO-nay ay kohr-tay-ZEE-ah.
politely and more courteously.

— Portrebbe farmi un favore?
Po-TREHB-bay FAHR-mee oon fa-VO-ray?
Could you do me a favor?

Le sarebbe possibile
Lay sa-REHB-bay pohs-SEE-bee-lay
Would it be possible for you

prestarmi cinque mila lire?
pray-STAHR-mee CHEEN-kway MEE-la LEE-ray?
to lend me five thousand liras?

Potrei restituirgliele fra una settimana.
Po-TRAY ray-stee-TWEER-l'yay-lay fra OO-na seht-tee-MA-na.
I would be able to give them back to you within a week.

Pronouns attached to infinitives
Notice how three words are written together as one: *restituire, gli* and *le*, after the conditional of *potere*. When pronouns are attached to the infinitive in some constructions, the final -e drops from the infinitive. Although *gli* means "to him" when used separately, it can mean "to him," "to her," or "to you" when written together with a direct object pronoun, as in this case, and an extra -e- is added between the two pronouns *gli* and *le* to make it easier to say.

— Lo farei volentieri,
Lo fa-RAY vo-lent-YAY-ree,
I would do it willingly,

ma non ho denaro con me.
ma no-NO day-NA-ro kohn may.
but I don't have any money with me.

— Non avrebbe almeno mille lire?
No-nahv-REHB-bay ahl-MAY-no MEEL-lay LEE-ray?
Wouldn't you have at least a thousand liras?

Ci si serve del condizionale anche
Chee see SEHR-vay del kohn-deets-yo-NA-lay AHN-kay
The conditional is also used

per raccontare ciò che è stato detto
pehr rahk-kohn-TA-ray cho kay ay STA-toh DEHT-toh
to tell what was said

> **Ciò che**
> *Ciò che* is equivalent to "what," as a relative
> clause, in the sense of "that which."
> "Give me what you have" — *Mi dia ciò che
> ha.*

nel passato su progetti futuri.
nel pahs-SA-toh soo pro-JET-tee foo-TOO-ree.
in the past about future plans.

> **He said he would — etc.**
> Another important use of the conditional is to
> tell what someone said in the past about their
> future plans. Compare:
> > *Dice che verrà domani.* — He says that he
> > will come tomorrow.
> > *Ha detto che verrebbe domani.* — He said
> > that he would come tomorrow.

— Le ha domandato il padrone
Lay ah doh-mahn-DA-toh eel pa-DRO-nay
Did the boss ask you

quando prenderebbe le Sue vacanze?
KWAHN-doh pren-day-REHB-bay lay SOO-ay va-KAHNT-say?
when you would take your vacation?

Vacation is plural in Italian.

— No, ma mi ha detto che egli
No, ma mee ah DEHT-toh kay ELL-yee
No, but he told me that he

sarebbe assente in luglio,
sa-REHB-bay ahs-SEN-tay een LOOL-yo,
would be away in July,

e che in agosto sarebbe in America
ay kay ee-na-GO-sto sa-REHB-bay ee-na-MAY-ree-ka
and that in August he would be in America

per una conferenza.
pehr OO-na kohn-fay-RENT-sa.
for a conference.

— In quel caso, sarebbe meglio per Lei
Een kwel KA-zo, sa-REHB-bay MELL-yo pehr Lay
In that case, it would be better for you

prendere le Sue vacanze più tardi.
PREN-day-ray lay SOO-ay va-KAHNT-say p'yoo TAHR-dee.
to take your vacation later.

Dovrebbe domandargli se Lei
Dohv-REHB-bay doh-mahn-DAHRLL-yee say Lay
You should ask him if you

"Dovere" in the conditional

Dovere means "to be obliged to" and also "to owe," but, in its conditional form, it means "ought" or "should" in the sense of obligation, necessity, or urging someone to do something.

You ought to read that book — *Dovrebbe leggere quel libro.*

We really ought to leave now — *Dovremmo veramente andare adesso.*

potrebbe prenderle in settembre.
po-TREHB-bay PREN-dehr-lay een seht-TEM-bray.
could take them (it) in September.

Così non avrebbe nessuna difficoltà
Ko-ZEE no-nahv-REHB-bay nehs-SOO-na deef-fee-kohl-TA
That way you wouldn't have any difficulty

a trovare posto negli alberghi.
ah tro-VA-ray PO-sto NELL-yee ahl-BEHR-ghee.
in finding room in hotels.

INSTANT CONVERSATION: LEAVING A TELEPHONE MESSAGE

— Pronto? Potrei parlare
PROHN-toh? Po-TRAY pahr-LA-ray
Hello? Could I speak

> **Per le conversazione per telefono**
> *Pronto,* literally "ready," is the accepted way of answering the phone. Some other telephone expressions:
>
> > *Rimanga in linea* — "Hold the line."
> > *La linea è occupata* — "The line is busy."
> > *L'utente non risponde* — "The party doesn't answer."
> > *Ha sbagliato il numero* — "You've got the wrong number."
> > *Con chi parlo?* — "With whom am I speaking?"

con la signora Giuliani?
kohn la seen-YO-ra Jool-YA-nee?
with Mrs. Giuliani?

— Non c'è, signore; è uscita.
Nohn chay, seen-YO-ray; ay oo-SHEE-ta.
She is not in, sir; she went out.

— Ma mi ha detto che sarebbe
Ma mee ah DEHT-toh kay sa-REHB-bay
But she told me that she would be

a casa a quest'ora!
ah KA-za ah kwess-TOH-ra!
at home at this time!

Non ha detto quando ritornerebbe?
No-NA DEHT-toh KWAHN-doh ree-tor-nay-REHB-bay?
She didn't say when she would come back?

— Ha lasciato detto che forse
Ah la-SHA-toh DEHT-toh kay FOHR-say
She left word that maybe

sarebbe in ritardo,
sa-REHB-day een ree-TAHR-doh,
she would be late,

che avrebbe delle compere da fare prima,
kay ahv-REHB-bay DEL-lay KOHM-pay-ray da FA-ray PREE-ma,
that she would do some shopping first,

e che, dopo, sarebbe andata
ay kay, DOH-po, sa-REHB-bay ahn-DA-ta
and that, after, she would go

a prendere una tazza di caffè
a PREN-day-ray OO-na TAHTS-sa dee kahf-FAY
to take a cup of coffee

in casa di un'amica,
een KA-za dee oo-na-MEE-ka,
at a friend's house,

e che rientrerebbe a casa verso le otto.
ay kay ree-en-tray-REHB-bay ah KA-za VEHR-so lay OHT-toh.
and that she would come home at about eight o'clock.

Avrebbe la gentilezza di telefonare più tardi?
Ahv-REHB-bay la jen-tee-LEHTS-sa dee tay-lay-fo-NA-ray p'YOO TAHR-dee?
Would you be so kind as to call later?

> **La cortesia**
> *Avrebbe la gentilezza* really means "would you have the kindness' or "would you be so kind"

— Certamente. Ma potrebbe dire alla signora Giuliani
Chehr-ta-MEN-tay. Ma po-TREHB-bay DEE-ray AHL-la seen-YO-ra
Jool-YA-nee
Certainly. But could you tell Mrs. Giuliani

che il signor Bianchini
kay eel seen-YOHR B'yahn-KEE-nee
that Mr. Bianchini

ha telefonato?
ah tay-lay-fo-NA-toh?
telephoned?

Prego, le dica di chiamarmi.
PRAY-go, lay DEE-ka dee k'ya-MAR-mee.
Please, ask her to call me.

TEST YOUR ITALIAN

Translate the following sentences into Italian. Score 10 points for each correct answer. See answers below.

1. You should visit Villa Borghese.

2. He said that he would come at eight.

3. How much time would it take?

4. Would you have something to drink?

5. I would like to buy some stamps.

6. Could I take a picture?

7. It would be better to leave right now.

8. We would like to see the Catacombs.

9. Could I speak to Claudia?

10. Could you do it?

Answers: 1. Lei dovrebbe visitare Villa Borghese. 2. Ha detto che verrebbe alle otto. 3. Quanto tempo prenderebbe? 4. Vorrebbe qualche cosa da bere? 5. Vorrei comprare dei francobolli. 6. Potrei prendere una fotografia? 7. Sarebbe meglio andare via adesso. 8. Vorremmo vedere le Catacombe. 9. Potrei parlare con Claudia? 10. Potrebbe farlo?

SCORE _____%

step 22

THE IMPERFECT — A TENSE TO USE WHEN TELLING A STORY

Quando usiamo espressioni come
KWAHN-doh oos-YA-mo ay-spress-YO-nee KO-may
When we use expressions like

"Mio padre diceva sempre . . ."
"MEE-oh PA-dray dee-CHAY-va SEM-pray . . ."
"My father always used to say . . ."

o "Quando ero giovane . . ."
oh **"KWAHN-doh AY-ro JO-va-nay . . ."**
or "When I was young . . ."

o "Quando abitavamo in Lombardia . . ."
oh "KWAHN-doh ah-bee-ta-VA-mo een Lohm-bahr-DEE-ah . . ."
or "When we used to live in Lombardy . . ."

o "Quando eravamo al Liceo . . ."
oh **"KWAHN-doh ay-ra-VA-mo ahl Lee-CHAY-oh . . ."**
or "When we were in high school . . ."

o altre frasi per descrivere azioni
oh AHL-tray FRA-zee pehr day-SKREE-vay-ray ahts-YO-nee
or other phrases describing actions

ripetute o continuate nel passato
ree-pay-TOO-tay oh kohn-tee-NWA-tay nel pahs-SA-toh
repeated or continued in the past

bisogna usare l'imperfetto.
bee-ZOHN-ya oo-ZA-ray leem-pehr-FEHT-toh.
we must use the imperfect.

When to use the imperfect
The imperfect is equivalent to the English "used to" in the sense of a continued action in the past whether or not "used to" is specifically

261

used. For instance, to say you were living somewhere for a period of time, use the imperfect, to express this continued action as this was a continued action. The imperfect is also used for something that was going on at a certain time.

I was singing	*cantavo*
I used to sing	*cantavo*
You were dancing	*ballava*
You used to dance	*ballava*
They were living	*vivevano*
They used to live	*vivevano*

Per riconoscere l'imperfetto
Pehr ree-ko-NO-shay-ray leem-pehr-FEHT-toh
To recognize the imperfect

in conversazione, si noti
een kohn-vehr-sahts-YO-nay, see NO-tee
in conversation, note

la lettera -*v*- nelle terminazioni
la LEHT-tay-ra *vee* NEL-lay tehr-mee-nahts-YO-nee
the letter "-v-" in the endings

di tutte le persone di questo tempo.
dee TOOT-tay lay pehr-SO-nay dee KWESS-toh TEM-po.
of all the persons of this tense.

How to form the imperfect
The imperfect endings for the three conjugations are as follows:

FIRST CONJUGATION	SECOND CONJUGATION
-*avo*	-*evo*
-*avi*	-*evi*
-*ava*	-*eva*
-*avamo*	-*evamo*
-*avate*	-*evate*
-*avano*	-*evano*

THIRD CONJUGATION
-*ivo*
-*ivi*
-*iva*

-ivamo
-ivate
-ivano

Here is how they look applied to the three conjugations:

parlare	*scrivere*	*finire*
parlavo	*scrivevo*	*finivo*
parlavi	*scrivevi*	*finivi*
parlava	*scriveva*	*finiva*
parlavamo	*scrivevamo*	*finivamo*
parlavate	*scrivevate*	*finivate*
parlavano	*scrivevano*	*finivano*

The only exception to this rule is *essere*, whose six imperfect forms are:

ero	—	I was
eri	—	you were
era	—	he, she, you were
eravamo	—	we were
eravate	—	you were
erano	—	they, you were

Essempi del imperfetto:

La nonna ci diceva sempre
La NOHN-na chee dee-CHAY-va SEM-pray
Grandmother always used to tell us

che, quando era giovane lei,
kay, KWAHN-doh AY-ra JO-va-nay lay,
that, when she was young,

tutto era differente.
TOOT-toh AY-ra deef-fay-REN-tay.
everything was different.

Se due giovani volevano uscire insieme,
Say DOO-ay JO-va-nee vo-LAY-va-no oo-SHEE-ray eens-YAY-may,
If two young people wanted to go out together,

dovevano prima fidanzarsi,
doh-VAY-va-no PREE-ma fee-dahnt-SAHR-see,
they had to get engaged first,

e poi potevano incominciare
ay poy po-TAY-va-no een-ko-meen-CHA-ray
and then they could start

a vedersi, ma mai da soli.
ah vay-DEHR-see, ma MA-ee da SO-lee.
seeing each other, but never alone.

Ci doveva sempre essere
Chee doh-VAY-va SEM-pray EHS-say-ray
There always had to be

qualcuno con loro. Secondo lei,
kwahl-KOO-no kohn LO-ro. Say-KOHN-doh lay,
somebody with them. According to her,

che credeva di avere sempre ragione,
kay kray-DAY-va dee ah-VAY-ray SEM-pray ra-JO-nay,
who thought she was always right,

nei tempi moderni tutto stava andando
nay TEM-pee mo-DEHR-nee TOOT-toh STA-va ahn-DAHN-doh
in modern times everything was going (changing)

per il peggio, e che la miglior cosa
pehr eel PEHDJ-jo, ay kay la meel-YOHR KO-za
for the worse, and that the best thing

era di ritornare ai costumi dei tempi passati.
AY-ra dee ree-tohr-NA-ray AH-ee ko-STOO-mee day TEM-pee
pahs-SA-tee.
was to go back to the customs of past times.

Noi, invece, le dicevamo che pensava
Noy, een-VAY-chay, lay dee-chay-VA-mo kay pen-SA-va
We, instead, used to tell her that she thought

all'antica e che aveva torto,
ahl-lahn-TEE-ka ay kay ah-VAY-va TOHR-toh,
in an old-fashioned way and that she was wrong,

che le cose oggidì andavano molto bene
kay lay KO-zay ohdj-jee-DEE ahn-DA-va-no MOHL-toh BAY-nay
that things nowadays were going very well

e che a noi piacevano proprio come erano.
ay kay ah noy p'ya-CHAY-va-no PRO-pr'yo KO-may AY-ra-no.
and that we liked them just as they were.

INSTANT CONVERSATION: A FAMILY REUNION — RECALLING THE PAST

LUI:
LOO-ee:
HE:

Oggi andremo a pranzo
OHDJ-jee ahnd-RAY-mo ah PRAHNT-so
Today we are going to have dinner

dai miei nonni.
DA-ee m'yay NOHN-nee.
at my grandparents'.

Ti parleranno molto di me.
Tee pahr-lay-RAHN-no MOHL-toh dee may.
They will talk to you a lot about me.

Ti racconteranno certamente
Tee rahk-kohn-tay-RAHN-no chehr-ta-MEN-tay
They will certainly tell you

come ero e tutto ciò che facevo
KO-may AY-ro ay TOOT-toh cho kay fa-CHAY-vo
how I was and all that I used to do

quando ero piccolo . . .
KWAHN-doh AY-ro PEEK-ko-lo . . .
when I was small . . .

Dai nonni
Dye NOHN-nee
At the grandparent's

LA NONNA:
La NOHN-na:
THE GRANDMOTHER:
Sapete, Riccardo sempre
Sa-PAY-tay, Reek-KAHR-doh SEM-pray
You know, Richard always

passava tutte le estati da noi in Toscana.
pahs-SA-va TOOT-tay lay ay-STA-tee da noy een Toh-SKA-na.
used to spend all the summers with us in Tuscany.

A question of formality
The grandmother in talking to her granddaughter-in-law, uses *voi*, instead of *tu*, which would be too familiar for someone that she has not met yet, even though they are of the same family, or of *Lei* which would be somewhat too formal.

Era un bellissimo ragazzino,
AY-ra oon bel-LEES-see-mo ra-gahts-SEE-no,
He was a very beautiful little boy,

ed era molto intelligente,
ay-DAY-ra MOHL-toh een-tel-lee-JEN-tay,
and he was very intelligent,

ma ci dava tanti problemi . . .
ma chee DA-va TAHN-tee prohb-LAY-mee . . .
but he used to give us so many problems . . .

tanti mal di testa . . .
TAHN-tee mahl dee TAY-sta . . .
so many headaches . . .

IL NONNO:
Eel NOHN-no:
THE GRANDFATHER:
Se ne andava senza dirci dove andava.
Say nay ahn-DA-va SENT-sa DEER-chee DOH-vay ahn-DA-va.
He used to leave without telling us where he was going.

Delle volte, faceva da solo
DEL-lay VOHL-tay fa-CHAY-va da SO-lo
At times, he would take by himself

delle pericolose camminate in montagna.
DEL-lay pay-ree-ko-LO-zay kahm-mee-NA-tay een mohn-TAHN-ya.
some dangerous walks in the mountains.

LA NONNA:
Non potevamo mai sapere
Nohn po-tay-VA-mo MA-ee sa-PAY-ray
We could never know

dove poteva essere.
DOH-vay po-TAY-va EHS-say-ray.
where he could be.

Eravamo sempre preoccupati.
Ay-ra-VA-mo SEM-pray pray-ohk-koo-PA-tee.
We were always worried.

Inventava dei giochi violenti.
Een-ven-TA-va day JO-kee v'yo-LEN-tee.
He used to invent violent games.

Aveva la sua banda di ragazzi,
Ah-VAY-va la SOO-ah BAHN-da dee ra-GAHTS-see,
He had his boys' gang,

e giocavano alla guerra . . .
ay jo-KA-va-no AHL-la GWAY-rra . . .
and they used to play war . . .

si gettavano pietre e petardi
see jeht-TA-va-no P'YAY-tray ay pay-TAHR-dee
they threw stones and firecrackers at each other

senza nessuna cautela.
SENT-sa nehs-SOO-na ka-oo-TAY-la.
without any caution.

I vicini protestavano . . .
Eee vee-CHEE-nee pro-tay-STA-va-no . . .
The neighbors used to protest . . .

IL NONNO:

Al cinema, gli piacevano
Ahl CHEE-nay-ma, ll'yee p'ya-CHAY-va-no
At the movies, he liked

soprattutto i westerns.
so-pra-TOOT-toh ee WEHS-tehrns.
most the Westerns.

Voleva andare in America
Vo-LAY-va ahn-DA-ray ee-na-MAY-ree-ka
He wanted to go to America

per vedere i cow-boy
pehr vay-DAY-ray ee cow-boy
to see the cowboys

ed i pellirossa.
ayd ee pel-lee-ROHS-sa.
and Indians (literally, "redskins").

LA NONNA:

Ma con noi era sempre
Ma kohn noy AY-ra SEM-pray
But with us he was always

così affettuoso.
ko-ZEE ahf-feht-T'WO-zo.
so affectionate.

Quando è partito per gli Stati Uniti,
KWAHN-doh ay pahr-TEE-toh pehr ll'yee STA-tee Oo-NEE-tee,
When he left for the United States,

credevamo che andava semplicemente
kray-day-VA-mo kay ahn-DA-va sem-plee-chay-MEN-tay
we thought that he was simply

a visitare il paese
ah vee-zee-TA-ray eel pa-AY-zay
going to visit the country

e che ritornerebbe fra poco.
ay kay re-tor-nay-REB-bay fra PO-ko.
and that he would come back soon.

> **Si ricordi**
> Note the use of the conditional to express future intention that was stated in the past.

Naturalmente, non sapevamo
Na-too-rahl-MEN-tay, nohn sa-pay-VA-mo
Naturally, we did not know

che doveva andare a sposarsi
kay doh-VAY-va ahn-DA-ray ah spo-ZAHR-see
that he was going to get married

con un'americana.
kohn OO-na-may-ree-KA-na.
to an American girl.

IL NONNO:
Ma con un'americana molto affascinante.
Ma ko-NOO-na-may-ree-KA-na MOHL-toh ahf-fa-shee-NAHN-tay.
But with a very fascinating American.

Volevamo fare la vostra conoscenza
Vo-lay-VA-mo FA-ray la VO-stra ko-no-SEHNT-sa
We wanted to meet you

da tanto tempo.
da TANH-toh TEM-po.
for so long.

LA NONNA:
Venite, ragazzi.
Vay-NEE-tay, ra-GAHTS-see.
Come, children.

Il pranzo è servito.
Eel PRAHNT-so ay sehr-VEE-toh.
Dinner is served.

Abbiamo testina d'agnello.
Ahb-B'YA-mo tay-STEEE-nah dahn-YEL-lo.
We have lamb's head.

A Riccardo gli piaceva tanto
Ah Reek-KAHR-doh ll'yee p'ya-CHAY-va TAHN-toh
Richard used to like it so much

quando era piccolo . . .
KWAHN-doh AY-ra PEEK-ko-lo . . .
when he was a boy . . .

LEI:
Lay:
SHE:

Ebbene, oggi ho saputo
Ehb-BAY-nay, OHDJ-jee oh sa-POO-toh
Well, today I have learned

molte cose sudi te
MOHL-tay KO-zay soo-dee tay
many things about you

che ancora non sapevo.
kay ahn-KO-ra nohn sa-PAY-vo.
that I did not know yet.

Ma dimmi, dovrei adesso imparare
Ma DEEM-mee, doh-VRAY ah-DES-so eem-pa-RA-ray
But tell me, should I now learn how

a cucinarti la testina d'agnello?
ah koo-chee-NAR-tee la tes-TEE-na dahn-YEL-lo?
to cook you lamb's head?

TEST YOUR ITALIAN

Translate the following sentences into Italian using the imperfect (*imperfetto*). Score 10 points for each correct answer. See answers below.

1. My mother always used to say. . . .
   _____

2. When we were in Florence. . . .
   _____

3. Everything was different then.
   _____

4. When I was young. . . .
   _____

5. We used to tell her that she was wrong.
   _____

6. He was very intelligent.
   _____

7. We were always worried.
   _____

8. We never knew where he was.
   _____

9. He used to like to go to the movies.
   _____

10. He never used to do anything.
   _____

Answers: 1. Mia madre diceva sempre . . . 2. Quando eravamo a Firenze . . . 3. Tutto era differente allora. 4. Quando ero giovane . . . 5. Le dicevamo che aveva torto. 6. Era molto intelligente. 7. Eravamo sempre in pensiero. 8. Non sapevamo mai dove era. 9. Gli piaceva andare al cinema. 10. Non faceva mai niente.

SCORE _____%

HOW TO USE THE
"REMOTE PAST"

Il passato remoto, come indica il suo nome,
Eel pahs-SA-toh ray-MO-toh, KO-may EEN-dee-ka eel SOO-oh NO-may,
The remote past, as its name indicates,

> **Il passato remoto**
> The *passato remoto* corresponds exactly to the English past tense, i.e. "did," "spoke," "went," "saw," etc. However, in Steps 19 and 20, you will remember that the *passato prossimo* also expressed the English past or the perfect, such as "have done," "have spoken," "have gone," "have seen," etc. What happens in Italian is that the *passato prossimo* is used in everyday speech to express the perfect or the past, while the *passato remoto*, the true past tense, is used for the past events that happened a long time ago, and is also employed when one recounts a story of something that happened in the past.

si usa per esprimere un'azione
see OO-za pehr es-SPREE-may-ray oo-nahts-YO-nay
is used to express an action

che avvenne molto tempo fà.
kay ahv-VEN-nay MOHL-toh TEM-po fa.
that happened a long time ago.

Dante Alighieri nacque a Firenze
DAHN-tay Ah-leeg-YAY-ree NAHK-kway ah Fee-RENT-say
Dante Alighieri was born in Florence

nel milleduecentosessantacinque,
nel MEEL-lay doo-ay-CHEN-toh-sehs-SAHN-ta-CHEEN-kway,
in twelve sixty-five,

e morì a Ravenna
ay mo-REE ah Ra-VEN-na
and died in Ravenna

nel milletrecentoventuno.
nel MEEL-lay-tray-CHEN-toh ven-TOO-no.
and thirteen twenty-one.

Visse soltanto cinquantasei anni,
VEES-say sohl-TAHN-toh cheen-KWAHN-ta-SAY AHN-nee,
He lived only fifty-six years,

ma lasciò un capolavoro eterno.
ma la-SHO oon ka-po-la-VO-ro ay-TEHR-no.
but he left an eternal masterpiece.

Il passato remoto si usa anche
Eel pahs-SA-toh ray-MO-toh see OO-sa AHN-kay
The remote past is used also

How to form the "passeto remoto"
The *passato remoto* is formed by adding a series of endings to the verb stem, which is obtained by dropping the infinitive endings -*are*, -*ere*, and -*ire*. The forms for the three conjugations are:

parlare	vendere	dormire
parlai	*vendei*	*dormii*
parlasti	*vendesti*	*dormisti*
parlò	*vendè* (or)	
	vendette	*dormì*
parlammo	*vendemmo*	*dormimmo*
parlaste	*vendeste*	*dormiste*
parlarono	*venderono*	
	(or)	
	vendettero	*dormirono*

For the second conjugation, the *io, egli* and *loro* forms have alternate endings: -*etti*, -*ette*, and -*ettero*. Thus, the three forms could also be: *io vendetti, egli (ella, Lei) vendette,* and *loro (Loro) vendettero.*

Verbs that are irregular in the *passato remoto* are usually irregular only in the first person sin-

gular (*io*), and the third person — singular (*egli,*
ella, Lei) and plural (*loro, Loro*). These three
persons have the same irregular stem, so that
by knowing the *io* form of a verb, the other two
forms can be deduced by adding respectively
the endings *-i, -e*, and *-ero* to the irregular
stem. Thus, for the verb *fare*, the three forms
would be *feci, fece* and *fecero*. The *tu, noi* and
voi forms of a verb are always regular, except
that for some verbs, like *fare*, use the old form
of the infinitive — *facere* — for the stem of the
three *regular* persons. Thus, these three forms
would be *facesti, facemmo*, and *faceste*. The
whole *passato remoto* of *fare* would look like
this:

    feci, facesti, fece, facemmo, faceste, fecero

Here are the first person forms for some of
the most common verbs that are irregular in the
passato remoto:

Infinitive	Passato Remoto
prendere	*presi*
chiudere	*chiusi*
avere	*ebbi*
chiedere	*chiesi*
conoscere	*conobbi*
venire	*venni*
stare	*stetti*
vedere	*vidi*
sapere	*seppi*
dare	*diedi*
volere	*volli*
perdere	*persi, or, perdetti*
piacere	*piacqui*
nascere	*nacqui*
mettere	*misi*
correre	*corsi*
leggere	*lessi*
scrivere	*scrissi*
vivere	*vissi*
rimanere	*rimasi*
potere	*potei, or, potetti*

per descrivere un'azione che avvenne
pehr day-SKREE-vay-ray oo-nahts-YO-nay kay ahv-VEN-nay
to describe an action that happened

mentre un'altra azione stava succedendo.
MEN-tray oo-NAHL-tra ahts-YO-nay STA-va soot-chay-DEN-doh.
while another action was happening.

Stavo dormendo profondamente,
STA-vo dohr-MEN-doh pro-fohn-da-MEN-tay,
I was sleeping deeply,

quando qualcuno suonò alla porta.
KWAHN-doh kwahl-KOO-no swo-NO AHL-la POHR-ta.
when somebody rang at the door.

The "passato remoto" in a narration

The use of the *passato remoto* is illustrated here as the person telling the story *was* sleeping, a continuing action which calls for the imperfect, but was suddenly interrupted by the doorbell, an isolated single action which takes the *passato remoto* in a narration such as this. In conversation form, however, you could still use the "passato prossimo." (see Step 19)

Mi alzai di malavoglia,
Mee ahld-zye dee ma-la-VOHL-ya,
I unwillingly got up,

e andai ad aprire.
ah ahn-dye ah-da-PREE-ray.
and I went to open it.

Ma mentre andavo verso la porta,
Ma MEN-tray ahn-DA-vo VEHR-so la POHR-ta,
But while I was going toward the door,

squillò anche il telefono.
skweel-LO AHN-kay eel tay-LAY-fo-no.
the telephone rang also.

Lasciai squillare il telefono,
La-SHY skweel-LA-ray eel tay-LAY-fo-no,
I let the telephone ring,

e continuai verso la porta.
ay kohn-tee-NWA-ee VEHR-so la POHR-ta.
and I continued toward the door.

Quando finalmente l'aprii,
KWAHN-doh fee-nahl-MEN-tay la-PREE-ee,
When I finally opened it,

non c'era più nessuno.
nohn CHAY-ra p'YOO nehs-SOO-no.
there was no longer anybody (there).

Poi corsi al telefono,
Poy KOHR-see ahl tay-LAY-fo-no,
Then I ran to the telephone,

ma quando staccai il ricevitore,
ma KWAHN-doh stahk-KA-ee eel ree-chay-vee-TOH-ray,
but when I picked up the receiver,

nemmeno lì c'era più nessuno.
nem-MAY-no LEE CHAY-ra p'YOO nehs-SOO-no.
there was no longer anybody there either.

Ritornai a letto,
Ree-tohr-NYE ah LEHT-toh,
I went back to bed,

ma a quel punto ero così nervoso
ma ah kwel POON-toh AY-ro ko-ZEE nehr-VO-zo
but at that point I was so nervous

che non potetti più dormire.
kay nohn po-TEHT-tee p'YOO dohr-MEE-ray.
that I could not sleep any more.

Per raccontare fatti storici,
Pehr rahk-kohn-TA-ray FAHT-tee STO-ree-chee,
To tell historic happenings,

si usa il passato remoto
see OO-za eel pahs-SA-to ray-MO-toh
the remote past is used

insieme con l'imperfetto.
eens-YAY-may kohn leem-pehr-FEHT-toh.
together with the imperfect.

Secondo la leggenda,
Seh-KOHN-doh la lehdh-JEN-da,
According to the legend,

i fondatori di Roma furono
ee fohn-da-TOH-ree dee RO-ma FOO-ro-no
the founders of Rome were

> **Essere**
> The verb *essere* is extremely irregular in the
> *passato remoto*. It is as follows: *fui, fosti, fu,*
> *fummo, foste, furono.*

i gemelli Romolo e Remo.
ee jay-MEL-lee RO-mo-lo ay RAY-mo.
the twins Romulus and Remus.

Quando erano bambini,
KWAHN-doh AY-ra-no bahm-BEE-nee,
When they were children,

furono abbandonati in una foresta.
FOO-ro-no ahb-bahn-doh-NA-tee ee-NOO-na fo-RAY-sta.
they were abandoned in a forest.

Una lupa li trovò e se ne prese cura.
OO-na LOO-pa lee tro-VO ay say nay PRAY-zay KOO-ra.
A she-wolf found them and took care of them.

Da grande, Romolo decise
Da GRAHN-day, RO-mo-lo day-CHEE-zay
When he was grown up, Romulus decided

di fondare una città.
dee fohn-DA-ray OO-na cheet-TA.
to found a city.

Così marcò i limiti del territorio che voleva,
Ko-ZEE mahr-KO ee LEE-mee-tee del tay-rree-TOHR-yo kay vo-LAY-va,
Thus he marked the limits of the territory that he wanted,

e disse al fratello
ay DEES-say ahl fra-TEL-lo
and told his brother

di non attraversare la linea.
dee no-naht-tra-vehr-SA-ray la LEE-nay-ah.
not to cross the line.

Ma Remo non lo prese sul serio
Ma RAY-mo nohn lo PRAY-zay sool SEHR-yo
But Remus did not take him seriously

e attraversò la linea.
ay aht-tra-vehr-SO la LEE-nay-ah.
and crossed the line.

Allora Romolo lo uccise.
Ahl-LO-ra RO-mo-lo lo oot-CHEE-zay.
So Romulus killed him.

Però dopo, sentì del rimorso
Peh-RO DOH-po, sen-TEE del ree-MOHR-so
But afterwards, he felt remorseful

e mise alla nuova città il nome del fratello —
ay MEE-zay AHL-la NWO-va cheet-TA eel NO-may del fra-TEL-lo —
and he gave to the new city his brother's name —

la chiamò Roma.
la k'ya-MO RO-ma.
he called it Rome.

Una propaganda antica
Although Romulus is given legendary credit for calling the city after his brother, it seems plausible that, given the similarity of his own name to that of the eternal city, this may not be the case.

Spesso il passato remoto si usa
SPEHS-so eel pahs-SA-toh ray-MO-toh see OO-za
Often the remote past is used

con il trapassato prossimo.
kohn eel tra-pahs-SA-toh PROHS-see-mo.
with the past perfect.

Il trapassato prossimo si usa
Eel tra-pahs-SA-toh PROHS-see-mo see OO-za
The past perfect is used

per descrivere un'azione nel passato
pehr day-SKREE-vay-ray oo-nahts-YO-nay nel pahs-SA-toh
to describe an action in the past

che avvenne prima di un'altra azione
kay ahv-VEN-nay PREE-ma dee oo-NAHL-tra ahts-YO-nay
that happened before another action

anche nel passato.
AHN-kay nel pahs-SA-toh.
also in the past.

The past perfect — "had been" etc.
The *trapassato prossimo* corresponds to the English past perfect, as in "had been," "had had," "had come," "had left," "had finished," etc. All you have to do to make the *trapassato prossimo* is to use the past participle of the verb combined with the imperfect tense of *avere* or *essere*. For a review, take another look at Steps 19 and 20, which indicate which verbs take *essere* and which take *avere*. Here are two examples of the *trapassato prossimo* — *mangiare* which takes *avere*, and *arrivare* which takes *essere*.

> *avevo mangiato*, etc. — I had eaten, etc.
> *ero arrivato* (-a), etc. — I had arrived, etc.

And remember, in compound tenses, past participles of verbs which take *essere* always agree with the subject.

Quando venni a casa tua ieri sera,
KWAHN-doh VEN-nee ah KA-za TOO-ah YAY-ree SAY-ra,
When I came to your house last night,

mi dissero che eri uscita con qualc'un altro.
mee DEES-say-ro kay AY-ree oo-SHEE-ta kohn kwahl-KOON
AHL-tro.
they told me that you had gone out with someone else.

Quando arrivammo alla stazione,
KWAHN-doh ah-rree-VAHM-mo AHL-la stahts-YO-nay,
When we arrived at the station,

il treno era già partito.
eel TRAY-no AY-ra ja pahr-TEE-toh.
the train had already left.

Avevo appena finito di scriverle una lettera,
Ah-VAY-vo ahp-PAY-na fee-NEE-toh dee SKREE-vehr-lay OO-na
LEHT-tay-ra,
I had just finished writing her a letter,

quando mi telefonò.
KWAHN-doh mee tay-lay-fo-NO.
when she telephoned me.

INSTANT CONVERSATION: RELATING AN INCIDENT

Già avevamo finito la cena
Ja ah-vay-VA-mo fee-NEE-toh la CHAY-na
We had already finished supper

ed eravamo nel salotto,
ay-day-ra-VA-mo nel sa-LOHT-toh,
and we were in the living room,

quando tutto ad un tratto
KWAHN-doh TOOT-toh ah-DOON TRAHT-toh
when all of a sudden

sentimmo un grido che veniva dal balcone.
sen-TEEM-mo oon GREE-doh kay vay-NEE-va dahl bahl-KO-nay.
we heard a scream that was coming from the balcony.

Past tenses compared
This short narrative incident illustrates the relationship between the different past tenses. The *imperfetto* sets a stage for what is going on in the past. The *trapassato prossimo* indicates what had gone on before, and specific actions which happened once take the *passato remoto*.

Quando andammo lì, trovammo la domestica tutta spaventata.
KWAHN-doh ahn-DAHM-mo lee, tro-VAHM-mo la doh-MAY-stee-ka TOOT-ta spa-ven-TA-ta.
When we got there, we found the maid completely terrified.

Ci disse che aveva visto
Chee DEES-say kay ah-VAY-va VEE-sto
She told us that she had seen

un'ombra dietro un albero.
oo-NOHM-bra D'YAY-tro oo-NAHL-bay-ro.
a shadow behind a tree.

Continuava ad essere molto nervosa —
Kohn-tee-NWA-va ah-DEHS-say-ray MOHL-toh nehr-VO-sa —
She kept on being very nervous —

pareva che aveva letto un articolo nel giornale
pa-RAY-va kay ah-VAY-va LEHT-toh oo-nahr-TEE-ko-lo nel johr-NA-lay
it seemed that she had read an article in the newspaper

su un ladro che usava entrare
soo oon LA-dro kay oo-SA-va en-TRA-ray
about a thief who was in the habit of entering

nelle case di notte
NEL-lay KA-zay dee NOHT-tay
houses at night

salendo dai balconi,
sa-LEN-doh DA-ee bahl-KO-nee,
by climbing over balconies,

e credeva che era qualcuno
ay kray-DAY-va kay AY-ra kwahl-KOO-no
and she thought that it was somebody

che voleva intrudersi nella casa.
kay vo-LAY-va een-TROO-dehr-see NEL-la KA-za.
who wanted to get into the house.

La poveretta aveva molta paura
La po-vay-REHT-ta ah-VAY-va MOHL-ta pa-OO-ra
The poor girl was very much afraid

e anche se l'assicuravamo
ay AHN-kay say lahs-see-koo-ra-VA-mo
and even though we kept assuring her

che non c'era nessuno lì,
kay nohn CHAY-ra nehs-SOO-no lee,
that there was nobody there,

continuava a tremare come una foglia.
kohn-tee-NWA-va ah tray-MA-ray KO-may OO-na FOLL-ya.
she kept trembling like a leaf.

Aiuto!

Speaking of emergencies, here are some key words:

help!	—	*aiuto!*
fire!	—	*fuoco!*
look out!	—	*attenzione!*
quickly!	—	*presto!*
stop thief!	—	*al ladro!*
there he goes!	—	*eccolo!*
stop!	—	*ferma!*
police!	—	*polizia!*

TEST YOUR ITALIAN

Translate the following sentences into Italian. Score 10 points for each correct answer. See answers on following page.

1. When was Dante born?

2. When did he die?

3. I was sleeping, when the telephone rang.

4. When I opened the door, there was nobody.

5. How long did she live?

6. When they were children, they were abandoned in a forest.

7. Romulus called the new city Rome.

8. When we arrived at the airport, the plane had already left.

9. We had just finished eating, when we heard a scream.

10. The maid had read an article in the newspaper.

SCORE _____%

Answers:
1. Quando nacque Dante?
2. Quando morì?
3. Stavo dormendo, quando squillò il telefono.
4. Quando aprii la porta, non c'era nessuno.
5. Quanto tempo visse?
6. Quando erano bambini, furono abbandonati in una foresta.
7. Romolo chiamò la nuova città Roma.
8. Quando arrivammo all'aeroporto, l'aeroplano era già partito.
9. Avevamo appena finito di mangiare, quando sentimmo un grido.
10. La domestica aveva letto un articolo nel giornale.

step 24

Il congiuntivo è facile
Eel kohn-joon-TEE-vo ay FA-chee-lay
The subjunctive is easy

perchè lei sa già come si forma.
pehr-KAY lay sa ja KO-may see FOHR-ma.
because you know already how it is formed.

Il verbo, al singolare,
Eel VEHR-bo, ahl seen-go-LA-ray,
The verb, in the singular,

ha la stessa forma
ah la STEHS-sa FOHR-ma
has the same form

che si usa per dare ordini.
kay see OO-za pehr DA-ray OHR-dee-nee.
that is used to give orders.

Come: *Entri! Venga qui! Si sieda!*
KO-may: EN-tree! VEN-ga kwee! See S'YAY-da!
Like: "Come in!" "Come here!" "Sit down!"

Prenda una sigaretta! Mi dica!
PREN-da OO-na see-ga-REHT-ta! Mee DEE-ka!
"Have a cigarette" "Tell me!"

Il congiuntivo si usa
Eel kohn-joon-TEE-vo see OO-za
The subjunctive is used

quando si vuole o si desidera
KWAHN-doh see VWO-lay oh see day-SEE-day-ra
when one wishes or desires

che un'altra persona
kay oo-NAHL-tra pehr-SO-na
that another person

faccia qualche cosa.
FAHT-cha KWAHL-kay KO-za.
do something.

Il congiuntivo è preceduto
Eel kohn-joon-TEE-vo ay pray-chay-DOO-toh
The subjunctive is preceded

sempre dalla parola *che.*
SEM-pray DAHL-la pa-RO-la kay.
always by the word ''that.''

The subjunctive mood

The subjunctive is not a tense but a mood, which includes several tenses. You have been familiar with the third person of the present subjunctive since Step 10, where you learned the polite imperative, such as *parli!, venga!, dica!, finisca!,* etc. You learned this construction as an example of how to give commands, since *venga* really means ''may you come.''

In like manner, *viva!,* as in *viva l'Italia!* — ''long live Italy!,'' really means ''may Italy live!.''

The subjunctive is important in Italian, because you must use it in expressions such as ''I want you to come,'' which literally is expressed by ''I want *that* you come.'' In fact, in expressions indicating that you want, desire or wish *another* person to do something, or that somebody else wants *you* to do something, you must use the subjunctive.

A further use of the subjunctive is in the case of when a person is looking for something that he has not yet found.

I am looking for a girl who knows how to take care of children.

Sto cercando una ragazza che sappia prendersi cura dei bambini.

Non voglio che egli venga.
Nohn VOHLL-yo kay ELL-yee VEN-ga.
I don't want him to come, (or, that he come).

Vuole che noi ritorniamo domani.
VWO-lay kay noy ree-tohrn-YA-mo doh-MA-nee.
He wants us to come back (or, that we come back) tomorrow.

Si noti l'uso del congiuntivo
See NO-tee LOO-so del kohn-joon-TEE-vo
Note the use of the subjunctive

in frasi che esprimono emozioni
een FRA-zee kay ay-SPREE-mo-no ay-mohts-YO-nee
in phrases that express emotion

o sentimenti, dopo la parola *che.*
oh sen-tee-MEN-tee, DOH-po la pa-RO-la *kay.*
or sentiments, after the word "that."

How to form the subjunctive
Here are the subjunctive forms for the present tense of six persons of the three conjugations:

parlare	scrivere
(*che*) *io parli*	(*che*) *io scriva*
(*che*) *tu parli*	(*che*) *tu scriva*
(*che*) *egli parli*	(*che*) *egli scriva*
(*che*) *noi parliamo*	(*che*) *noi scriviamo*
(*che*) *voi parliate*	(*che*) *voi scriviate*
(*che*) *loro parlino*	(*che*) *loro scrivano*

partire	finire
(*che*) *io parta*	(*che*) *io finisca*
(*che*) *tu parta*	(*che*) *tu finisca*
(*che*) *egli parta*	(*che*) *egli finisca*
(*che*) *noi partiamo*	(*che*) *noi finiamo*
(*che*) *voi partiate*	(*che*) *voi finiate*
(*che*) *loro partino*	(*che*) *loro finiscano*

Irregular verbs, similarly to regular verbs, also form their subjunctive from the first form of the

289

present indicative, as in the case of *faccio* —
che io faccia; vengo — *che io venga; leggo* —
che io legga; dico — *che io dica; esco* —
che io esca; etc.

We have prefaced the examples by *che* to re-
mind you that *che* is used like a signal to show
that the following verb takes the subjunctive.

Some verbs that form their subjunctive completely irregularly are as follows:

avere	essere
(che) io abbia	*(che) io sia*
(che) tu abbia	*(che) tu sia*
(che) egli abbia	*(che) egli sia*
(che) noi abbiamo	*(che) noi siamo*
(che) voi abbiate	*(che) voi siate*
(che) loro abbiano	*(che)* loro siano

sapere	dare
(che) io sappia	*(che) io dia*
(che) tu sappia	*(che) tu dia*
(che) egli sappia	*(che) egli dia*
(che) noi sappiamo	*(che) noi diamo*
(che) voi sappiate	*(che) voi diate*
(che) loro sappiano	*(che) loro diano*

Still others are:
devo — *che io debba;*
sto — *che io stia.*

— Sono contento che Lei sia qui,
SO-no kohn-TEN-toh kay Lay SEE-ah kwee,
I am happy that you are here,

ma mi dispiace che Sua moglie
ma mee dees-p'YA-chay kay SOO-ah MOHL-yay
but I regret that your wife

sia malata.
SEE-ah ma-LA-ta.
is ill.

Emotions and the subjunctive
The subjunctive is also used after expressions indicating wishing, doubt, emotion, uncertainty, emotions of fear, anger, happiness, etc.

— Sì, è un peccato che non abbia
See, ay oon pehk-KA-toh kay no-NAHB-b'ya
Yes, it is a sin that she has not

Note the difference between

I am sorry she cannot come.
Mi dispiace che (ella) non possa venire.

and

I am sorry she could not come.
Mi dispiace che (ella) non abbia potuto venire.

The second example is in the past subjunctive (*il passato congiuntivo*) which is formed simply by using the present subjunctive of *essere* or *avere*, plus the past participle.

potuto venire, ma il dottore
po-TOO-toh vay-NEE-ray, ma eel doht-TOH-ray
been able to come, but the doctor

non vuole che ella esca.
nohn VWO-lay kay EL-la AY-ska.
does not want her to go out.

Il congiuntivo si usa
Eel kohn-joon-TEE-vo see OO-za
The subjunctive is used

in espressioni impersonali
ee-nay-spress-YO-nee eem-pehr-so-NA-lee
in impersonal expressions

e con certi avverbi.
ay kohn CHEHR-tee ahv-VEHR-bee.
and with certain adverbs.

The subjunctive with impersonal expressions
The subjunctive is used after certain impersonal
expressions, such as:

it is necessary that — *è necessario che*
it is important that — *è importante che*
it is possible that — *è possible che*
(one) must. . . . — *bisogna che*. . . .
it is not certain that — *non è certo che*

Bisogna che gli parli.
Bee-SOHN-ya kay ll'yee PAHR-lee.
I must speak to him.

Bisogna che voi visitiate la Calabria.
Bee-SOHN-ya kay voy vee-seet-YA-tay la ka-LAHBR-ya.
You must visit Calabria.

Peccato che io non possa andarci.
Pehk-KA-toh kay EE-oh nohn POHS-sa ahn-DAHR-chee.
It is a shame that I cannot go.

Bisogna che Marta parta adesso.
Bee-SOHN-ya kay MAHR-ta PAHR-ta ah-DESS-so.
It is necessary that Martha leave now.

— È necessario che ci chiamino presto,
Ay nay-chehs-SAHR-yo kay chee K'YA-mee-no PRAY-sto,
It is necessary that they call us early,

cosi che abbiamo tempo
koh-SEE kay ahb-B'YA-mo TEM-po
so that we have time

per fare le valigie.
pehr FA-ray lay va-LEE-jay.
to pack (our) suitcases.

È importante che arriviamo
Ay eem-pohr-TAHN-tay kay ah-rreev-YA-mo
It is important that we arrive

all'aeroporto
ahl-la-ay-ro-POHR-toh
at the airport

una mezz'ora prima della partenza.
OO-na mehts-SO-ra PREE-ma DEL-la pahr-TENT-sa.
half an hour before departure.

Prima che possiamo salire
PREE-ma kay pohs-S'YA-mo sa-LEE-ray
Before we can board

nell'aeroplano, bisogna
nel-la-ay-ro-PLA-no, bee-SOHN-ya
the plane, it is necessary

che pesino i bagagli,
kay PAY-zee-no ee ba-GAHL-lyee,
that they weigh the luggage,

e che noi passiamo per il controllo di sicurezza.
ay kay noy pahs-YA-mo pehr eel kohn-TRO-lo dee see-koo REHT-sa.
and that we pass through security control.

— Ma perchè tanta fretta?
Ma pehr-KAY TAHN-ta FREHT-ta?
But why so much rush?

Anche se arriviamo tardi,
AHN-kay say ah-rreev-YA-mo TAHR-dee,
Even if we arrive late,

è possibile che ci sia
ay pohs-SEE-bee-lay kay chee SEE-ah
it is possible that there is

un altro volo più tardi.
oo-NAHL-tro VO-lo p'yoo TAHR-dee.
another flight later.

— Crede? Può anche essere
KRAY-day? Pwo AHN-kay EHS-say-ray
Do you think so? It may also be

che non ce ne sia.
kay nohn chay nay SEE-ah.
that there isn't any.

The importance of the subjunctive

Some students of Italian wonder why the subjunctive mood is used at all, since it has practi-
cally disappeared from English. It is quite
important in Italian, however, where the ending
of a verb is a key to its precise meaning, and
the correct use of tenses and moods is a proof
of your ability to speak Italian with style and
brio (animation.)

INSTANT CONVERSATION:
THE GENERATION GAP

IL PADRE:
Eel PA-dray:
THE FATHER:
Mi dispiace che Giancarlo
Mee deesp-YA-chay kay Jahn-KAR-lo
I am sorry that Giancarlo

riceva dei voti tanto bassi
ree-CHAY-vee day VO-tee TAHN-toh BAHS-see
is receiving such low grades

a scuola. Ho paura
ah SKWO-la. Oh pa-OO-ra
in school. I am afraid

che abbia difficoltà
kay AHB-b'ya deef-fee-kohl-TA
that he may have difficulty

quando verranno gli esami.
KWAHN-doh vay-RRAHN-no l'yay-ZA-mee.
when the examinations come.

È importante che studi di più
Ay eem-pohr-TAHN-tay kay STOO-dee dee p'YOO
It is important that he study more

e che non passi tutto il suo tempo
ay kay nohn PAHS-see TOOT-toh eel SOO-oh TEM-po
and that he not spend all his time

al cinema o al teatro.
ahl CHEE-neh-ma oh ahl tay-AH-tro.
in the movies or at the theater.

295

LA MADRE:
La MA-dray:
THE MOTHER:

Ma perchè ti preoccupi tanto?
Ma pehr-KAY tee pray-OHK-koo-pee TAHN-toh?
But why do you worry so much?

Dubiti che egli riesca
DOO-bee-tee kay ELL-yee ree-AY-ska
Do you doubt that he will succeed

a passare tutti gli esami?
ah pahs-SA-ray TOOT-tee ll'yay-ZA-mee?
in passing all the examinations?

IL PADRE:
Non cercare di difenderlo.
Nohn chehr-KA-ray dee dee-FEN-dehr-lo.
Don't try to defend him.

Quando ritorna a casa
KWAHN-doh ree-TOHR-na ah KA-za
When he returns home

bisogna che tu gli dica
bee-SOHN-ya kay too ll'yee DEE-ka
you must tell him

che voglio vederlo affinchè
kay VOHLL-yo vay-DEHR-lo ahf-feen-KAY
that I want to see him so that

mi spieghi la sua ultima pagella.
mee SP'YAY-gee la SOO-ah OOL-tee-ma pa-JEL-la.
he can explain his last report card to me.

Non posso permettere che egli
Nohn POHS-so pehr-MEHT-tay-ray kay ELL-yee
I cannot allow him

continui ad essere tanto svogliato
kohn-TEE-nwee ah-DEHS-say-ray TAHN-toh zvohl-YA-toh
to continue being so lazy

nei suoi studi, e nemmeno
nay SWO-ee STOO-dee, ay nehm-MAY-no
in his studies, and not even

che sia tanto negligente.
kay SEE-ah TAHN-toh nay-glee-JEN-tay.
that he be so negligent.

LA MADRE:
Ascolta, Giancarlo —
Ah-SKOHL-ta, Jahn-KAR-lo —
Listen, Giancarlo —

Tuo padre è molto adirato
TOO-oh PA-dray ay MOHL-toh ah-dee-RA-toh
Your father is very angry

che tu non abbia ricevuto
kay too no-NAHB-b'ya ree-chay-VOO-toh
that you have not received

voti migliori.
VO-tee meel-YO-ree.
better grades.

È necessario che tu vada a vederlo.
Ay nay-chehs-SAHR-yo kay too VA-da ah vay-DEHR-lo.
It is necessary that you go see him.

IL FIGLIO:
Eel FEELL-yo:
THE SON:
Perchè? Quando mi vedrà,
Pehr-KAY? KWAHN-doh mee vay-DRA,
What for? When he sees me,

mi parlerà senza dubbio
mee pahr-lay-RA SENT-sa DOOB-b'yo
he will without a doubt speak to me

di ciò che egli vuole che io faccia,
dee cho kay ELL-yee VWO-lay kay EE-oh FAHT-cha,
about what he wants me to do,

297

della carriera che egli
DEL-la ka-RR'YAY-ra kay ELL-yee
about the career that he

vuole che io segua,
VWO-lay kay EE-oh SEHG-wa,
wants me to follow,

della vita che egli vuole
DEL-la VEE-ta kay ELL-yee VWO-lay
of the life that he wants

che io meni.
kay EE-oh MAY-nee.
me to lead.

La mia ambizione è di arrivare
La MEE-ah ahm-beets-YO-nay AY dee ah-rree-VA-ray
My ambition is to get

ad essere regista.
ah-DEHS-say-ray ray-JEE-sta.
to be a movie director.

Nella vita voglio fare
NEL-la VEE-ta VOHLL-yo FA-ray
In life I want to do

ciò che voglio io.
cho kay VOHLL-yo EE-oh.
what I want to do.

LA MADRE:
Oh, Dio mio!
Oh, DEE-oh MEE-oh!
Oh, goodness!

Non parlare così,
Nohn pahr-LA-ray ko-ZEE,
Don't talk like that,

figlio mio.
FEELL-yo MEE-oh.
my son.

Sai molto bene
SA-ee MOHL-toh BAY-nay
You know very well

che tuo padre
kay TOO-oh PA-dray
that your father

non vuole che il bene tuo
nohn VWO-lay kay eel BAY-nay TOO-oh
wants only your good

> **"Only" — "non . . . che"**
> Another way of expressing "only," besides *so-lamente*, is by putting *non* before the verb, and *che* after it.
>
> *Non viene che una volta la settimana.*
> *"He comes only once a week."*

e quello di Giacomo.
ay KWEL-lo dee JA-ko-mo.
and that of James.

Vuole che riceviate
VWO-lay kay ree-chehv-YA-tay
He wants you (both) to receive

il vostri diploma
eel VO-stri dee-PLO-ma
your degrees

dal liceo, e che continuiate
dahl lee-CHAY-oh, ay kay kohn-tee-nwee-YA-tay
from high school, and to continue

> **Tu — voi**
> In this scene the father and mother use *tu* to each other as is natural with a married couple. The mother uses *tu* to her son and, when she brings the brother into the conversation, shifts to *voi,* the plural form of *tu.* Sometimes, however, *voi* is used to only one person, for a relationship not too familiar — not too formal.

all'Università.
ahl-loo-nee-vehr-see-TA.
to the university.

Tuo padre ha sempre voluto
TOO-oh PA-dray ah SEM-pray vo-LOO-toh
Your father has always wanted

che Giacomo diventi
kay JA-ko-mo dee-VEN-tee
James to become

dottore, e che tu sia
doht-TOH-ray, ay kay too SEE-ah
a doctor, and you to be

avvocato come lui.
ahv-vo-KA-toh KO-may LOO-ee.
a lawyer like him.

IL FIGLIO:
Lo so bene.
Lo so BAY-nay.
I know it well.

Però fra ciò che io voglio diventare
Pay-RO fra cho kay EE-oh VOHLL-yo dee-ven-TA-ray
But between what I want to become

e quello che egli vuole che io diventi,
ay KWEL-lo kay ELL-yee VWO-lay kay EE-oh dee-VEN-tee,
and what he wants me to become,

> **"Che" — a key word.**
> Observe in this present example that English
> can get around the subjunctive by simply saying
> "He wants me to become," while Italian must
> use an expression equivalent to "He wants that
> I become."

c'è un mare di differenza.
chay oon MA-ray dee deef-fay-RENT-sa.
there is a sea of difference.

Che mi lasci in pace!
Keh mee LA-shee een PA-chay!
Let him leave me in peace!

LA MADRE:
Cielo! Che parole!
CHAY-lo! Kay pa-RO-lay!
Heavens! What words!

Com'era differente la vita
Ko-MAY-ra deef-fay-REN-tay la VEE-ta
How different life was

quando io ero giovane!
KWAHN-doh EE-oh AY-ro JO-va-nay!
when I was young!

Non si parlava mai così
Nohn see pahr-LA-va mye ko-ZEE
One never spoke like that

ai propri genitori.
AH-ee PRO-pree jay-nee-TOH-ree.
to one's own parents.

How things were . . .
At the end of this dialogue relevant to the generation gap, the mother, in her aside, shifts into the imperfect, the tense indicated for speaking of things that once were or used to be.

301

TEST YOUR ITALIAN

Fill in the missing verb in each sentence in the subjunctive mood. Score 10 points for each correct answer. See answers below.

1. I hope that he will not see me.
   Spero che egli non mi _____.

2. They want us to arrive at eight.
   Vogliono che _____ alle otto.

3. I want him to go.
   Voglio che egli _____.

4. He insists that I play.
   Insiste che io _____.

5. Do you want me to stay?
   Vuole che io _____?

6. I am very sorry that you cannot go.
   Mi dispiace molto che Lei non _____ andare.

7. I hope that she will come tomorrow.
   Spero che ella _____ domani.

8. It is necessary that you study often.
   È necessario che tu _____ spesso.

9. What a shame that it is raining!
   Peccato che _____ piovendo!

10. What does he want me to tell him?
    Che cosa vuole che gli _____?

SCORE _____%

step 25   CONDITIONS AND SUPPOSITIONS

Frasi come:
FRA-zee KO-may:
Sentences like:

Se piove domani, non andremo alla spiaggia.
Say P'YO-vay doh-MA-nee, no-nahn-DRAY-mo AHL-la SP'YADJ-ja.
If it rains tomorrow, we will not go to the beach.

Se viene, gli darò il messaggio.
Say V'YAY-nay, l'yee da-RO eel mes-SAHDJ-jo.
If he comes, I will give him the message.

Sono delle condizioni semplici.
SO-no DEL-lay kohn-deets-YO-nee SEM-plee-chee.
Are simple conditions.

Qualche volta, la supposizione
KWAHL-kay VOHL-ta, la soop-po-zeets-YO-nay
Sometimes, the supposition

è più evidente, come:
ay p'yoo ay-vee-DEN-tay, KO-may:
is more evident, like:

Se Lei fosse al posto mio,
Say Lay FOHS-say ahl PO-sto MEE-oh,
If you were in my place,

che cosa farebbe?
kay KO-za fa-REHB-bay?
what would you do?

Se vivessi nella regione alpina,
Say vee-VEHS-see NEL-la ray-JO-nay ahl-PEE-na,
If I lived in the Alpine region,

farei dello sci.
fa-RAY DEL-lo shee.
I would do some skiing.

Per questo genere di supposizioni,
Pehr KWESS-toh JAY-nay-ray dee soop-po-zeets-YO-nee,
For this kind of supposition,

bisogna usare l'imperfetto
bee-ZOHN-ya oo-SA-ray leem-pehr-FEHT-toh
we must use the imperfect

del congiuntivo dopo se
del kohn-joon-TEE-vo DOH-po say
of the subjunctive after "if"

How to form the imperfect subjunctive

In Step 24, we presented the present subjunctive and an example of the past subjunctive. There is still another subjunctive tense, the imperfect subjunctive, which is used in supposing something that is not true, as for example:

> If you were in my place — *Se Lei fosse al mio posto.*
> If you were I — *Se Lei fosse me.*

The imperfect subjunctive endings for the three conjugations are:

(che) io *parlassi*	*scrivessi*	*finissi*
(che) tu *parlassi*	*scrivessi*	*finissi*
(che) egli *parlasse*	*scrivesse*	*finisse*
(che) noi *parlassimo*	*scrivessimo*	*finissimo*
(che) voi *parlaste*	*scriveste*	*finiste*
(che) loro *parlassero*	*scrivessero*	*finissero*

Important irregular verbs in the imperfect subjunctive are *fare* — *facesse; dire* — *dicesse; dare* — *dessi; essere* — *fossi; stare* — *stessi; bere* — *bevessi.*

e mettere l'altro verbo
ay MEHT-tay-ray LAHL-tro VEHR-bo
and put the other verb

304

nel condizionale.
nel kohn-deets-yo-NA-lay.
in the conditional.

Si noti nel dialogo seguente:
See NO-tee nel D'YA-lo-go say-GWEN-tay:
Note in the following dialogue:

— Se Lei fosse nel deserto della Libia
Say Lay FOHS-say nel day-ZEHR-toh DEL-la LEEB-ya
If you were in the Libyan desert

e vedesse un leone,
ay vay-DESS-say oon lay-OH-nay,
and you saw a lion,

che cosa farebbe?
kay KO-za fa-REHB-bay?
what would you do?

— Ma non ci sono leoni in Libia.
Ma nohn chee SO-no lay-OH-nee een LEEB-ya.
But there are no lions in Libya.

— Allora supponiamo che Lei fosse
Ahl-LO-ra soop-pohn-YA-mo kay Lay FOHS-say
Then let's suppose that you were

in Etiopia, dove ci sono leoni,
ee-neht-YOHP-ya, DOH-vay chee SO-no lay-OH-nee,
in Ethiopia, where there are lions,

e ne incontrasse uno,
ay nay een-kohn-TRAHS-say OO-no,
and you met one,

che cosa farebbe?
kay KO-za fa-REHB-bay?
what would you do?

— Lo ucciderei col mio fucile.
Lo oot-chee-day-RAY kohl MEE-oh foo-CHEE-lay.
I would kill it with my rifle.

(col = con + il)

305

— E se Lei non avesse il fucile,
Ay say Lay no-na-VEHS-say eel-foo-CHEE-lay,
And if you didn't have a rifle,

come si difenderebbe?
KO-may see dee-fen-day-REHB-bay?
how would you defend yourself?

— Se non avessi il fucile,
Say no-na-VEHS-see eel foo-CHEE-lay,
If I didn't have a rifle,

salirei su un albero.
sa-lee-RAY soo oo-NAHL-bay-ro.
I would climb a tree.

— E se non ci fossero alberi,
Ay say nohn chee FOHS-say-ro AHL-bay-ree,
And if there were no trees,

come scapperebbe via?
KO-may skahp-pay-RAYB-bay VEE-ah?
how would you escape?

— Se non ci fossero alberi,
Say nohn chee FOHS-say-ro AHL-bay-ree,
If there were no trees,

mi metterei a correre.
mee meht-tay-RAY ah KO-rray-ray.
I would start running.

— Hmm . . . Credo che il leone
Hmm . . . KRAY-doh kay eel lay-OH-nay
Hmm . . . I think that the lion

La acchiapperebbe facilmente.
La ahk-k'yahp-pay-REHB-bay fa-cheel-MEN-tay.
would catch you easily.

— Ma, senta un po',
Ma, SEN-ta oon po,
But, listen here,

Lei è amico mio o per caso
Lay ay ah-MEE-ko MEE-oh oh pehr-KA-so
are you a friend of mine or by chance

amico del leone?
ah-MEE-ko del lay-OH-nay?
a friend of the lion's?

Apparte queste supposizioni, ci sono
Ahp-PAHR-tay KWESS-tay soo-po-zeets-YO-nee, chee SO-no
Besides these suppositions, there are

altre supposizioni
AHL-tray soop-po-zeets-YO-nee
other suppositions

che si riferiscono a cose
kay see ree-fay-REE-sko-no ah KO-zay
that refer to things

che non sono mai avvenute:
kay nohn SO-no MA-ee ahv-vay-NOO-tay:
that have never happened:

Se la Regina Isabella non avesse aiutato
Say la rey-JEE-na Ee-za-BEL-la no-na-VEHS-say ah-yoo-TA-toh
If Queen Isabella had not helped

Cristoforo Colombo,
Kree-STO-fo-ro Ko-LOHM-bo,
Christopher Columbus,

chi avrebbe scoperto il Nuovo Mondo?
kee ahv-REHB-bay sko-PEHR-toh eel NWO-vo MOHN-doh?
who would have discovered the New World?

Se Roma non fosse mai
Say RO-ma nohn FOHS-say MA-ee
If Rome had never

caduta, parleremmo tutti
ka-DOO-ta, pahr-lay-REM-mo TOO-tee
fallen, would we all be speaking

latino adesso?
la-TEE-no ah-DESS-so?
Latin now?

The final supposition

So far in Step 25, we have been considering ordinary contrary to fact suppositions which use the imperfect subjunctive with "if" and the conditional with the "would" clause. An even more pronounced supposition is concerned in wondering how things *would have been,* if something else had happened or never had happened. The examples given in the text illustrate this, because actually Queen Isabella did help Columbus, and ancient Rome, however eternal, did finally decline and fall. In cases like the above, the *trapassato congiuntivo,* the past perfect of the subjunctive — which is simply the imperfect subjunctive of *essere* or *avere* with the past participle, is used in the "if" clause, and the past or present conditional is used in the other clause.

Compound tenses, despite their difficult names, are really quite easy, as the only changes occur in *avere* and *essere,* the forms of which you already know, while the past participle remains the same.

Congratulazioni! You have just attained the top step in understanding verb constructions. There is nothing further. But don't forget to review the steps you have already passed!

INSTANT CONVERSATION: WHAT WOULD YOU DO IF YOU WON THE LOTTERY?

— Che cosa farebbe Lei
Kay KO-za fa-REHB-bay Lay
What would you do

se vincesse il gran premio
say veen-CHEHS-say eel grahn PREM-yo
if you won the big prize

alla lotteria?
ahl-la loht-tay-REE-ah?
in the lottery?

— Prima di tutto, sloggeremmo,
PREE-ma dee TOOT-toh, zlohdj-jay-REM-mo,
First of all, we would move,

e andremmo ad abitare
ay ahn-DREM-mo ah-da-bee-TA-ray
and we would go to live

in una casa più grande.
ee-NOO-na KA-za p'YOO GRAHN-day.
in a bigger house.

Questo renderebbe contenta mia moglie.
KWESS-toh ren-day-REHB-bay kohn-TEN-ta MEE-ah MOHLL-yay.
This would make my wife happy.

Secondo, comprerei una nuova automobile.
Say-KOHN-doh, kohm-pray-RAY OO-na NWO-va
           ah-oo-toh-MO-bee-lay.
Secondly, I would buy a new car.

Questo mi renderebbe contento.
KWESS-toh mee ren-day-REHB-bay kohn-TEN-toh.
This would make me happy.

Dopo, andremmo nelle Puglie,
DOH-po, ahn-DREM-mo NEL-lay POOLL-yay,
After, we would go to Puglie,

e faremmo visita ai miei genitori.
ay fah-RAY-moh VEE-see-tah i m'yay jay-nee-TOH-ree.
and we would pay a visit to my parents.

(*ai* = *a* + *i*)
Darei loro del macchinario moderno
Da-RAY LO-ro del mahk-kee-NAHR-yo mo-DEHR-no
I would give them modern machinery

per il loro podere.
pehr eel LO-ro po-DAY-ray.
for their farm.

Così non avrebbero da lavorare più tanto,
Ko-ZEE no-nahv-REHB-bay-ro da la-vo-RA-ray p'yoo TAHN-toh,
In that way they wouldn't have to work so much any more,

e la vita sarebbe più facile per loro.
ay la VEE-ta sa-REHB-bay p'YOO FA-chee-lay pehr LO-ro.
and life would be easier for them.

— E dopo, che farebbe?
Ay DOH-po, kay fa-REHB-bay?
And afterwards, what would you do?

— Ritorneremmo qui a Milano.
Ree-tohr-nay-REM-mo kwee ah Mee-LA-no.
We would return here to Milan.

— E continuerebbe a lavorare?
Ay kohn-tee-nweh-REHB-bay ah la-vo-RA-ray?
And would you continue working?

— Sicuro. Dovrei lavorare per forza.
See-KOO-ro. Dohv-RAY la-vo-RA-ray pehr FOHRT-sa.
Sure. I would have to work.

Il denaro della lotteria
Eel day-NA-ro DEL-la loht-tay-REE-ah
The lottery money

non durerebbe mica per sempre.
nohn doo-ray-REHB-bay MEE-ka pehr SEM-pray.
would not really last forever.

— Però, sarebbe molto bello
Pay-RO, sa-REHB-bay MOHL-toh BEL-lo
But it would be very nice

mentre questo durerebbe, no?
MEN-tray KWESS-toh doo-ray-REHB-bay, no?
while it lasted, no?

— Certo. Usciamo subito
CHEHR-toh. Oo-SHA-mo SOO-bee-toh
Certainly. Let's go out right now

a comprare un biglietto.
ah kohm-PRA-ray oon beell-YEHT-toh.
to buy a ticket.

(La domenica seguente)
(La doh-MAY-nee-ka seh-GWEN-tay)
(The following Sunday)

— Che delusione! Non ho vinto niente.
Kay day-loos-YO-nay! No-NO VEEN-toh N'YEN-tay.
What a disappointment! I didn't win anything.

— Meno male! Se avesse vinto
MAY-no MA-lay! Say ah-VEHS-say VEEN-toh
It is just as well! If you had won

qualche cosa, avrebbe subito
KWAHL-kay KO-za, ahv-REHB-bay SOO-bee-toh
something, you would have soon

speso tutto.
SPAY-zo TOOT-toh.
spent everything.

— Forse. Ma almeno
FOHR-say. Ma ahl-MAY-no.
Maybe. But at least

avrei avuto il gusto
ahv-RAY ah-VOO-toh eel GOO-sto
I would have had the pleasure

di averlo speso.
dee ah-VEHR-lo SPAY-zo.
of having spent it.

È un piacere
Here is an example of the infinitive and the past participle. Compare:

It is a pleasure to meet you.
È un piacere fare la Sua conoscenza.
It is a pleasure to have met you.
È un piacere aver fatto la Sua conoscenza.

TEST YOUR ITALIAN

Fill in the missing words with the proper forms of the conditional or the imperfect subjunctive. Score 10 points for each correct answer. See answers below.

1. If I had the money, I would buy a new car.
   Se avessi il denaro, _____ una nuova automobile.

2. If you told it to me, I wouldn't tell it to anyone.
   Se me lo dicesse, non glielo _____ a nessuno.

3. What would you do if you missed the train?
   Che cosa _____ se perdesse il treno?

4. What would you buy if you won the lottery?
   Che cosa comprerebbe se _____ alla lotteria?

5. If I were able to I would do it.
   Se _____ farlo, lo farei.

6. He would come with me if you permitted it.
   Verrebbe con me se Lei glielo _____.

7. If I wanted to, I could stop smoking.
   Se lo volessi, _____ smettere di fumare.

8. If there was no police, would there be an increase in crimes?
   Se non ci _____ la polizia, ci sarebbe un aumento del crimine?

9. If I had the time, I would go to Italy.
   Se avessi il tempo, _____ in Italia.

10. If Hannibal had conquered Rome, would history have been different?
    Se Annibale avesse conquistato Roma, _____ _____ differente la storia?

SCORE _____%

313

step 26 HOW TO READ ITALIAN

Ecco alcuni consigli per facilitare
Here is some advice to make

le vostre letture in italiano.
your reading in Italian easier.

Nella corrispondenza commerciale troverete spesso
In business correspondence you will often find

che il condizionale e il congiuntivo
that the conditional and the subjunctive

si usano molto. Per esempio:
are very much used. For example:

Gentilissimi Signori:
Dear Sirs:

Vi saremmo molto grati se ci poteste mandare
We would be very grateful to you if you could send us

il Vostro ultimo catalogo e il Vostro elenco dei prezzi.
your latest catalogue and your list of prices.

Apprezzeremmo molto se ci rispondeste
We would appreciate it very much if you answered us

al più presto possibile.
as soon as possible.

Ci scusiamo per il disturbo.
We thank you for your trouble.

Con distinti saluti, . . .
With best regards, . . .

For ending letters
Con distinti saluti and *con distinti ossequi* are
two ways of ending a business letter. A personal letter can be ended with *con affettuosi sa-*

luti — "with affectionate greetings," or even more affectionately — *con baci ed abbracci,* "with hugs and kisses."

Nei giornali vedrete
In newspapers you will see

che si usa essere molto brevi
that they are accustomed to being very brief

nei titoli degli articoli:
in the headlines of the articles:

"Geloso ammazza sua moglie —
"Jealous (man) kills his wife —

altro delitto d'onore"
another crime of honor"

"Impiegati postali
"Post office workers

fanno sciopero generale"
on general strike"

"Milan batte Bologna —
"Milan beats Bologna —

vince lo scudetto"
wins the trophy."

Headlines and announcements
Newspaper headlines and radio–TV announcements often drop articles and superfluous pronouns. Adjectives are sometimes used as subjects without the noun; as *un geloso* is masculine, it would mean "a jealous man," and *una gelosa* — "a jealous woman."

In reading Italian newspapers and magazines, certain contemporary words and references have to be learned as they occur, as sometimes they are words of very recent actuality, or peculiar to certain sports, as *scudetto* — "little shield," or "trophy," is to *calcio* (soccer).

315

La letteratura italiana
Italian literature

è bellissima ed è anche molto ricca.
is very beautiful and it is also very rich.

L'opera immortale di Dante —
The immortal work of Dante —

La Divina Commedia —
The Divine Comedy —

è conosciuta in tutto il mondo.
is known throughout the world.

Fin dai primi versi
From the very first verses

sono evidenti l'armonia
are evident the harmony

e la bellezza della sua poesia.
and the beauty of his poetry.

Ecco il principio della *Commedia:*
Here is the beginning of the *Comedy:*

Nel mezzo del cammin di nostra vita
In the middle of the walk of our life

mi ritrovai per una selva oscura,
I found myself in a dark forest,

chè la diritta via era smarrita.
because the right way had been lost.

Ah quanto a dir qual era è cosa dura,
Ah how hard it is to tell what it was like,

Dropping the "e"
In literary style, especially in poetry and in
songs, the final -e is often dropped from the infinitive and from the adjective.

esta selva selvaggia e aspra e forte,
this savage and harsh and strong forest,

Esta
Esta is poetic usage for *questa*.

che nel pensier rinnova la paura!
that even in thought renews the fear!

Tant'è amara che poco è più morte.
It is so bitter that death itself is only a little more so.

Nelle vostre letture italiane,
In your Italian readings,

troverete degli interessanti
you will find interesting

e divertenti esempi di prosa,
and entertaining examples of prose,

a cominciare dai racconti del Boccaccio, fino
beginning with the tales of Boccaccio, up to

agli autori dei tempi moderni.
the authors of modern times.

L'opera italiana —
Italian opera —

letteratura musicale —
musical literature —

L'italiano è la lingua internazionale della musica.
It is fitting that Italian, being such a musical language itself, is also the language of music. The musical directions on sheet music are the same words one uses in spoken Italian:

piano — softly, gently, slowly
pianissimo — very softly
adagio — smoothly
poco a poco — little by little
allegretto — somewhat cheerful
allegro — cheerful, lively
forte — strongly, loudly
fortissimo — very strongly
crescendo — increasing, to a climax

Some musical terms have an additional meaning in Italian: *Opera,* for example, means a "work" in the sense of a musical, artistic or literary composition. *Andante,* in music, "not fast nor slow" means both "current" and also "cheap." *Scherzo,* a "light touch" in music, is also the word for a "joke."

sarà per voi più interessante
will be more interesting for you

perchè potrete riconoscere le parole,
because you will be able to recognize the words,

come queste del *Rigoletto* di Giuseppe Verdi:
like these from (the) *Rigoletto* by Giuseppe Verdi:

La donna è mobile
Woman is as changeable

qual piuma al vento,
as a feather in the wind,

muta d'accento
she changes her meaning

e di pensiero.
and her thoughts.

Sempre un amabile
Always a lovable

leggiadro viso,
(a) beautiful face,

in pianto o in riso,
in tears or in laughter,

è menzognero.
is a false one.

Tutto quello che leggete in italiano,
All that you read in Italian,

che siano delle commedie, dei romanzi,
whether it is plays, novels,

dei libri di storia o d'arte,
books of history or art,

aumenterà la vostra conoscenza dell'italiano
will increase your knowledge of Italian

e sarà una fonte inesauribile di distrazione.
and will be an inexhaustible source of entertainment.

Però, la cosa più importante è di parlare
However, the most important thing is to speak

e di ascoltare gli altri parlare,
and to listen to others speak,

perchè, per imparare bene una lingua,
because, to learn a language well,

bisogna praticarla in tutte le occasioni.
one must practice it on all occasions.

UN CONSIGLIO BUONO — SOME GOOD ADVICE

While you have learned up to now the essential elements for speaking Italian, you will encounter, when reading Italian books, magazines, and newspapers, many words not included in this book. You will be aided, however, in your understanding and use of new words by the fact that there are so many words in English which are similar in Italian, in meaning, and *almost* in spelling.

This is because Italian belongs to the group of romance languages, meaning it is descended from Latin, the language of ancient Rome, as are Spanish, French, Portuguese, and several other languages. A large part of the English language, perhaps more than 40%, comes from Latin and French through the Norman-French conquest of England in 1066, and is therefore similar to Italian in much of its vocabulary. You will find as you learn more and more Italian that there are thousands of words that are almost the same as English. All you have to do is get used to their Italian pronunciation.

When you read new material in Italian, or when you hear Italian spoken, you will constantly encounter many words that you may not have studied but that *you already know.* Therefore, if you have a two way dictionary, use the English/Italian part frequently for making up your own sentences, but do not use the Italian/English section, except in rare cases. Let the meaning and construction become evident to you through context and your own initiative — and, above all, read *aloud* at every chance you get. It is suggested that you read Italian material onto cassettes, or copy spoken material in your own voice, and compare your entries from day to day. As you progress, you will be surprised at how soon you will sound as if you were speaking your own language.

DICTIONARY
ENGLISH — ITALIAN

This dictionary contains numerous words not in the preceding text, but which will complete your ability to use current Italian. It is an interesting linguistic fact that most people use less than 2,000 words in their daily conversation in any language. In this dictionary, you have over 2,600 words chosen especially for frequency of use.

N. B.   1. Masculine and feminine gender of nouns is shown only when the noun does not end in -*o* (masc.) or -*a* (fem.)

2. Adjectives must agree in number and gender with the nouns they describe. Adjectives ending in -*o* change to -*i* when masculine plural is used, and to -*a* for feminine singular and -*e* for feminine plural. When an adjective already ends in -*e* in the singular, the plural is -*i* for masculine and feminine.

3. Adjectives ending in a letter other than -*o* remain the same for masculine and feminine (unless otherwise indicated) and form the plural for both genders by adding -*i* or -*e*.

4. Only the most important adverbs are given. But remember that most adjectives become adverbs by adding -*mente* to the feminine form.
Adjective: *fortunato* — fortunate
Adverb: *fortunatamente* — fortunately

5. When a choice of meaning is approximately equal between two frequently used words or expressions, both are given, separated by a comma. This will help to increase your comprehension of the words you will hear or see in Italian.

A

a, an (*m*) un, uno (*f*) una, un'
(*to be*) able potere
about (*concerning*) circa
above su
absence assenza
absent assente (*m* & *f*)
accent accento
(*to*) accept accettare
accident incidente (*m*)
according to secondo
account conto
accurate esatto
(*to*) accuse accusare
ache dolore (*m*)
across attraverso
act atto
actor attore
actress attrice
(*to*) add aggiungere
address indirizzo
(*to*) admire ammirare
admission ammissione (*f*)
(*to*) advance avanzare
adventure avventura
advertisement annuncio
advice consiglio

affectionate affettuoso
(*to be*) afraid avere paura
Africa Africa
African africano
after dopo (*di*)
afternoon pomeriggio
again di nuovo, un'altra volta
against contro
age età
agency agenzia
agent agente (*m*)
ago fa
agreeable gradevole
(*to*) agree essere d'accordo
ahead avanti
air aria
air-conditioning aria condizionata
air mail posta aerea
airplane aeroplano, aereo
airport aeroporto
alcohol alcool (*m*)
all tutto
    That's all questo è tutto
(*to*) allow permettere
all right va bene, sta bene
almost quasi
alone solo
alphabet alfabeto

already già
also anche
always sempre
(*I*) am sono
(*I*) am (*for the progressive
tense*) sto
America America
American americano
among fra, tra
amount quantità
amusing divertente
and e, ed
anesthetic anestetico
angry arrabbiato
(*to be*) angry essere in collera
animal animale (*m*)
ankle caviglia
anniversary anniversario
(*to*) annoy annoiare
annoying noioso
another un altro
answer risposta
(*to*) answer rispondere
ant formica
antiseptic antisettico
any qualunque, qualsiasi
anyone, anybody qualcuno,
qualcheduno
anyone (*at all*) qualsiasi
anything qualunque cosa, qualche
cosa
anywhere in qualsiasi luogo,
ovunque
apartment appartamento
(*to*) apologize scusarsi, chiedere
scusa
appetite appetito
apple mela
appointment appuntamento

(*to*) appreciate apprezzare
(*to*) approve approvare
April aprile
architect architetto
architecture architettura
are siamo, sono (*pl.*)
(*you, sing.*) are (*Lei*) é
(*we*) are (*noi*) siamo
(*they, you, pl.*) are (*loro,
Loro*) sono
are (*for the progressive*)
(*you, sing.*) are (*Lei*) sta
(*we*) are (*noi*) stiamo
(*they, you, pl.*) are (*loro,
Loro*) stanno
(*there*) are ci sono
area area
argument argomento
arithmetic aritmetica
arm braccio (*pl. -le braccia*)
army esercito
around (*surrounding*) nella vicinanza di, vicino a
around (*approximately*) circa, più
o meno
(*to*) arrange accomodare
(*to*) arrest arrestare
(*to*) arrive arrivare
art arte (*f*)
article articolo
artificial artificiale
artist artista (*m & f*)
as come
Asia Asia
(*to*) ask (*a question*) domandare,
fare una domanda
(*to*) ask (*for*) chiedere,
domandare
asleep addormentato

asparagus asparago (*pl. asparagi*)
aspirin aspirina
ass asino
assortment assortimento
astronaut astronauta (*m*)
at (*location*) in, a
at (*time*) a
Atlantic Atlantico
atmosphere atmosfera
atomic atomico
(*to*) **attend** essere presente a
attention attenzione
August agosto
aunt zia
Australia Australia
Australian australiano
Austria Austria
Austrian austriaco
author autore (*m*)
author autrice (*f*)
authority autorità
automatic automatico
automobile automobile, macchina
autumn autunno
avenue viale
average medio
(*to*) **avoid** evitare
away (*not here*) assente
    far away lontano
    right away! subito!

B

baby bambino
bachelor scapolo
back (*part of body*) schiena
bacon lardo, pancetta
bad male, cattivo

bag borsa
baggage bagaglio
bakery panetteria
ballerina ballerina
ballet balletto
banana banana
band (*musical*) banda
bandage benda, fascia
bank banca
banquet banchetto
bar bar (*m*)
barber barbiere (*m*)
(*at a*) **bargain** a buon mercato
basement sottosuolo
basket cesta
bath bagno
bathing suit costume da bagno
    (*m*)
bathroom stanza da bagno
battery batteria
battle battaglia
bay baia
(*to*) **be** essere
(*to*) **be** (*for progressive*)
    stare
beach spiaggia
beans fagioli
bear (*animal*) orso
beard barba
beautiful bello
beauty bellezza
beauty shop salone di bellezza (*m*)
because perchè
bed letto
bedroom camera da letto
bedspread coperta da letto
bee ape (*f*)
beef manzo
been stato

beer birra
before prima (*di*), davanti (*a*)
beggar mendicante (*m & f*)
(*to*) begin cominciare, iniziare
behind dietro (*di*)
(*to*) believe credere
Belgian belga (*m & f*)
Belgium Belgio
bell campana, campanello
(*to*) belong appartenere
below sotto (*a*)
belt (*men*) cinghia
belt (*women*) cintura
bench banco, panca
(*to*) bend piegare
beside al lato di
besides inoltre
best (*adj.*) il (*la*) migliore
best (*adv.*) il meglio
bet scommessa
better migliore, meglio
between fra, tra
bicycle bicicletta
big grande
bill conto
bird uccello
birthday compleanno
black nero
blanket coperta
blond biondo
blood sangue (*m*)
blouse blusa
(*to*) blow soffiare
blue blù, azzurro
boarding house pensione (*f*)
boat barca
body corpo
boiled bollito
bomb bomba

book libro
bookstore libreria
boot stivale (*m*)
border frontiera
born nato
(*to*) borrow prendere in prestito
boss capo
both tutti e due, entrambi
(*to*) bother disturbare
bottle bottiglia
bottom fondo
bowl coppa
box scatola
boy ragazzo
bracelet braccialetto
brain cervello
brake freno
brand marca
brandy cognac
brass ottone (*m*)
brassiere reggiseno
brave coraggioso
Brazil Brasile
Brazilian brasiliano
bread pane (*m*)
(*to*) break rompere
breakfast colazione (*f*)
breast seno, petto
(*to*) breathe respirare
breeze brezza, venticello
bride sposa
bridegroom sposo
bridge ponte (*m*)
brief breve
briefcase valigetta
bright chiaro
(*to*) bring portare
broken rotto
broom scopa

brother fratello
brother-in-law cognato
brown marrone
brunette bruna, brunetta
brush spazzola
brute bruto
(*to*) **build** costruire
building edificio
bull toro
bullet pallottola
bureau comò
(*to*) **burn** ardere
bus autobus (*m*)
bus stop fermata dell'autobus
business gli affari
businessman uomo d'affari
busy occupato
but ma, però
butcher macellaio
butcher's macelleria
butter burro
button bottone (*m*)
(*to*) **buy** comprare, acquistare
by da
by the way a proposito

C

cab tassì (*m*)
cabaret cabaret (*m*)
cabbage cavolo
cable cablogramma (*m*)
cake torta, dolce (*m*)
calendar calendario
calf (*animal*) vitello
(*to*) **call** chiamare, telefonare
calm calmo, tranquillo
camera macchina fotografica

camp campo
can (*to be able*) potere
can (*container*) lattina
can opener apriscatole (*m*)
candle candela
candy caramella
cap berretto
cabable capace
cape (*clothing*) cappa
capital (*geographic*) capitale (*f*)
capital (*financial*) capitale (*m*)
captain capitano
car automobile (*f*), macchina
carburetor carburatore (*m*)
card biglietto
(*to take*) **care of** avere cura di
careless trascurato
carpet tappeto
carrot carota
(*to*) **carry** portare
cash denaro contante
cashier cassiere (*m*)
castle castello
cat gatto
catalogue catalogo
cathedral cattedrale (*f*)
catholic cattolico
cattle bestiame (*m*)
cave caverna
ceiling soffitto
celebration celebrazione (*f*)
cellar cantina
cement cemento
cemetery cimitero
cent centesimo
center centro
central centrale
century secolo

cereal cereale (*m*)
certain certo
certainly certamente, come no
certificate certificato
(*to*) certify certificare
chain catena
chair sedia
chandelier candelabro
change (*money*) cambio
(*to*) change cambiare
chapel capella
character carattere (*m*)
charming grazioso
(to) chat chiacchierare
chauffeur autista (*m*)
cheap a buon mercato
cheaper meno caro, più
   economico
check assegno
checkroom guardaroba (*m*)
cheerful allegro
cheese formaggio
chest petto
chicken pollo
child bambino
children bambini
chimney camino
chin mento
China Cina
Chinese cinese (*m & f*)
chocolate cioccolata
(*to*) choose scegliere
chop costoletta
Christmas Natale (*m*)
church chiesa
cigar sigaro
cigarette sigaretta
city città

class classe (*f*)
classroom classe, aula (*f*)
(*to*) clean pulire
clear chiaro
clerk impiegato
clever abile
client cliente (*m & f*)
climate clima (*m*)
(*to*) climb salire
clock orologio
close vicino
(*to*) close chiudere
closed chiuso
closet armadio
clothes vestiti, abiti
cloud nuvola
club (*social*) club (*m*), circolo
coast costa
coat cappotto
cocktail cocktail (*m*)
cocoa cacao
coffee caffè (*m*)
coin moneta
coincidence coincidenza
cold freddo
cold (*sickness*) raffreddore (*m*)
(*to*) collect (*money*) riscuotere
college università
color colore (*m*)
comb pettine (*m*)
combination combinazione (*f*)
(*to*) come venire
(*to*) come back ritornare
comedy commedia
comfortable comodo
comment commento
commentary commentario
commercial commerciale

commercial (*T.V.*) annuncio
  pubblicitario
commission commissione (*f*)
common comune
communist comunista (*m & f*)
company compagnia
company (*business*) compagnia,
  società
(*to*) **compare** paragonare
comparison paragone (*m*)
competition competizione (*f*)
complete completo
compliment complimento
composer compositore (*m*)
computer macchina calcolatrice
concert concerto
condition condizione (*f*)
congratulations congratulazioni
  (*f*)
conservative conservativo
(*to*) **consider** considerare
consul console (*m*)
contented contento
continent continente (*m*)
(*to*) **continue** continuare
(*to*) **control** controllare
convenient conveniente
conversation conversazione (*f*)
(*to*) **converse** conversare
(*to*) **convince** convincere
cook cuoco
(*to*) **cook** cucinare
cookie biscotto
cool fresco
copy copia
cork tappo
corkscrew cavatappi (*m*)
corn grano

corner angolo
corporation corporazione (*f*)
correct corretto
(*to*) **correspond** corrispondere
(*to*) **cost** costare
cost costo
cotton cotone (*m*)
cough tosse (*f*)
(*to*) **cough** tossire
(*to*) **count** contare
country (*nation*) paese (*m*)
countryside campagna
course corso
cousin cugino
(*to*) **cover** coprire
cow vacca
crazy pazzo
cream crema
credit credito
crime crimine (*m*)
criminal criminale (*m & f*)
crisis crisi (*f*)
(*to*) **criticize** criticare
cross croce (*f*)
(*to cross*) attraversare
crossing attraversamento
crossroads incrocio
crowd folla
cruel crudele (*m & f*)
(*to*) **cry** piangere
crystal cristallo
cup tazza
(*to*) **cure** curare
curve curva
custom (*habit*) costume (*m*), abitudine (*f*)
customer cliente (*m & f*)
customs (*office*) dogana

customs form formulario di dogana
(to) cut tagliare

D

daily quotidiano
dairy latteria
damp umido
(to) dance ballare
danger pericolo
dangerous pericoloso
dark scuro
darling caro
date (*calendar*) data
date (*appointment*) appuntamento
daughter figlia
daughter-in-law nuora
dawn alba
day giorno, giornata
dead morto
dear caro
debt debito
December dicembre
(to) decide decidere
deck (*boat*) coperta
deep profondo
(to) defend difendere
delay ritardo
delighted felicissimo
delicious delizioso
(to) deliver consegnare
democracy democrazia
dentist dentista (*m*)
(to) depart partire
departure partenza
(to) deposit depositare
(to) descend scendere

(to) describe descrivere
desert deserto
(to) deserve meritare
design disegno
(to) desire desiderare
desk scrittoio, scrivania
dessert dolci, frutta
(to) destroy distruggere
detective detective (*m*)
detour svolta
(to) develop sviluppare
dialect dialetto
dialogue dialogo
diamond diamante (*m*)
dictionary dizionario
(to) die morire
diet dieta
difference differenza
different differente
difficult difficile
(to) dine pranzare, cenare
dining room sala da pranzo
dinner pranzo, cena
dinner jacket smoking (*m*)
direct diretto
(to) direct dirigere
direction direzione (*f*)
director direttore (*m*)
directly direttamente
dirty sporco
disadvantage svantaggio
disappointed deluso
disappointment delusione (*f*)
discount sconto
(to) discover scoprire
discreet discreto
(to) discuss discutere
disease malattia

dish piatto
dishonest disonesto
(*to*) disinfect disinfettare
(*to*) dismiss licenziare
(*to*) disobey disubbidire
distance distanza
(*to*) distrust non fidarsi di
(*to*) disturb disturbare
diverse diverso
divine divino
divorced divorziato
(*to*) do fare
dock molo
doctor dottore (*m*)
dog cane (*m*)
doll bambola
dollar dollaro
done fatto
donkey asino
door porta sportello
dose dose (*f*)
double doppio
doubt dubbio
doubtful dubbioso
dove colombo
down giù, sotto
downtown centro della città
dozen dozzina
draft corrente d'aria (*f*)
drawer cassetto
dream sogno
dress vestito, abito
(*to*) dress oneself vestirsi
dressmaker sarta
(*to*) drink bere
(*to*) drive guidare
driver autista (*m*)
driver's license patente di guida
(*f*)

(*to*) drown annegare
drugstore farmacia
drunk ubriaco
dry secco
dry cleaner tintoria
duck anitra
during durante
dust polvere (*f*)

E

each ciascuno, ognuno
ear orecchio
early presto
(*to*) earn guadagnare
earrings orecchini
earth terra
earthquake terremoto
east est (*m*)
Easter Pasqua
easy facile
easily facilmente
(*to*) eat mangiare
economical economico
edge orlo
education istruzione (*f*)
egg uovo (*pl. le uova*)
eight otto
eighteen diciotto
eight hundred ottocento
eighty ottanta
either ... or o ... o
either (*one*) l'uno o l'altro
elastic elastico
elbow gomito
elderly anziano
election elezione (*f*)
electric electtrico
electricity elettricità

elegant elegante (*m & f*)
elephant elefante (*m*)
elevator ascensore (*m*)
eleven undici
(*to*) embark imbarcarsi
embarrassed imbarazzato
embassy ambasciata
(*to*) embrace abbracciare
embroidery ricamo
emerald smeraldo
emergency emergenza
emotion emozione (*f*)
employee impiegato
employer padrone (*m*)
empty vuoto
encore ancora
end fine (*f*)
(*to*) end finire, terminare
enemy nemico
engaged (*busy*) occupato
engaged (*to be married*) fidanzato
engine motore (*m*)
engineer ingegnere (*m*)
England Inghilterra
English inglese (*m & f*)
enough abbastanza
(*to*) enter entrare
enter! entri!
(*to*) entertain divertire, ospitare
entertaining divertente
entertainment divertimento
enthusiastic entusiastico
enthusiasm entusiasmo
entire intero
entrance entrata
envelope busta
(*to*) envy invidiare
equal uguale, medesimo
equator equatore (*m*)

error errore, sbaglio (*m*)
(*to*) escape (*something*) scappare da
especially specialmente
et cetera eccetera
Europe Europa
European europeo
even anche
evening sera, serata
ever sempre
every ogni
everybody tutti
everything tutto
everywhere dappertutto, ovunque
evidently evidentemente
exact esatto
exactly esattamente
examination esame (*m*)
(*to*) examine esaminare
example esempio
excellent eccellente
except eccetto
(*to*) exchange scambiare
excited eccitato
excursion escursione (*f*)
excuse scusa
(*to*) excuse scusare
excuse me! mi scusi!
exercise esercizio
exhausted esausto
exhibition esibizione (*f*), esposizione (*f*)
exit uscita
(*to*) expect attendere
expedition spedizione (*f*)
expenses spese (*f pl.*)
expensive caro
experience esperienza
experiment esperimento

expert esperto
(*to*) **explain** spiegare
explanation spiegazione (*f*)
(*to*) **explode** esplodere
explorer esploratore (*m*)
(*to*) **export** esportare
exposition esposizione (*f*)
express espresso
expression espressione (*f*)
exquisite squisito
(*to*) **extend** estendere
extra extra
extraordinary straordinario
extravagant stravagante (*m & f*)
eye occhio
eyesight vista

F

fabric tessuto
face faccia, volto, viso
fact fatto
factory fabbrica
(*to*) **fade** scolorire
(*to*) **fail** fallire, mancare
failure fallimento, mancanza
(*to*) **faint** svenire
fair (*show*) fiera
fall caduta
(*to*) **fall** cadere
fall (*season*) autunno
false falso
family famiglia
famous famoso
fan ventilatore (*m*)
far lontano, distante
fare tariffa
farewell addio
farm fattoria

farmer contadino
farther più lontano, più distante
fashion moda
fast veloce (*m & f*)
(*to*) **fasten** assicurare
fat grasso
fate destino, sorte (*f*)
father padre (*m*)
father-in-law suocero
fault colpa
favor favore (*m*)
(*to*) **fear** temere, aver paura di
feather piuma
february febbraio
fee onorario
(*to*) **feel** sentire
feeling sentimento
feet piedi
female femmina
feminine femminile
fender parafango
festival festival (*m*)
fever febbre (*f*)
few pochi
fewer di meno
fiancé fidanzato
field campo
fifteen quindici
fifty cinquanta
fig fico
fight lotta
(*to*) **fight** lottare
(*to*) **fill** riempire
filling (*tooth*) impiombatura
film film
final finale
finally finalmente
(*to*) **find** trovare
(*to*) **find out** scoprire

fine (*delicate*) fine
fine (*good*) bene
finger dito (*pl. le dita*)
(*to*) finish finire, terminare
fire fuoco
fireman pompiere (*m*)
first primo
fish pesce (*m*)
fisherman pescatore (*m*)
fishing pesca
fishmarket pescheria
fist pugno
fitting prova
five cinque
(*to*) fix aggiustare
flag bandiera
flame fiamma
flashlight lampadina tascabile
flat (*level*) piatto
flat tire gomma a terra
flavor sapore (*m*)
flight volo
flood inondazione (*f*)
floor (*of a room*) pavimento
floor (*of a building*) piano
Florence Firenze
florist fioraio
flour farina
flower fiore (*m*)
fly (*insect*) mosca
(*to*) fly volare
fog nebbia
(*to*) follow seguire
following seguente
food cibo
foot piede (*m*)
for per
(*to*) forbid proibire, vietare
force forza

foreign estero
foreigner straniero
forest foresta
forever sempre
(*to*) forget dimenticare
(*to*) forgive perdonare
fork forchetta
form forma
(*to*) form formare
formal formale
formula formula
fortunate fortunato
fortunately fortunatamente
fortune fortuna
forty quaranta
forward avanti
fountain fontana
four quattro
fourteen quattordici
fourth quarto
fox volpe (*f*)
fragile fragile
France Francia
free libero
free (*of charge*) gratis
freedom libertà
French francese (*m & f*)
frequent frequente
frequently frequentemente
fresh fresco
Friday venerdì
fried fritto
friend amico
friendly amichevole
frog rana
from da
front fronte (*m*)
(*in*) front (*of*) di fronte a
frozen congelato

frozen (*food*) surgelati
fruit frutta
full pieno
fun divertimento
funeral funerale (*m*)
funny comico, divertente
fur pelliccia
furniture mobilia (*f sing.*)
further oltre
fuse fusibile (*m*)
futile futile
future futuro, avvenire (*m*)

G

(*to*) gain guadagnare
gallon gallone (*m*)
(*to*) gamble giocare
game giuoco
garage autorimessa
garbage mondezza
garden giardino
garlic aglio
gas gas (*m*)
gasoline benzina
gas station stazione di servizio (*f*)
gate cancello
gay gaio
gear ingranaggio
gender genere (*m*)
general (*mil.*) generale (*m*)
generally generalmente
generation generazione (*f*)
generous generoso
gentle gentile
gentleman signore
genuine genuino
geography geografia
German tedesco

Germany Germania
(*to*) get (*obtain*) ottenere
(*to*) get (*receive*) ricevere, avere
(*to*) get (*become*) diventare
(*to*) get (*off*) scendere
(*to*) get (*on*) salire
(*to*) get (*out*) uscire
(*to*) get (*up*) alzarsi
(*to*) get (*down*) scendere
(*to*) get (*to*) arrivare
(*to*) get married sposarsi
gift regalo, dono
gin gin (*m*)
girl ragazza
(*to*) give dare
give me mi dia
glad contento
glass (*material*) vetro
glass window vetrina
glass (*drinking*) bicchiere (*m*)
glasses (*eye*) occhiali
glove guanto
glue colla
(*to*) go andare
(*to*) go away andarsene
go away! se ne vada! vada via!
(*to*) go back ritornare
(*to*) go in entrare
(*to*) go on continuare
(*to*) go out uscire
(*to*) go to bed andare a letto, coricarsi
goat capra
God Dio
goddaughter figlioccia
godfather padrino
godmother madrina
godson figlioccio
gold oro

golf golf (*m*)
good buono
goodbye arrivederci, addio
good looking bello, benfatto
gossip pettegolezzo
government governo
graceful grazioso
gradually gradualmente
graduate laureato
grandchild nipote (*m* & *f*)
granddaughter nipote (*f*)
grandfather nonno
grandmother nonna
grandparents nonni
grandson nipote (*m*)
grapes uva
grapefruit pompelmo
grass erba
grateful grato, riconoscente
gravy salsa
gray grigio
great grande
green verde
greetings saluti
groceries alimentari
ground terra
group gruppo
(*to*) grow crescere
guaranteed garantito
guest ospite (*m* & *f*)
guide guida (*f*)
guilty colpevole
guitar chitarra
gymnasium palestra
gypsy zingaro

H

habit costume (*m*), abitudine (*f*)
hair capelli

hairbrush spazzola
hairdresser parrucchiere (*m*)
hiarpin forcina
half metà
ham prosciutto
hammer martello
hand mano (*f*)
handbag borsetta
handkerchief fazzoletto
handmade fatto a mano
handsome bello
(*to*) happen succedere
happy felice (*m* & *f*)
harbor porto
hard duro
(*to*) harm (*oneself*) farsi male
(*to*) harm far male a
harmful dannoso
haste fretta
hat cappello
(*to*) hate odiare
(*to*) have avere
he egli, lui
head testa
headache mal di testa
(*to*) heal curare
health salute (*f*)
(*to*) be healthy essere sano
(*to*) hear udire, sentire
heart cuore (*m*)
heating calorifero
heaven cielo
heavy pesante
Hebrew ebreo
heel (*shoe*) tacco
heel (*foot*) tallone (*m*)
heir erede (*m* & *f*)
helicopter elicottero
hell inferno

hello! ciao!
Hello! (*on the telephone*) Pronto!
(*to*) help aiutare
help! aiuto!
helpful utile
hen gallina
her la, lei
her (poss.) suo, il suo
to her le, a lei
here qui
hero eroe (*m*)
heroine eroina
hers suo, il suo
(*to*) hesitate esitare
(*to*) hide nascondere
high alto
highway autostrada
hill collina
him lo, lui
to him gli, a lui
hip fianco
(*to*) hire noleggiare
(*to*) hire (*a person*) assumere
his suo, il suo
historical storico
history storia
(*to*) hit colpire
(*to*) hold tenere
hole buco
holiday giorno festivo
holy santo
home casa
honest onesto
honey miele (*m*)
honeymoon luna di miele
honor onore (*m*)
hope speranza
(*to*) hope sperare

horizon orizzonte (*m*)
horn (*auto*) claxon (*m*)
horn (*cattle*) corno
horrible orribile
horse cavallo
horseback a cavallo
hospitable ospitale (*m & f*)
hospital ospedale (*m*)
hospitality ospitalità
host padrone di casa (*m*)
hostess padrona di casa (*f*)
hot caldo
hotel hotel (*m*), albergo
hour ora
house casa
how come
    how far? quanto lontano?
    how many? quanti?
    how much? quanto?
however comunque
hug abbraccio
(*to*) hug abbracciare
huge enorme (*m & f*)
human umano
humid umido
humorous spiritoso
hundred cento
hunger fame (*f*)
(*to be*) hungry avere fame
hunting caccia
(*to*) hunt andare a caccia
hunter cacciatore (*m*)
hurricane uragano
hurry fretta
(*to*) be in a hurry essere in fretta,
    aver fretta
hurry up! fà presto!
(*to*) hurt far male
husband marito

I

i io
ice ghiaccio
ice cream gelato
idea idea
identical identico
identification identificazione (f)
identity identità
idiot idiota (m & f)
if se
ignorant ignorante (m & f)
ill malato
illegal illegale (m & f)
illness malattia
illustration illustrazione (f)
imagination immaginazione (f)
(to) imagine immaginare
(to) imitate imitare
imitation imitazione (f)
immediate immediato
immediately immediatamente
immigrant immigrante (m & f)
impatient impaziente
importance importanza
important importante (m & f)
imported importato
impossible impossibile (m. & f)
(to) improve migliorare
improvement miglioramento
in in
incident avvenimento
(to) include includere
included incluso, accluso
income reddito
income tax tassa sul reddito
incomplete incompleto
inconvenient sconveniente

incorrect incorretto
increase aumento
(to) increase aumentare
incredible incredibile
indeed davvero
indefinite indefinito
independence indipendenza
independent indipendente (m & f)
India India
Indian indiano
(to) indicate indicare
indication indicazione (f)
indigestion indigestione (f)
indirect indiretto
indiscreet indiscreto
individual individuo
indoors dentro
industrial industriale (m & f)
industry industria
inefficient inefficiente
inexpensive economico
infant neonato
infection infezione (f)
infectious infettivo
inferior inferiore
infinitive infinito
influence influenza
informal informale
information informazione (f)
inhabitant abitante (m & f)
injection iniezione (f)
injury danno
inn taverna
innocent innocente (m & f)
in order to per
(to) inquire informarsi
insane pazzo
insect insetto

inside dentro
(*to*) **insist** insistere
(*to*) **inspect** ispezionare
instead invece
institution istituzione (*f*)
(*to*) **instruct** istruire
instructor istruttore (*m*)
instrument strumento
insurance assicurazione (*f*)
(*to*) **insure** assicurare
intact intatto
intelligent intelligente (*m & f*)
intense intenso
intention intenzione (*f*)
interested interessato
interesting interessante
interior interiore
interior decorator arredatore (*m*)
intermission intervallo
internal interno
international internazionale
(*to*) **interpret** interpretare
interpreter interprete (*m & f*)
interview intervista
intestines intestino
into in
(*to*) **introduce** presentare
introduction introduzione (*f*)
invention invenzione (*f*)
(*to*) **investigate** investigare
invitation invito
(*to*) **invite** invitare
iodine tintura di iodio
iron (*metal*) ferro
iron (*for ironing*) ferro da stiro
(*to*) **iron** stirare
irregular irregolare
is è, sta

island isola
Israel Israele
Israeli israelano
it (*object of verb*) la, lo
Italian italiano
Italy Italia
(*to*) **itch** prudere
its suo, il suo
ivory avorio

J

jacket giacca
jail carcere (*m*)
January gennaio
Japan Giappone (*m*)
Japanese giapponese (*m & f*)
jar barattolo
jaw mandibola
jealous geloso
jewelry gioielli
jewelry store gioielleria
Jewish ebreo
job lavoro
joke scherzo
journey viaggio
joy gioia
judge giudice (*m*)
(*to*) **judge** giudicare
juice succo
July luglio
(*to*) **jump** saltare
June giugno
jungle giungla
jury giuria
just giusto
just (*only*) solo, solamente
just now proprio adesso
justice giustizia

K

(to) **keep** mantenere
key chiave (f)
kid (*animal*) capretto
kid (*child*) ragazzo
kidneys reni (f pl.)
(to) **kill** uccidere
kind (*nice*) gentile (*m & f*)
kind (*type*) tipo
king re (*m*)
kiss bacio
(to) **kiss** baciare
kitchen cucina
knee ginocchio
(to) **kneel** inginocchiarsi
knife coltello
(to) **knock** bussare
(to) **know** (*a person*) conoscere
(to) **know** (*a fact or how to*) sapere
   I don't know Non so

L

laboratory laboratorio
laborer lavoratore (*m*)
lace merletto
ladder scala
ladies' room toletta
lady signora
lake lago
lamb agnello
lame zoppo
lamp lampada
land terra
(to) **land** (*from a ship*) sbarcare
(to) **land** (*from a plane*) atterrare
landlord, landlady proprietario, -a
landscape paesaggio
language lingua

large grande
last ultimo
(to) **last** durare
late tardi
later più tardi
(to) **laugh** ridere
laundress lavandaia
laundry lavanderia
law legge (f)
lawyer avvocato
laxative lassativo
lazy pigro
lead (*metal*) piombo
(to) **lead** guidare
leader capo, guida
leading principale
leaf foglia
leak perdita
(to) **leak** gocciolare
(to) **learn** imparare
(to) **lease** affittare
least minimo
leather cuoio
(to) **leave** (*something*) lasciare
(to) **leave** (*depart*) partire
lecture conferenza
left (*direction*) sinistra
(*to the*) **left** a sinistra
leg gamba
legal legale
leisure ozio
leisure time tempo libero
lemon limone (*m*)
lemonade limonata
(to) **lend** prestare
leopard leopardo
less meno
lesson lezione (f)
(to) **let** lasciare

letter lettera
lettuce lattuga
level livello
liar bugiardo
liberal liberale
liberty libertà
library biblioteca
license licenza
(*drivers*) **license** patente di guida (*f*)
lie (*untruth*) bugia
(*to*) **lie down** coricarsi
lieutenant tenente (*m*)
life vita
(*to*) **lift** sollevare
light (*weight*) leggero
light (*illumination*) luce (*f*)
light (*color*) chiaro
lightning lampo
like (*as*) come
like this così
(*to*) **like** piacere
   I like it mi piace
likewise egualmente
limit limite (*m*)
line linea
linen lino
lingerie biancheria
lion leone (*m*)
lip labbro (*pl. le labbra*)
liquor liquore (*m*)
list elenco
(*to*) **listen** ascoltare
little piccolo
a little bit un poco
(*to*) **live** vivere
liver fegato
living room salotto
(*to*) **load** caricare

(*a*) **loan** prestito
lobby salone (*m*)
lobster aragosta
local locale
location località
(*to*) **lock** chiudere a chiave
locomotive locomotiva
logical logico
long lungo
(*to*) **look** guardare
look! guardi!
look out! attenzione!
loose sciolto
(*to*) **lose** perdere
loss perdita
lost perduto
lot (*much*) molto
loud forte
love amore (*m*)
(*to*) **love** amare
lovely bello, carino
lover innamorato, amante (*m* & *f*)
low basso
   in a low voice sottovoce
luck fortuna
luggage bagagli (*m pl.*)
lunch seconda colazione (*f*)
lung polmone (*m*)
luxurious lussuoso
luxury lusso

M

machine macchina
mad (crazy) pazzo
madam signora
made fatto
magazine rivista

magic (*n*) magia (*f*)
magic (*adj.*) magico
maid cameriera
mail posta
mailbox cassetta postale
mailman postino, portalettere
main principale
main course piatto principale
main (*principal*) maggiore
major maggiore (*m*)
majority maggioranza
(*to*) make fare
male maschio
man uomo
manager gerente (*m*)
manicure manicure (*f*)
manner maniera, modo
(*to*) manufacture fabbricare
manufactured fabbricato
many molti
map carta (*geografica*)
marble marmo
March marzo
mark marca
market mercato
married sposato
marvelous meraviglioso
masculine maschile
mass (*religious*) messa
massage massaggio
masterpiece capolavoro
match fiammifero
material materiale (*m*)
(*to*) matter importare
  What's the matter? Che c'è?
  It doesn't matter Non importa
May maggio
may (*to be able to*) potere
  May I? Posso?

maybe forse, chissà
mayonnaise maionese (*f*)
me (*before the verb*) mi
me (*after the verb*) me
  to me (*before the verb*) mi
  to me (*after the verb*) a me
meal pasto
(*to*) mean significare, voler dire
(*to*) measure misurare
meat carne (*f*)
mechanic meccanico
medal medaglia
medical medico
medicine medicina
Mediterranean Mediterraneo
(*to*) meet incontrare
meeting riunione (*f*)
melon melone (*m*)
member (*of group*) membro
member (*of company*) socio
men uomini
(*to*) mend rammendare
men's room toletta per uomini
menu lista
merchant commerciante (*m*)
message messaggio
messenger messaggero
metal metallo
meter metro
Mexican messicano
Mexico Messico
middle mezzo
midnight mezzanotte (*f*)
midway a metà strada
mile miglio (*pl. le miglia*)
milk latte (*m*)
million milione (*m*)
mind mente (*f*)
mine (*belonging to me*) mio, il mio

mine (*for minerals*) miniera
mineral minerale (*m*)
mineral water acqua minerale
minister ministro
mink visone (*m*)
minus meno
minute minuto
mirror specchio
misfortune disgrazia, sfortuna
Miss signorina
(*to*) miss (*a train, etc.*) perdere
(*to*) miss (*sentiment*) mancare
I miss you tu mi manchi
mission missione (*f*)
mistake sbaglio, errore (*m*)
mistaken sbagliato
Mister signore
misunderstanding malinteso
(*to*) misunderstand malintendere
(*to*) mix mescolare
mixed mescolato
model modello
modern moderno
modest modesto
moment momento
monastery monastero
Monday lunedì
money denaro, soldi (*m pl.*)
monkey scimmia
month mese (*m*)
monument monumento
moon luna
moonlight chiaro di luna
more più
more or less più o meno
morning mattina
mortgage ipoteca
mosquito zanzara
most il più, la più

most of la maggior parte di
mother madre (*f*), mamma
mother-in-law suocera
motor motore (*m*)
motorcycle motocicletta
mountain montagna
mouse topo
mouth bocca
(*to*) move muovere
movies cinema (*m*)
Mrs. signora
much molto
how much? quanto?
mud fango
mule mulo
municipal municipale
murder omicidio
muscle muscolo
mushroom fungo
music musica
musician musicista (*m & f*)
must dovere
mustache baffi (*m pl.*)
mustard mostarda
my mio, il mio
myself io stesso
myself (*obj.*) me stesso
mysterious misterioso
mystery mistero

N

nail (*on finger*) unghia
nail (*for hammer*) chiodo
naked nudo
name nome (*m*)
(*last*) name cognome (*m*)
Naples Napoli
narrow stretto

nation nazione (*f*)
national nazionale
nationality nazionalità
natural naturale
naturally naturalmente
navy marina
Neapolitan napoletano
near vicino
nearly circa
necessary necessario
neck collo
necklace collana
necktie cravatta
(*to*) need aver bisogno
needle ago
neighbor vicino
neighborhood quartiere, (*m*)
neither ... nor ... nè ... nè ...
nephew nipote (*m*)
nerve nervo
nervous nervoso
never mai
    Never mind non importa
nevertheless tuttavia
neutral neutrale
new nuovo
news notizia
newspaper giornale (*m*)
New Year Anno Nuovo
next prossimo
nice simpatico
niece nipote (*f*)
night notte (*f*)
nightclub locale notturno (*m*)
nightgown camicia da notte
nine nove
nineteen diciannove
ninety novanta
no no

nobody nessuno
noise rumore (*m*)
noisy rumoroso
none nessuno, niente
nonsense sciocchezza
noon mezzogiorno
normal normale
north nord (*m*)
northeast nord-est (*m*)
northwest nord-ovest (*m*)
Norway Norvegia
Norwegian norvegese (*m & f*)
nose naso
not no, non
not yet non ancora
note nota
notebook quaderno
nothing niente
notice avviso
(*to*) notice notare
(*to*) notify notificare
noun nome (*m*)
novel (*book*) romanzo
novelty novità
November novembre
now ora, adesso
nowhere in nessuna parte
nuisance noia
number numero
numerous numeroso
nurse infermiera
nut noce (*f*)

O

(*to*) obey obbedire, ubbidire
object oggetto
(*to*) oblige obbligare
(*to*) obtain ottenere

obvious ovvio
occasion occasione (*f*)
occasionally ogni tanto
occupation occupazione (*f*)
(*to*) occupy occupare
ocean oceano
October ottobre
odd (*unusual*) raro
odd (*uneven*) dispari
of di
of course naturalmente, come no
offer offerta
(*to*) offer offrire
office ufficio
officer ufficiale (*m*)
official ufficiale
often spesso
oil olio
oil (*for industry*) petrolio
oil well pozzo di petrolio
o.k. va bene, sta bene
old vecchio
    How old are you? Quanti
    anni ha?
olive oliva
olive oil olio d'oliva
omelet frittata
on su, sopra
once una volta
at once subito, immediatamente
one uno
one way (*traffic sign*) senso unico
on time a tempo
onion cipolla
only soltanto, solo
open aperto
(*to*) open aprire
opera opera
operation operazione (*f*)

operator (*telephone*) telefonista
    (*m* & *f*)
opinion opinione (*f*)
opportunity opportunità
opposite opposto
optician ottico
or o
orange arancia
orangeade aranciata
orchard frutteto
orchestra orchestra
orchid orchidea
order ordine (*m*)
    out of order fuori uso
(*to*) order ordinare
    in order to per
ordinary ordinario
organization organizzazione (*f*)
oriental orientale (*m* & *f*)
original originale (*m* & *f*)
ornament ornamento
orphan orfano
orthodox ortodosso
other altro
ought dovere (*used in the
    conditional*)
ounce oncia
our, ours nostro, il nostro
outdoors all'aperto, all'aria aperta
outside fuori
oven forno
over (*above*) sopra
over (*finished*) finito, terminato
overcharge prezzo eccessivo
overcoat soprabito
overhead avanti
(*to*) owe dovere
own proprio
owner proprietario, padrone (*m*)

ox bue (*m*)
oxygen ossigeno
oyster ostrica

P

(*to*) **pack** impaccare
(*to*) **pack** (*suitcases*) fare le valigie
package pacco, pacchetto
pack of cards mazzo di carte
page pagina
paid pagato
pail secchio
pain dolore (*m*)
painful doloroso
paint, painting pittura
(*to*) **paint** dipingere
painter pittore (*m*)
pair paio
pajamas pigiama (*m*)
palace palazzo
pale pallido
palm (*tree*) palma
palm (*hand*) palmo
pants pantaloni (*m pl.*)
paper carta
parade parata
parcel pacco
pardon scusa
    Pardon me! Mi scusi!
parents genitori
Paris Parigi
park parco
(*to*) **park** (*a car*) parcheggiare,
  posteggiare
parkway autostrada
parsley prezzemolo
part parte (*f*)
part (*of a machine*) pezzo

participle participio
partner (*business*) socio
party festa
(*to*) **pass** passare
passage passaggio
passenger passeggero
past passato
pastries paste (*f pl.*), dolci (*m pl.*)
patience pazienza
patient paziente (*m & f*)
pay (*salary*) salario
(*to*) **pay** pagare
(*to*) **pay cash** pagare in contanti
payment pagamento
pea pisello
peace pace (*f*)
peaceful pacifico
peach pesca
pear pera
pearl perla
peasant contadino
peculiar strano
pen penna
penalty pena
pencil matita
people gente (*f*)
pepper pepe (*m*)
percent percento
perfect perfetto
perfume profumo
perhaps forse
period periodo
permanent permanente
(*to*) **permit** permettere
permitted permesso
Persian persiano
person persona
personal personale
personality personalità

perspiration sudore (*m*)
persuade persuadere
petrol petrolio
pharmacy farmacia
philosopher filosofo
philosophy filosofia
phone telefono
photo foto (*f*)
photographer fotografo
photostatic copy copia fotostatica
piano piano
(*to*) **pick up** prendere
picture quadro
picture film (*m*)
pie torta
piece pezzo
pier molo
pig maiale (*m*)
pigeon piccione (*m*)
pilgrim pellegrino
pill pillola
pillar pilastro
pillow guanciale (*m*)
pilot pilota (*m*)
pin (*brooch*) spilla
pin (*sewing*) spillo
pineapple ananasso
pink rosa
pipe (*for water*) tubo
pipe (*for smoking*) pipa
pistol pistola
place luogo
in the first place in primo luogo
plain (*simple*) semplice
plan piano
planet pianeta (*m*)
plant (*garden*) pianta
plant (*factory*) fabbrica
plastic (*n*) plastica

plastic (*adj.*) plastico
plate piatto
play (*theater*) commedia
(*to*) **play** (*games*) giocare
(*to*) **play** (*an instrument*) suonare
pleasant piacevole
please per piacere, per favore, prego
pleasure piacere (*m*)
plenty (*enough*) abbastanza
plenty (*quantity*) abbondante
plum susina
plural plurale (*m*)
pneumonia polmonite (*f*)
pocket tasca
pocketbook (*for men*) portafogli (*m*)
pocketbook (*for women*) borsellino
poem poesia
poet poeta (*m*)
point punto
(*to*) **point** (*out*) segnalare
poison veleno
poisonous velenoso
police polizia
policeman poliziotto, carabiniere (*m*)
polite cortese (*m & f*)
political politico
politics politica
pool piscina
poor povero
pope papa (*m*)
popular popolare
pork porco
port porto
portrait ritratto
Portugal Portogallo

position posizione (*f*)
position (*job*) posto
positive positivo
possible possibile
possibly possibilmente
postage stamp francobollo
postcard cartolina
postoffice ufficio postale
(*to*) **postpone** posporre
potato patata
pound (*weight*) libbra
(*to*) **pour** versare
powder (*cosmetic*) cipria
power potere (*m*)
powerful potente (*m & f*)
practical pratico
(*to*) **practice** praticare
prayer preghiera
precious prezioso
(*to*) **prefer** preferire
preferable preferibile
pregnant incinta
premier primo ministro
preparation preparazione (*f*)
(*to*) **prepare** preparare
prescription ricetta
present (*time*) presente
present (*gift*) regalo, dono
(*to*) **present** (*a gift*) regalare
president presidente (*m*)
(*to*) **press** (*clothes*) stirare
press (*news etc.*) la stampa
pretty carino, bello
(*to*) **prevent** prevenire
previous precedente
previously precedentemente
price prezzo
priest sacerdote (*m*)
prince principe (*m*)

princess principessa
principal principale
prison prigione (*f*), carcere (*m*)
prisoner prigioniero
private privato
prize premio
probable probabile
probably probabilmente
problem problema (*m*)
(*to*) **produce** produrre
production produzione (*f*)
profession professione (*f*)
professor professore (*m*)
profit profitto
program programma (*m*)
progressive progressivo
promenade passeggiata
promise promessa
(*to*) **promise** promettere
prompt pronto
(*to*) **pronounce** pronunciare
pronunciation pronuncia
proof prova
propaganda propaganda
property proprietà
proposal proposta
prosperity prosperità
(*to*) **protect** proteggere
protection protezione (*f*)
(*to*) **protest** protestare
protestant protestante (*m & f*)
proud orgoglioso, fiero
(*to*) **prove** provare
province provincia
provincial provinciale
psychiatrist psichiatra (*m*)
psychologist psicologo
public pubblico
publicity pubblicità

(*to*) **publish** pubblicare
publisher editore (*m*)
publishing house casa editrice
(*to*) **pull** tirare
(*to*) **punish** punire
punishment castigo
pupil alunno
(*to*) **purchase** comprare
pure puro
purple porpora
purse borsetta
(*to*) **push** spingere
(*to*) **put** mettere
(*to*) **put on** mettersi, indossare

Q

quality qualità
quantity quantità
quarrel lite (*f*)
(*to*) **quarrel** litigare
quarter quarto
queen regina
queer strano
question domanda
quick rapido, svelto
quickly rapidamente, alla svelta
quiet quieto

R

rabbi rabbino
rabbit coniglio
race (*human*) razza
race (*contest*) corsa
radio radio (*f*)
rag straccio
railroad ferrovia
railroad car vagone (*m*)
rain pioggia

raincoat impermeabile (*m*)
(*to*) **raise** sollevare
rank grado
rapid rapido, svelto
rapidly rapidamente, alla svelta
rare (*uncommon*) raro
rarely raramente
rat topo
rather piuttosto
raw crudo
razor rasoio
razorblade lametta (*per la barba*)
(*to*) **reach** raggiungere
(*to*) **read** leggere
ready pronto
real vero
(*to*) **realize** rendersi conto
really veramente
rear di dietro
reason ragione (*f*)
reasonable ragionevole
receipt ricevuta
(*to*) **receive** ricevere
recent recente
recently recentemente, di recente
recipe ricetta
(*to*) **recognize** riconoscere
(*to*) **recommend** raccomandare
record (*phono*) disco
(*to*) **recover** guarire
red rosso
Red Cross Croce Rossa (*f*)
(*to*) **reduce** ridurre
reduction riduzione (*f*)
red wine vino rosso
refrigerator frigorifero
(*to*) **refund** rimborsare
(*to*) **refuse** rifiutare
region regione (*f*)

register registro
(to) register registrare
(to) register (a letter) fare una raccomandata
registration (car) immatricolazione (f)
(to) regret dispiacersi
regular regolare
regulation regolamento
relative parente (m & f)
religion religione (f)
(to) remain rimanere
remark osservazione (f)
(to) remark osservare
remedy rimedio
(to) remember ricordare
rent affitto
(to) rent affittare
(to) repair riparare
repair riparazione (f)
(to) repay ricompensare
(to) repeat ripetere
reply risposta, replica
(to) reply rispondere
reporter cronista (m)
(to) represent rappresentare
representative rappresentante (m)
reproduction riproduzione (f)
republic repubblica
reputation reputazione (f)
(to) request richiedere
(to) rescue salvare
(to) resemble assomigliare a
reserved prenotato
residence residenza
resident residente (m & f)
(to) resist resistere
rest (remainder) il resto
(to) rest riposare

restaurant ristorante (m)
restless irrequieto
result risultato
(to) retire ritirare
retired ritirato
(to) return (to a place) ritornare
(to) return (give back) restituire
revolution rivoluzione (f)
reward ricompensa
rib costola
ribbon nastro
rice riso
rich ricco
ride corsa, passeggiata
rifle fucile (m)
right (direction) a destra
right (correct) esatto, corretto
(to be) right aver ragione
right away subito, immediatamente
right now proprio adesso
ring anello
riot tumulto
(to) rise sorgere
risk rischio
(to) risk rischiare
river fiume (m)
road strada
roast arrosto
roasted arrostito
(to) rob rubare
robber ladro
rock roccia
roll (bread) panino
Roman romano
romantic romantico
Rome Roma
roof tetto
room (space) spazio

room (*in a house*) stanza, camera
rope corda
rose rosa
rough ruvido
round rotondo
round trip andata e ritorno
royal reale (*m & f*)
rubber gomma
ruby rubino
rude rude, rozzo
ruin rovina
rum rum (*m*)
(*to*) **run** correre
Russia Russia
Russian russo

S

sack sacco
sad triste
saddle sella
sadness tristezza
safe salvo, sicuro
safe (*box*) cassaforte (*f*)
safety pin spilla di sicurezza
(*to*) **sail** navigare
sail vela
sailor marinaio
saint santo
salad insalata
salary salario
sale vendita
salesman commesso
saleswoman commessa
salmon salmone (*m*)
salt sale (*m*)
same stesso
sand sabbia

sandwich sandwich, panino imbottito
sanitary sanitario
sapphire zaffiro
sarcasm sarcasmo
sarcastic sarcastico
satisfactory soddisfacente
satisfied soddisfatto
(*to*) **satisfy** soddisfare
Saturday sabato
sauce salsa, sugo
sausage salsiccia
savage selvaggio
(*to*) **save** (*rescue*) salvare
(*to*) **save** (*money*) economizzare
savior salvatore (*m*)
saw (*tool*) sega
(*to*) **say** dire
scale bilancia
scar cicatrice (*f*)
scarce scarso
(*to*) **scare** spaventare
scarf sciarpa
scarlet scarlatto
scene scena
scenery paesaggio
schedule (*time*) orario
school scuola
science scienza
scientific scientifico
scientist scienziato
scissors forbici (*f pl.*)
(*to*) **scold** rimproverare
Scotch scozzese (*m & f*)
Scotland Scozia
(*to*) **scratch** graffiare
scratch graffio
scream grido

(*to*) **scream** gridare
screw vite (*f*)
sea mare (*m*)
seasickness mal di mare (*m*)
seam cucitura
(*to*) **search** ricercare
season stagione (*f*)
seat posto, sedile (*m*)
second secondo
secret segreto
secretary segretario
section sezione (*f*)
secure sicuro
(*to*) **see** vedere
seed seme (*m*)
(*to*) **seem** parere, sembrare
    it seems to me that ... mi
    pare che ...
seen visto, veduto
seldom di rado, raramente
(*to*) **select** selezionare, scegliere
self stesso
selfish egoista (*m & f*)
(*to*) **sell** vendere
(*to*) **send** mandare
sensation sensazione (*f*)
sensible ragionevole (*m & f*)
sensitive sensitivo
sentence sentenza
sentimental sentimentale
separate separato
(*to*) **separate** separare
September settembre
series serie (*f*)
serious serio
servant servo
service servizio
seven sette

seventeen diciassette
seventh settimo
seventy settanta
several vari, molti
severe severo
(*to*) **sew** cucire
shade ombra
shampoo shampoo
shape forma
shark pescecane (*m*)
sharp (*pain*) acuto
sharp (*knife*) affilato
shave barba
(*to*) **shave** fare la barba
(*to*) **shave oneself** farsi la barba
she ella, essa, lei
sheep pecora
sheet (*of paper*) foglio
sheet (*of bed*) lenzuolo (*m sing*),
    lenzuola (*f pl*)
shell conchiglia
shelter rifugio
sherry sherry
(*to*) **shine** brillare
(*to*) **shine** (*shoes*) lustrare
ship nave (*f*)
(*to*) **ship** (*goods*) spedire
shock colpo
shoe scarpa
(*to*) **shoot** sparare
shop negozio
short corto
shoulder spalla
(*to*) **shout** gridare
shovel pala
(*to*) **show** mostrare
    show me mi mostri
show (*theater*) spettacolo

shower (*bath*) doccia
shrimp gambero
(*to*) shut chiudere
shy timido
Sicilian siciliano
Sicily Sicilia
sick malato
(*to become*) sick ammalarsi
side lato, fianco
side dish contorno
sidewalk marciapiede (*m*)
sight vista
sign insegna
(*to*) sign firmare
signature firma
silence silenzio
silent silenzioso
silk seta
silly sciocco
silver argento
similar simile
simple semplice
since da
sincerely sinceramente
(*to*) sing cantare
singer cantante (*m & f*)
single (*unmarried*) (*man*) scapolo,
　(*woman*) nubile
sir signore
sister sorella
sister-in-law cognata
(*to*) sit sedersi
situation situazione (*f*)
six sei
sixteen sedici
sixth sesto
sixty sessanta
size misura
size (*clothes*) taglia, misura

(*to*) skate pattinare
(*to*) ski sciare
skin pelle (*f*)
skirt gonna
sky cielo
slave schiavo
(*to*) sleep dormire
sleeve manica
slice fetta
slight leggero
slippers pantofole (*f pl.*)
slippery sdrucciolevole
slow lento
slowly lentamente, piano
small piccolo
smaller più piccolo
smell odore (*m*)
(*to*) smell odorare
smile sorriso
(*to*) smile sorridere
smoke fumo
(*to*) smoke fumare
smooth liscio
snail lumaca
snake serpente (*m*)
sneeze starnuto
(*to*) sneeze starnutire
(*to*) snore russare
snow neve (*f*)
(*to*) snow nevicare
snowstorm nevicata
so (*thus*) così
soap sapone (*m*)
social sociale
sock calzino
soda soda
sofa sofà (*m*), divano
soft soffice
sold venduto

soldier soldato
solid solido
some qualche (*sing.*)
    alcuni (*pl.*)
some (*sing.*) un poco di, del, dello, della
some (*pl.*) dei, degli, delle
somebody qualcuno
something qualche cosa, qualcosa
sometimes qualche volta
somewhere da qualche parte, in qualche posto
son figlio
son-in-law genero
song canzone (*f*)
soon presto
sore throat mal di gola
sorrow pena
(*I am*) sorry mi dispiace
soul anima
sound suono, rumore (*m*)
sour agro
south sud (*m*)
South America Sud America
South American sudamericano
souvenir ricordo
space spazio
spaghetti spaghetti
Spain Spagna
Spanish spagnuolo
spark scintilla
(*to*) speak parlare
special speciale
specialty specialità
speed velocità
(*to*) spend spendere
splendid splendido
spoiled guasto
spoon cucchiaio

sport sport (*m*)
spot (*stain*) macchia
spring (*season*) primavera
square (*measure*) quadrato
square (*street*) piazza
(*to*) stab pugnalare
stairs scale (*f pl.*)
stamp francobollo
(*to*) stand (*up*) alzarsi
standing in piedi
star stella
starch amido
(*to*) start cominciare
state stato
station stazione (*f*)
statue statua
(*to*) stay stare
steak bistecca
(*to*) steal rubare
steam vapore (*m*)
steel acciaio
stenographer stenografo
step passo
sterilized sterilizzato
steward cameriere (*m*)
stiff rigido
still (*adv.*) ancora
still (*adj.*) fermo, immobile
stimulant stimolante (*m*)
sting puntura
stocking calza
stockmarket borsa
stocks (*shares*) azioni (*f pl.*)
stomach stomaco
stone pietra
(*to*) stop fermare
stop! alt!, ferma!
store negozio, bottega
storm tempesta

story storia
straight diritto
strange strano
stranger straniero
street strada
streetcar tram (*m*)
strength forza
strike (*labor*) sciopero
string corda
strong forte
student studente (*m*)
studio studio
(*to*) study studiare
stupid stupido
style stile (*m*)
subway metropolitana
success successo
such tale
suddenly improvvisamente,
    d'improvviso
(*to*) suffer soffrire
sufficient sufficiente
sugar zucchero
suit (*clothes*) vestito, abito
suitcase valigia
summer estate (*f*)
sun sole (*m*)
Sunday domenica
sure sicuro
surely di sicuro, sicuramente,
    certamente
surprise sorpresa
(*to*) surround circondare
surroundings dintorni (*m pl.*), vi-
    cinanze (*f pl.*)
sweater pullover (*m*) golf
Sweden Svezia
(*to*) sweep spazzare

sweet dolce
sweetheart innamorato
(*to*) swim nuotare
swimming pool piscina
Switzerland Svizzera
swollen gonfio
sword spada
symptom sintomo
system sistema (*m*)

T

table tavola
tablecloth tovaglia
tail coda
tailor sarto
(*to*) take prendere
take it! lo prenda!
(*to*) take away portare via
(*to*) take a walk (*a ride*) fare una
    passeggiata
talent talento
(*to*) talk parlare
tall alto
tank cisterna
tape (*magnetic*) nastro magnetico
tape recorder registratore (*m*)
taste gusto
tax tassa
taxi tassì (*m*)
tea té (*m*)
(*to*) teach insegnare
teacher maestro
team squadra
tear lacrima
teaspoon cucchiaino
telegram telegramma (*m*)
telephone telefono

telephone operator telefonista (*m* & *f*)
television televisione (*f*)
(*to*) tell dire
tell me! mi dica!
temple tempio
temperature temperatura
temporary temporaneo
ten dieci
tenant inquilino
tennis tennis (*m*)
tenor tenore (*m*)
(*past*) tense tempo passato
(*future*) tense tempo futuro
tenth decimo
terrace terrazza
terrible terribile
test prova
test (*exam*) esame (*m*)
(*to*) test provare
than di, che
thank you grazie
thankful grato
that che
the (*sing*) il, lo, la, l'
the (*pl*) i, gli, le
theater teatro
their loro
theirs il loro
them loro (*for persons*)
them li, le (*for things*)
then allora
there là, lì
there is c'è
there are ci sono
therefore perciò
thermometer termometro
these questi, queste

they loro (*for persons only*)
they essi, esse (*for persons, animals or things*)
thick doppio
thief ladro
thin sottile
thing cosa
(*to*) think pensare
third terzo
(*to be*) thirsty avere sete
thirteen tredici
thirty trenta
this questo, questa
those quelli, quelle
thousand mille
thread filo
three tre
throat gola
through (*finished*) finito
through per, attraverso
(*to*) throw lanciare
thunder tuono
Thursday giovedì
thus così
ticket biglietto
ticket window sportello
tie cravatta
tiger tigre (*f*)
tight stretto
till fino a
time tempo
what time is it? che ore sono?, che ora è?
at what time? a che ora?
tin stagno
tip (*money*) mancia
tire gomma
tired stanco
to (*direction*) a

to (*in order to*) per
toast (*bread*) pane tostato
toast (*wish*) brindisi (*m*)
tobacco tabacco
today oggi
toe dito del piede
together insieme
toilet toletta
tomato pomodoro
tomb tomba
tomorrow domani
tongue lingua
tonight questa notte, stanotte
too (*excessive*) troppo
too (*also*) anche
tooth dente (*m*)
toothache mal di denti
toothbrush spazzolino da denti
toothpaste dentifricio
top cima
torn strappato
total totale
(*to*) **touch** toccare
tough duro
tour giro
(*to*) **tow** rimorchiare
toward verso
towel asciugamano
tower torre (*f*)
town città
toy giocattolo
trade commercio
traffic traffico
train treno
tragedy tragedia
(*to*) **transfer** trasferire
transit transito
(*to*) **translate** tradurre
translation traduzione (*f*)

transportation trasporto
(*to*) **travel** viaggiare
traveler viaggiatore (*m*)
treasure tesoro
tree albero
trip viaggio
trolley-car tranvai, tram
tropical tropicale
trouble guaio, problema (*m*)
trousers pantaloni
truck autocarro
true vero
trunk baule (*m*)
truth verità
(*to*) **try** provare
(*to*) **try** (*on*) provarsi, indossare
Tuesday martedì
tulip tulipano
tune tono
tunnel tunnel, traforo
Turkey Turchia
turkish turco
turkey tacchino
(*to*) **turn** voltare
(*to*) **turn off** spegnere
(*to*) **turn on** accendere
turtle tartaruga
Tuscany Toscana
twelve dodici
twenty venti
twice due volte
twin gemello
(*to*) **twist** torcere
two due
type tipo
typewriter macchina da scrivere
typical tipico
typist dattilografo

U

ugly brutto
umbrella ombrello
uncle zio
uncomfortable scomodo
unconscious inconscio
under sotto
underneath di sotto
(to) understand capire
(to) undertake intraprendere
underwear biancheria intima
(to) undress svestirsi
unemployed disoccupato
unequal ineguale
unexpected inaspettato
unfair ingiusto
unfortunate sfortunato
unfortunately sfortunatamente
ungrateful ingrato
unhappy infelice
unhealthy malsano
uniform uniforme (f)
union unione (f)
united unito
(to) unite unire
United Nations Nazioni Unite (f pl.)
United States Stati Uniti (m pl.)
university università
unless a meno che
unlucky sfortunato
(to) unpack disfare le valigie
unpleasant spiacevole
unsafe non sicuro, pericoloso
until fino a
untrue falso
unusual insolito
up su

upstairs sopra
urgent urgente
us noi, ci
use uso
(to) use usare
used to (in habit of) abituato, accostumato
useful utile
useless inutile
usual usuale, solito
usually usualmente, di solito
utensil utensile (m)

V

vacant libero, vuoto
vacation vacanze (f pl.)
vaccination vaccinazione (f)
valid valido
valley valle (f)
valuable prezioso
value valore (m)
vanilla vainiglia
variety varietà
various vari (pl.)
Vatican Vaticano
veal vitello
vegetables legumi (m pl.)
velvet velluto
vengeance vendetta
Venice Venezia
very molto
very well molto bene
vest panciotto, gilet
veterinarian veterinario
vicinity vicinanza
victory vittoria
view veduta
village villaggio

vinegar aceto
violence violenza
violent violento
violets violette
violin violino
visit visita
(*to*) **visit** far visita
visiting in visita
vivid vivido
voice voce (*f*)
volcano vulcano
voyage viaggio

W

waist vita
(*to*) **wait** aspettare
waiter cameriere (*m*)
waiting room sala d'aspetto
waitress cameriera
(*to*) **wake up** svegliarsi
(*to*) **walk** camminare
walk passeggiata
(*to take a*) **walk** fare una
  passeggiata
wall muro, parete (*f*)
wallet portafogli (*m*)
(*to*) **want** volere, desiderare
war guerra
warm caldo
was ero, era
was fui, fu
(*to*) **wash** lavare
washable lavabile
(*to*) **waste** sciupare
watch orologio
(*to*) **watch** guardare
    Watch out! Attenzione!

water acqua
waterfall cascata
wave (*ocean*) onda
way (*road*) via, strada
way (*manner*) maniera, modo
we noi
weak debole
weapon arma
(*to*) **wear** indossare
weather tempo
wedding matrimonio
Wednesday mercoledì
week settimana
weekend week-end, fine di
  settimana
(*to*) **weigh** pesare
weight peso
welcome benvenuto
(*to*) **welcome** dare il benvenuto
    you're welcome prego
well bene
(*there*) **were** c'erano
west ovest (*m*)
wet bagnato
whale balena
what? che? che cosa?
what else? che altro?
what of it? che importa?
wheel ruota
when quando
where dove
wherever dovunque
where to? per dove?
whether se
which? quale?
while mentre
(*a*) **while** un tratto
white bianco

why? perchè?
who (*relative pronoun*) chi, che
who? chi?
whole intero
whom chi, che
whose? di chi? di che?
why? perchè?
why not? perchè no?
wide largo
widow vedova
widower vodovo
wife moglie (*f*)
wig parrucca
wild selvaggio
will (*see Step 17*)
will (*legal*) testamento
willing disposto
(*to*) win vincere
wind vento
window finestra
wine vino
wing ala
winter inverno
wire filo
wise saggio
wish desiderio
(*to*) wish desiderare
   Best wishes! Auguri!
with con
without senza
witness testimonio, testimone (*m*)
wolf lupo
woman donna
(*to*) wonder domandarsi
wonderful meraviglioso
wonderfully meravigliosamente
wood legno
woods bosco

wool lana
word parola
work lavoro
(*to*) work lavorare
world mondo
worried preoccupato
(*to*) worry preoccuparsi
   Don't worry! Non si
   preoccupi!
worse peggiore
would (*see Steps 21 & 25*)
(*to*) wrap avvolgere
wrist polso
(*to*) write scrivere
writer scrittore (*m*)
writing scrittura
wrong sbagliato
(*to be*) wrong aver torto

X

X-Rays Raggi X

Y

yacht panfilo
year anno
yellow giallo
yes sì
yesterday ieri
yet ancora
you (*subject*) (*formal*) Lei (*sing.*),
   Loro (*pl.*)
      (*informal*) tu (*sing.*),
   voi (*pl.*)
you (*formal*) (*subject*) Lei, Loro
   (*object*) La, Le, Loro
you (*informal*) (*subject*) tu, voi
   (*object*) te, vi

young giovane
your suo
your (*formal*) il suo, il Loro
your (*informal*) il tuo, il vostro
yours il suo
yourself (*formal*) se stesso
youth giovinezza, gioventù

Z

zebra zebra
zero zero
zipper chiusura lampo
zone zona
zoo zoo, giardino zoologico